MOUNTING
PRAISE FOR
THE TURNING

D1021874

is more important than families. In *The Turning*, Linda and Richard Eyre give us solid tips for making our family cultures stronger than all the other cultures that swirl around our kids. And they also have the moxie to urge these other cultures to do more to help and strengthen families."

—**Johnny and Linda Miller, professional golfer and commentator,**
parents of six and grandparents of twenty-two

"The Eyres are right—when families become stronger and more stable, both individual businesses and the whole economy benefit. Count me in for a movement to get all of our institutions to pay more attention to the needs of families."

—**Bill Marriott, Chairman and CEO of Marriott Corporation**

"*The Turning* reveals America's, indeed the world's, blind spot which is preventing progress and prosperity. This blind spot is the centrality of family to the human experience. In *The Turning*, Richard and Linda Eyre carefully and thoroughly remove society's cataract covering the family. As they have for forty years, the Eyres open our eyes to the obvious: family is the fundamental unit of society."

—**Paul Mero, President of Sutherland Institute and Administrator,**
World Congress of Families 2015

"More than ever before, our world needs deliberate, effective parents. And in order to be effective, we need (1) help and support from our "village" of schools, churches, neighborhoods and communities, and (2) family systems and traditions that help teach our children responsibility and ownership that will help them become contributing adults. This book advocates the first and provides a great framework for formulating the second within each of our own unique families."

—**Shawni Pothier, 2013 National Mother of the Year**
and Founder of 71toes.com

"Developing countries and post-communist nations all over the world are copying the mistakes of America—putting ideas of materialism, entitlement, and selfish personal options ahead of responsibility and commitment to family. It is classic short-range thinking that will let us all down—individuals and countries—in our later years. I see *The Turning* as a warning, and one we had all better heed!"

—Przemek Gacek, CEO of Grupa Pracuj SA (Poland)
and YPO Regional Officer, Europe CEO

"Just as *In Defense of Food: An Eater's Manifesto* opened our eyes to the undesirable effects of an industrialized food chain, and *Disrupting Class* gave us hope for reigniting the curiosity lost to the industrialized classroom, *The Turning* illuminates the negative influences of industrialization upon the ultimate institution—our families—while providing parents with the power to do something about it!"

—Adam Timothy, Young Entrepreneur and father of three

"The biggest problems of today's world are not caused by economics. Rather, they stem from a seismic shift of demographics and priorities. *The Turning*, more clearly than any other writing I have read, sorts out these shifts and suggests not how we can reverse them but how we can turn them onto positive paths as parents make their family culture stronger than all competing cultures."

—Santiago Sanchez Reynoso, CEO of COA Internacional (Columbia) and
Chair of the International Family Committee, Young Presidents Association

"The Eyres urge enlightened religious, educational, business, and government leaders—who disagree about many things—to at least agree about this: institutional policies should bolster life-long trust and responsibility between caring children, parents, and grandparents."

—C. Randall Paul, President of the Foundation for Religious Diplomacy

"Moms will love this book because it recognizes their pivotal role and gives practical ideas for their own families. I hope that policy makers in the public and private sectors will also read it and understand that the support of parents and families is critical to the long-term vitality of the companies and governments they represent. Strong families need to be nurtured and supported from the inside out and from the outside in."

—Saren Loosli, Co-Founder of PowerOfMoms.com

"There have been a number of books in recent years documenting what is happening to marriages and families these days. The difference here is that the Eyres go beyond just documenting the trends by suggesting specific steps that different societal stakeholders can take to actually do something about it."

—Jason S. Carroll, PhD, Family Life Specialist
and author of *Sexual Wholeness in Marriage*

"Schools need to focus on their critical role of providing support and back-up for parents in the all-important task of raising the next generation. And this is one of the many things that the Eyres get right in their landmark book, *The Turning*."

—Ken Peterson, President of Peterson International Schools of Mexico

"For the high level group of entrepreneurs I interact with, we're always looking for thoughtful and proven solutions to parenting. The Eyres have a distinctive way of providing real solutions to significant issues facing twenty-first-century families. This material can be a real turning point and rallying cry for intentional leaders raising impactful children and even the institutions we entrust with this critical role."

—Yanik Silver, Founder of Maverick1000

"The largest threat to modern society is the dissolution of the family, and this is a disease for which Richard and Linda Eyre have a cure. *The Turning* comes at a crucial time for kids and parents everywhere. As someone who focuses on social media, I can tell you that the our society is getting better and better at creating content, but this book contains true knowledge that can help change the way parents look at their most important job, that of raising a family prepared to take on all the challenges society throws at them. Every parent today needs to read this book."

—Adrian Dayton, Founder of ClearView Social, named the #1 social media consultant in the legal industry by the *National Law Journal*

"The Family should not be a wedge issue. *Family* is not a word owned by one end of the political spectrum. Regardless of political or religious affiliation, we should all be concerned about what is happening to the traditional family and its resultant impact on children's well-being, repeated cycles of inner-generational poverty, and overall community stability. *The Turning* is well conceived and smartly written. Richard and Linda Eyre bring a wealth of insight and expertise on this important topic."

—Clark Gilbert, Publisher and CEO of *Deseret News*

THE
Turning

BOOKS BY LINDA AND/OR RICHARD EYRE

(Partial List)

Teaching Your Children Values

The Entitlement Trap

3 Steps to a Strong Family

Teaching Children Responsibility

How to Talk to Your Child about Sex

The Happy Family

Teaching Children Joy

A Joyful Mother of Children

Teaching Children Sensitivity

LifeBalance

Spiritual Serendipity

Stewardship of the Heart

I Didn't Plan to Be a Witch

Empty Nest Parenting

The Book of Nurturing

The Mother's Book of Secrets

5 Spiritual Solutions for Parents

On the Homefront

The Awakening (a novel)

The Thankful Heart

Published by Familius LLC, www.familius.com

Familius books are available at special discounts for bulk purchases for sales promotions, family or corporate use. Special editions, including personalized covers, excerpts of existing books, or books with corporate logos, can be created in large quantities for special needs. For more information, contact Premium Sales at 559-876-2170 or email specialmarkets@familius.com

Library of Congress Catalog-in-Publication Data

2014941872   pISBN 9781939629265   eISBN 9781939629548

Printed in the United States of America

Edited by Sheila Curry Oakes and Brooke Jorden
Cover design and layout by David Miles

10 9 8 7 6 5 4 3 2 1
First Edition

THE
Turning

Why the State of

the Family Matters,

and What the World

Can Do About It

NEW YORK TIMES #1 BESTSELLING AUTHORS

RICHARD AND LINDA EYRE

FAMILIUS

"... turn the heart of the fathers to the children, and the heart of the children to their fathers, lest I come and smite the earth with a curse."

—MALACHI, 4:6, THE FINAL WORDS OF THE BIBLE'S OLD TESTAMENT

Where are our hearts turning?
What is the curse?
Who are the culprits?

"Family, the core and the crux of all society, is in an unprecedented crisis that will destroy this world unless we can discover and turn toward a cure."

—RICHARD AND LINDA EYRE,
KEYNOTE ADDRESS:
WORLD CONGRESS OF FAMILIES, 2015
(FORTHCOMING ADDRESS)

Where is the crux?
What causes the crisis?
How do we turn toward the cure?

CONTENTS

FOREWORD

When we try to understand our world, we instinctively reach for data, asking it to explain what is happening. But data is rarely so kind: when your analysis of data yields one result, it often initiates a reciprocal study by someone else using different data to prove the opposite. Data only converts the converted. This is the reason why scholars incessantly argue back and forth about why great nations fall, why the young can't find jobs, why prisons are bulging, why more people get divorced and fewer want to marry, and why schools fail to excite our children to learn. Analysts, data, and statistical packages have made little progress against these scourges. And they never will because their tools and methods are designed to describe, not explain.

Understanding makes progress against problems such as these only when researchers stop trying to understand all the data in all of its complexity, and instead try to understand one thing in all of its clarity. Whether in the physical or the social sciences, great science simplifies. It proposes not the many things that are correlated to the outcome of interest—instead it shows us the cause.

That is why this book is so important. Richard and Linda Eyre have spent their lives working with families, one at a time and in groups, in all of their complexity. They have studied families with faith, and those without; families that teach values and those that do not. And one at a time, in all of their complexity, they have studied children and parents within their families. This book gives us a common cause, and a clear way to frame and explain the causality of problems such as those listed above. *I could not read this book on a couch. It made me stand up and commit again that my family and our love of God are my work.*

Thank you, Richard and Linda. I have watched your family and the families of your children who have lived near us. You are master teachers in writing. They are master teachers in living. May God bless all of you for teaching us.

—Dr. Clayton Christensen, Harvard Business School professor, bestselling author, and recently named "The World's Most Influential Business Thinker" by *Forbes* and Thinkers50

AUTHOR'S NOTE

Consider reading this book *with* someone. If you're married, read it with your spouse. If you're a single parent—read it with another single parent or with a grandparent or someone else who loves your children. If you have not yet started your family, read it with a friend. Parenting is often a lonely and difficult business, as is trying to understand the world our kids are growing up in, and working at it and discussing it with another person can do wonders for our attitudes and our motivation—not to mention our commitment.

At the back of the book is a readers' guide with a number of discussion points and topics to use in a book club or in discussion with friends or to think about as you seek to understand the society around you and as you re-envision your family within it.

INTRODUCTION

WHERE WE ARE COMING FROM

LINDA:

We're going to say some fairly personal things in this book, so I want to use this introduction to tell you where we are coming from. Together and between the two of us, Richard and I have written forty books. And now, forty years after the publication of our first book, we look back and marvel at how much we have seen and learned from those books and from the travel and interactions that they spawned, including the rare opportunity to speak and lecture to parents and families in forty-five countries throughout the world, spanning the widest imaginable variety of cultures and economic and social classes. When the last of our children left for college, we essentially became full-time speakers and lecturers on family, parenting, and life-balance, responding to invitations that often resulted from our books. Thus, we have had the opportunity to see first-hand what is happening to families throughout the world—and what we see both encourages and scares us.

We have been invigorated by the wide array of family commitments and good parenting practices of so many parents and grandparents from the four

corners of the earth, but all too often we have also seen the entitlement attitudes created by some kinds of parenting and the fear and disruption caused
by other approaches. We have watched in horror the devastation of the
family culture in the leprosy colonies in India, and had our eyes opened to
unimaginable poverty as we walked through the slums of Smokey Mountain
in the Philippines—stunned to see happy and incongruously clean families
emerge from a literal mountain of garbage. We have seen the good as well
as the harm that can come from parents who are obsessively committed to
the education of their children at any cost in Korea or who push their single
child to be "the best" in China.

If there is one thing that has taught us more than our writing or our trav-
elling, it has been the blessing of raising nine children (one of every kind,
it seems). From the birth of our first child while we were at Harvard to the
birth of our latest grandchild this year, our children have lit our lives and
motivated our books.

When they were young, we took them with us on research and writing
and publicity trips; and since we could work anywhere so long as we had
paper and pen, we spent our summers living in places that provided contrast to our kids' suburban American experience. As our children learned,
we learned with them. During a summer in rural Mexico, they discovered
from their new friends that you don't need shoes to be happy, but you do
need a supportive family that believes in you. Another summer, in Japan,
they learned that twelve hours of academics a day makes a child smart, but
it severely limits precious family and friend time. And a year in England
taught them that entitlement attitudes exist on all levels, from families on
the dole thinking they deserve everything from the government to "peerage"
children who think Porsches and yachts come with their title.

Still another summer was spent working together as a family in a "hand-
icapped" orphanage in the Transylvanian mountains of Romania where our
kids tried to deal with the tragedy of babies labeled as outcasts for reasons as
trivial as low birth weight.

But more than the negatives, we hope our children learned from these experiences that vastly different family cultures can all, with commitment and love, produce the same thing—happy, responsible children.

As our sons and daughters grew, they inherited our love for travel and determined that, before they had families of their own, they wanted to go beyond where we had taken them. Instead of short "diversity summers," they each elected to break up their college and graduate school with major breaks for experience and service abroad. All studied in Jerusalem for a semester—perhaps the epicenter of religious and cultural diversity—and each had a two-year missionary and humanitarian experience, often in a very poor part of the world. Sometimes with us and sometimes on their own, they experienced humanitarian expeditions that allowed them to immerse themselves in the most critical and urgent of human needs. They took the family mission statement we had written together very seriously and literally: *Broaden and Contribute.* Somewhere along the line, we added the family mantra: *Hard Is Good.*

As missionaries, two of our sons learned to love families from the poverty-stricken areas of Campinas, Brazil, and Santiago, Chile, where both the problems and joys of those they worked with seemed always directly rooted in their families. Two of our daughters worked in orphanages in Bulgaria and Romania during the first months after the fall of the iron curtain, where they experienced the heartbreak of seeing children who were often placed there not because they had no parents but because they had disabilities or special needs or even difficult personalities that their parents were unwilling to deal with.

One of our daughters experienced a different culture right at home in the United States in a rehab center for teenagers of the wealthy whose drug and addiction problems almost always stemmed from the entitlement or abdication of their parents. Then she spent her mission in poor areas of London where she observed single teenage girls having babies to increase the amount of their welfare checks.

Another daughter cried with old women living in the gutters of Chennai, India, who had been deserted by their families. While our youngest son learned about the fascinating formality of family life in Japan, our oldest son was helping to build a water system in Ethiopia, surrounded by family-less children who were desperate for his love.

After ten years of working and burning out in New York City, another of our sons and his new wife decided to leave the "rat race" and go on a one-year humanitarian honeymoon to Mozambique and then India. Immersing themselves in both cultures, they were able to make a difference by focusing their humanitarian projects on sustaining families.

On the other end of the spectrum, one son and his wife, concerned by the materialism of families with "too much," have figured out a fun, alternative lifestyle and are raising five kids in Hawaii with little income but lots of creativity.

The point is that our grown children, through their own experience, have joined us in the conviction that the most meaningful kinds of success and happiness hinge on family life. And they share with us the common cause of doing all we can, individually and collectively, to strengthen families and to combat the family decline we see around us almost everywhere we travel in the world

Together, the eleven of us have come to some core conclusions: nothing is more responsible for the pain and suffering in the world than the breakdown of families; nothing can heal and renew the world like the revaluing of families; and there is not nearly enough focus on how dramatically the state of families affects the state of society.

In this book, we will use statistics and surveys and studies to back up our conclusions, but the conclusions themselves are based on our experience as a family, and on our personal observations.

One more thing you should know, because it is the true genesis of this book: My husband Richard has always been more interested in the "whys" of life than I have. I'm usually ready to take action on the "whats" and "hows" of a situation, but he keeps pulling me back to the "whys" and telling me that we'll never solve a problem until we completely understand it. During these last forty years, as we've worked with and written books for parents and families (mostly on the "hows" of raising children), Richard has become ever more troubled by the steadily increasing difficulty of raising responsible children, despite greater efforts being put forth by so many parents. We are both convinced that most of today's parents place their families in as high a priority as any parents ever have. So *why* are marriages and families breaking up at a record clip, and *why* are kids harder than ever to control and values harder than ever to teach?

It's these "whys" that Richard tries to address in Part 1, because he believes (as I have come to) that understanding the forces that work against families is the first step in saving families, whether we're acting individually as parents or working collectively as a society to stop the family breakdown that threatens our whole way of life.

We both see this book as a natural progression from our earlier writing. Many of our earlier books have sought to teach better parenting methods. But no matter how many parenting skills we have, it is harder and harder to practice them in a world that is increasingly hostile to families. This book will examine the causes of family breakdown and attempt to explain the forces that are working against the family—because understanding the problem is the first step toward solving it!

—LJE, PARK CITY, UTAH

WHAT WE BELIEVE

RICHARD:

To put it bluntly, we believe that turning our hearts toward our families and re-enshrining family as the crux of our culture is the only alternative to society's demise. Although this may sound extreme, it is not. Let me explain.

Unless our *hearts* (feelings, attention, priorities) are turned toward and centered more on families (marriage, children, commitments), we will continue to face the individual and societal *curse* of the expanding social problems that are crushing America and the world. Centering on the young, and ranging from teen pregnancy to drugs and alcohol and from crime to violence and abuse, this curse produces poverty and isolation, bloats our welfare and justice systems, and imposes oppressive taxes to pay for ineffective, finger-in-the-dike government "solutions."

Social problems are never adequately solved by social programs.

The burgeoning problems of today are a direct result of the deterioration of families. The vacuum created by disappearing families creates space for everything from gangs to excess government, which flourish within the hole the lack of family leaves behind. Our public and private sectors—from local officials and public education to big business and electronic media, the very groups which should be supporting, supplementing, and protecting families—instead seem to be trying either to substitute for them or to undermine them. Our newest, largest institutions, from giant corporations to information and entertainment industries, are creating misplaced loyalties and false paradigms that are destroying the oldest, smallest institution of family. And more and more parents, hot in pursuit of professional and financial success, can find neither the time nor the inclination to put family first.

Social problems and declining birth rates today threaten the demise of America and the West as much as economic problems and too many children threaten developing countries around the globe. So great are these curses, and so turned away are our hearts, that as we chug deeper into the twenty-first century, there is serious question about continuing economic progress and about whether society as we know it will survive.

Survive. Demise. These are extreme and desperate words—words we don't typically use when talking about America and other developed countries. But Alexis de Tocqueville, writing about America in the 1830s, predicted our eventual destruction from within.

The shiny surface of America is pockmarked by poverty, riddled by racism, gouged by gangs and guns. The greatest, richest land paradoxically contains some of the most dangerous and terrifying places on the planet, places where life is cheap and joy is scarce—more so than anywhere in the third world. Europe and developed Asia face similar problems, some more severe and some less than in the US.

The sickness is spreading from cities through suburbs (where there is supposed stability), and is incredibly expensive, seemingly incurable, unfixable by courts or welfare, and it is getting bigger every day. We benignly call the frightening statistics "social problems," but there is a better word. It is the word used in the prophecy from the last page of the Bible's Old Testament— the one that says that unless we turn our hearts to our families, the whole earth will be *cursed.*

The challenges that our culture faces are preventable and curable only if *family*, the smallest of organizations, is revived and supported. Family is the cornerstone and crux of all stable societies.

Individual families may never function exactly as we wish, but "the family" has functioned for millennia as the basic unit for caring for those too young or too old to care for themselves, for replacing and replenishing humanity, and for raising and rearing children by teaching and training them and integrating them into the broader society.

There is really no other entity that can take on these functions, and without them, our world is not sustainable.

Individual lives can teeter for quite a while on the edge, bereft of the ties of family and the anchor of faith and values. A whole society can do the same thing. But in order to keep from falling into the abyss, the family needs to be revalued. *Re·valu·ing* has a triple meaning:

1. Recognizing the transcending societal value of families,
2. Personally reprioritizing our families, and
3. Putting values back into our families.

Values are best defined as what matters, what counts, and what we care about—what's right, what's important, what's real. Values are more than philosophy or a pleasant placebo of belief. They are practical, practiced, personal principles. And family values (and family value) are anything but a right-wing conspiracy and a political football. They are the truest and most time-tested way to live, the single constant requirement of a safe and stable society, and the key underpinning of real happiness.

Most people know, intuitively and instinctively, what real values are and what family values are. The goal of this book is to help *rekindle* those values inside individual parents, and then in the broader culture, thus turning our hearts, protecting our families, and saving our world.

Part I is about why and how, on many levels, hearts have turned away from family. Part II is about how we can turn them back.

You may find Part I depressing, so before you start, let us offer a compensating hopeful thought: After more than three decades of writing and speaking to widely diverse people around the globe about their marriages, their children, their life-balance, and their family relationships, we continue to find wide-spread agreement among parents concerning both the dreams and the worries they have for their children and the values they want to teach them. We also find remarkably similar aspirations among most people for their partnerships and marriages. As speakers, we may have one of the few topics where our fundamental message does not need to be significantly adjusted according to what country or part of the world we happen to be visiting.

So perhaps the bottom-line conviction of this book is that humans, often divided and factionalized so radically by their politics, their religion, and their economic status, can come together on something that supersedes all these other differences—namely, their common desire to preserve their family ties and maximize their children's chances for happiness.

Instead of the ever deeper divides of ideology and competing cultures, our hope is for a movement toward a paradigm in which the strongest criteria for evaluating or judging most everything—a decision, a policy, a doctrine, a legislative bill, a movie, a technology, a business plan, a humanitarian initiative, an educational goal, a philosophy, a life-plan—is *"How does it affect families and children?"*

Thanks for reading, and please share your comments and feedback with us at www.The-Turning.com.

—RME, PARK CITY, UTAH

PART ONE

TURNING
AWAY

How and why are hearts and minds moving away

from the natural family?

CHAPTER ONE

THE CRUX

Everything Starts with Family, and

Everything Ends without Family

---

crux *noun* \ˈkrəks, ˈkrüks\

1. the main or central feature
2. a puzzling or difficult problem
3. an essential point requiring resolution or resolving an outcome

The family is the crux of society.

The decline of family is the crux that is re-shaping our world—often in negative directions.

Re-valu-ing the family is the crux of reviving both the micro of individual happiness and the macro of societal order and safety.

IT'S ALL ABOUT FAMILY

We are all born into family. And we hope that family will surround us when we exit this world. In between, family provides us with our greatest joys and deepest sorrows. Family has always been our main reference point and the basis for much of our terminology and metaphor.

- In theology, God is *father* and we are *children*.
- In history, the past is best understood and connected through extended *families*.
- In economics, markets and enterprise are driven by *family* needs, attitudes, and perceptions.
- In education, *parents* are the most influential teachers, and home environment is the most powerful factor in school success.
- In sociology and anthropology, we conclude that society doesn't form families; *families* form society.
- In politics, all issues reduce down to how public policy affects private *family*.
- In public opinion polls, we reveal that *family* commitments exceed all other commitments.
- In ethics or morality, *family* relationships teach the highest forms of selfless and empathetic values. Lack of those committed relationships promotes selfish and antisocial behavior.
- In media, the things that touch us most deeply or offend us most dramatically generally involve *family*.
- In nature, everything that grows is in a *family*, and some cultures living closest to nature speak of "mother earth" and "father sky."

Our similes, our semantics, and our symbols all use family as our frame of reference. Yet less than two decades into the third millennia, the family is our most threatened institution, and the fear, which we should all feel, is that if the family goes down, it will take *everything* else with it.

> *We were sitting in a small café in San Salvador, having lunch with a father of three who had introduced us the night before when we spoke to a group of parents and teachers about teaching values to children. "You know," he said, "I try so hard to be a good parent, but it almost seems like there is a sinister conspiracy working against me. How do I compete with the peer group, the Internet, the media? What is happening to families today, and can they even survive?"*

Defining "Family"

Before we can look objectively and constructively at what is happening to the family and where the family is going, we must have a clear understanding of what a family is.

Trying to define "family" can be a tricky proposition. It's a widely—and politically—used word and can mean different things to different people. We feel that the most useful approach, at least for our purposes in this book, is to define the family in terms of its essential and indispensable *functions* within society. Indeed, families have historically played at least seven critical societal *roles* that no other group or institution can fully or adequately perform.

1. The role of *procreation* (replenishing the population).
2. The role of *roles*. (Boys need a role model for becoming a man, and girls need a role model for becoming a woman.)
3. The role of *nurturing* (facilitating children's emotional growth and helping them develop into responsible adults).
4. The role of providing a lasting *identity*, something permanent

in our lives as everything else (employment, residences, and so on) changes.

5. The role of instilling *values*. (Other institutions may help, but the buck stops with the family wherein values are applied as well as taught.)

6. The role of offering love and *fulfillment* to individuals at a level beyond what is obtainable elsewhere. (Children should receive unconditional love within families, and parents are refined and completed as persons through the selfless love they give to their children.)

7. The role of *caring* for the elderly (ideally in a personal or direct manner, but if not, at least in connection with institutional care).

Two things are absolutely clear. First, society cannot survive, let alone prosper, without these seven functions. Second, no entity other than family can perform the full list of roles as well or as efficiently.

These seven roles or functions can also be thought of as the core *purposes* of family and, to some degree, as the measurements of a family's success. Parents who accomplish these seven things derive a satisfaction that is available nowhere else. By fostering and supporting these aspects of family life, they make an incomparable contribution to society.

The chart below gives some examples of what can happen if these functions are not fulfilled by families:

FAMILY FUNCTIONS	EXAMPLES OF EROSION	WHAT HAPPENS WHEN LARGER INSTITUTIONS TRY TO ASSUME THIS FUNCTION
Procreation	• Intentional "no child families"	• "Brave new world" scenarios
Roles	• Gay marriages	• Gender confusion, lack of identity
Nurturing	• Two or more careers • Excessive day care	• Impersonal, institutionalized care
Identity	• No permanence • No traditions	• Corporate identity; Commune identity (Marx model) • Gang identity
Values	• Poor parental examples • Amorality or conditional morality	• Confusion and destructive debates over "whose values"
Fulfillment	• Prioritizing career over families • Momentary pleasure rather than lasting joy	• Neither parents nor children finding peace and satisfaction in family
Elder Care	• Growing government welfare	• Loneliness, alienation, dissolution of family ties and loss of family tradition, narrative, and history

Four Essential Elements

In order to meet the last six of the above functions (and in an ideal world, the first one would not happen without the other six) families need, within them, four essential *elements*:

1. Love
2. Commitment
3. Time
4. Communication

It is difficult to imagine a family succeeding over time (or even staying together very long) without at least a basic level of each of these four elements.

When families lack any of the four essential elements, or when they fail to provide any of the seven critical roles or purposes, we always lose—both individually and societally. When larger institutions—from schools to businesses to government—try to assume these seven functions or provide these four elements, it alters the way we experience one another, diminishes relationships, and undermines human happiness.

ESSENTIAL ELEMENTS OF FAMILY	DETERIORATION	WHAT HAPPENS WHEN LARGER INSTITUTIONS TAKE OVER
Love	• Diluted by busyness and other priorities • Infidelity: love confused with lust	• Love of material possessions or position rather than love of people

Commitment	• Climbing divorce rates • Alternative cohabitation models	• Loyalty to corporate culture replacing family commitment
Time	• Family gets less and less • Work gets more and more	• Longer work hours and more time-consuming diversions
Communication	• More with machines, less with people • A widening "generation gap"	• "Communication" becomes information and data exchange rather than centering on feelings

Larger institutions simply do not work like families. *Love, commitment, time,* and *communication* are all defined differently in the corporate or government culture than they are in the family culture. As these larger entities grow, and as they increasingly dominate our lives, our families suffer.

As former Secretary of Education William Bennett put it, "The original and best Department of Health, Education, and Welfare . . . is the family."[1]

WORLD VIEWS

Some see the world geographically—continents and countries, latitude and locations. Others see it politically—groups and governments, ideas and ideologies. Still others see it economically—haves and have nots, producers and consumers.

We see the world concentrically: at the center is the most personal and important aspect of life (the bull's-eye of family), and the concentric rings around the family represent the voluntary, private, and public sectors.

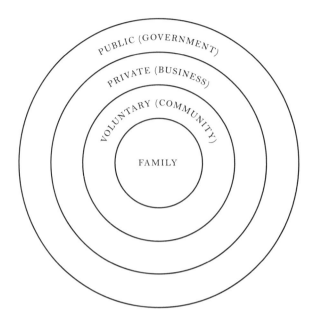

The family is the nucleus, like the center of an atom or the core of a tree, making everything else possible, providing the building blocks of procreation and nurturing from which all else is formed. In reality, the individual household is the basic unit, not only of society, but also of our markets and all of our larger institutions. The present and future well-being of all institutions—from corporations to schools and from communities to governments—relies on the strength of our families. All macro entities and institutions in the private, public, and voluntary sectors ultimately depend on the basic unit of families and thus should strongly support, financially and otherwise, well-conceived efforts to preserve and strengthen families and micro solutions.

The voluntary or community sector or "second ring" includes neighborhoods, churches, clubs, and all other elective elements that encompass and link families. The private or business sector or "third ring" is the economy—the goods and services and enterprises that both sustain us and employ us. The public "fourth ring" is government on all levels—all that our taxes pay for.

In an ideal society, the outer three rings protect, support, and supplement the core of families. Unfortunately, in our current society, they squeeze it, supplant and substitute for it, and sometimes undermine and destroy it.

Despite the pressures on families, we believe that if parents truly prioritize their children and their homes, families will be saved. And if every public policy, every business decision, and every community direction is set with parents and children in mind, families will improve and strengthen, and with them, the world.

Families, thought of as parent(s), child(ren), and sometimes grandparent(s) living in one household, are both the basic unit and the micro solution. When sound principles are not practiced and problems are not solved at this most basic level, they grow more complex and more expensive to understand and to solve. In our bull's-eye model, the second ring around the family should be the neighborhood, the church, and the school, which supports and supplements the family, and when necessary, substitutes for it. The third ring of the societal target is the whole private sector, from business to media, which should be ever conscious of the effects its actions and policies, its programming and promotions have on families. We should try to limit and contain government into the thin safety net of the outer fourth ring of the target.

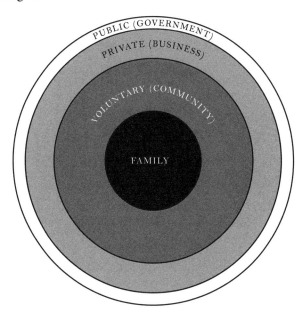

Once problems spill over past these inner rings and drip into the fourth ring of government, into the welfare and justice and juvenile systems, they become impossibly expensive and expensively impossible to solve.

Who Can Make a Difference— Why and How

When our kids were small, we fell into a silly little family tradition on my October birthday. We would rake up big piles of bright, dry autumn leaves and jump in them, stuff them down each other's backs, and bury ourselves in them.

I thought the ritual would die as the kids got older, but instead, it just got bigger—we had to go to the park where there were larger trees and more leaves, and then we had to jump out of the trees into the leaf piles.

One birthday came when, for the first time, our oldest son and our oldest daughter were gone—he to his first year of college and she to work as a volunteer in the poor areas and orphanages of Bulgaria. I was missing them on my birthday until the mailman came with what I thought were simply two birthday cards.

But when I opened the first, from my daughter, a leaf fell out. On it was a post-it note that said,

"Dear Dad,

Happy birthday. This is a Bulgarian leaf, and the orphans helped me honor your tradition. Don't forget, even though I'm far away, I'm still part of our family!"

Through my tears, I opened the second envelope, and out fell another leaf—no note on this one because it was from our son. I could imagine him in his dorm room thinking, I'll just send Dad a leaf, and he'll know what it means.

We all come from families. None of them are perfect, all have problems, and some seem to hardly exist at all. But families are what tie us to those who went before and to the rest of humanity. They give us our identity, and it is an identity that we can build on and improve before we pass it on to our own children.

The first objective of this book is not just to teach us *how* to reprioritize our families—but also to remind us and help us fully understand *why* we should.

A parent who has contemplated and understood (and felt) the vast importance of family relationships will find his or her own ways to improve them—and there will be different ways for different people. The goal of understanding the "whys" is to motivate parents and grandparents to reprioritize, even re-enshrine, their families; to help their children—and themselves—be more aware of and then escape the quicksand of the world's false paradigms and priorities.

> *The first objective of this book is not just to teach us how to reprioritize our families—but also to remind us and help us fully understand why we should.*

But we hope to do even more than that. This book hopes to contribute to a movement, a banner under which people who care about values, who live for their families, who are outraged by forces trying to destroy both—can unite, can support each other, and can reach out to the majority who have been conned into thinking that those who value families are a minority.

As mentioned in the introduction, de Tocqueville said, "If America is ever destroyed, *it will be destroyed from within.*" It is a forecast that can be applied to the whole developed world. The warning of this book is simple and frightening but by no means new: America's most basic institution, the family, is breaking down. This breakdown is the direct cause of steep increases in social problems: crime, violence, gangs, teen pregnancy, drugs, poverty, spouse abuse, child abuse, suicide, depression, homelessness, bankruptcies, latchkey kids, juvenile delinquency, school dropouts, declining test scores, and pretty much every other "curse" you can name.

If you doubt that thesis—if you're unconvinced that families in most of the developed world are breaking down as never before and that our burgeoning social problems are the direct result—we will seek to *convince* you of the cause and the effect and the connections between them.

If you already believe the thesis (or once you do), we will try to explain *why* it is happening and expose the "culprits" of misdirected larger institutions and commonly accepted false paradigms. When we understand what is happening and know who and what to blame, we can become part of the solution. Once we grasp *why* things are the way they are and *why* it is critical that we change, we will each find our individual ways to do so.

This world's current generations—our generations—parents and grandparents who are now raising children, running companies, creating media, making laws, teaching, writing, voting, consuming—essentially the adults of this current world—may be this world's last chance. If we continue to ignore (or accept temporary solutions for) the symptoms, and if we fail to understand or combat the cause, the world we have known will not exist for our children. But if we recognize and restore priorities of families and values, we can rescue our own happiness, even as we turn aside the forces that would destroy our children's future.

Besides parents, we are writing and appealing to anyone who has any influence in the public (government), private (business), voluntary (community), and individual (personal/family) sectors.

Parents have more influence over their children's destiny than anything or anyone else. And parents, collectively, have more influence over our culture's destiny than anything or anyone else. Thus, the center of this book's target is parents.

Our second most-hoped-for "hit" is those with influence in the voluntary and community sector—the teachers and trainers, coaches and counselors, ministers and mentors of the religious, recreational, social, cultural, and educational institutions that make up our neighborhoods. Next to home and parents, these community institutions and their leaders can do the most to turn the hearts and end the curse.

Besides parents, we are writing and appealing to anyone who has any influence in the public (government), private (business), voluntary (community), and individual (personal/ family) sectors.

To some extent at least, we also hope to reach business leaders and owners, especially those who have realized, or will through reading this book, that the strength and stability of their employees' families *is* the strength and future of their business—that when employees must choose between loyalty to work or loyalty to family, both sides lose.

Ideally, we would like to reach the policy makers at all levels of government whose unenlightened laws and interpretations can sabotage and substitute for family rather than support and supplement the family.

Coalitions and Movements

Toward the end of the book, we will recommend some coalition building that may assist the larger institutions of our society to become more effective in strengthening the most basic institution of the family. The coalition-building approach hearkens back to days when neighborhoods gathered in the village church or the town hall or the school auditorium to tackle problems, to teach sound principles, and to assist families in need. Today's gathering place may often be online, in social media, at the water cooler in the office, in the classroom, or within audiences of the media, but the solidarity and urgency and unity of purpose should be no different and no less than the proverbial town hall.

These coalitions can develop task forces and corporate support and fund-raising and even a public relations and image-building publicity arm that lets parents and families everywhere know that they are important and that their hope to raise responsible kids and to escape the misdirection, violence, amorality, and entitlement of the broader society is not the exception but the norm . . . and that help is on the way!

In family life, love is the oil that eases
friction, the cement that binds
closer together, and the music that
brings harmony.

—FRIEDRICH NIETZSCHE

CHAPTER TWO

THE CRISIS

How the Failure of

Families Fails Us All

cri·sis *noun* \ˈkrī-səs\

1. a difficult or dangerous situation that needs serious attention

2. a critical or decisive point or situation, a turning point, as in a story where a conflict reaches its highest tension and must be resolved

Families are at a tipping point, which is the edge of crisis.

The symptoms range from poverty to addiction, but the systemic illness is broken families.

Family, the core and the crux of all society, is in an unprecedented crisis that will destroy this world unless we can discover and turn toward a cure.

THE PERIL OF FAILING TO
TURN OUR HEARTS

We were the keynote speakers at a conference in Singapore where the government has a Ministry of Social and Family Development. We were introduced by the Speaker of the National Parliament who talked about how critical strong families are to a stable society. The audience was made up Buddhists, Muslims, Hindus, and Christians in roughly equal parts, but we began by quoting from the Old Testament—the passage that inspired the theme and title of this book.

The sharpest, most foreboding language in all of scripture comes in the Old Testament verse mentioned earlier, and it refers to what will happen to this whole earth if families fail. Prophesying of our time, the prophet Malachi warned that if families lose their cohesion— if the hearts of parents are not turned to their children and the hearts of children to parents, God will *"smite the earth with a curse."*

Whether you believe in scripture or in statistics, the signs and the evidence are ominous. Families, as the world has known them for millennia, are disappearing. Our hearts are turning elsewhere.

In the New Testament, the same strong language recurs . . . of *turning the hearts of fathers to children* (Luke 1:17). Still other scripture admonishes that our hearts must be with our families (Quran 55:82) and warns that if the hearts of parents are not turned to their children and the hearts of children to their parents *"the whole earth will be utterly wasted"* (Doctrine and Covenants 2:3). Buddhist and Hindu teachings also talk about turning our hearts to our families.

Whether you believe in scripture or in statistics, the signs and the evidence are ominous. Families, as the world has known them for millennia, are disappearing. Our hearts are turning elsewhere.

Tipping Points

In the last decade, the family (the core institution and cornerstone of our society) has suffered changes that have repercussions far beyond an individual family ending in divorce or partners choosing cohabitation instead of marriage. There is a critical mass of these negative changes in families across the United States and around the world that is undermining not only culture, but our economy and our society as a whole. Unless we can reverse these trends, we lose the powerful, positive influence that families have on the world.

Sometimes problems reach a kind of critical mass where majorities shift—when something that had tilted one way flips past vertical and begins to tilt in the opposite direction. Consider ten ratios that have changed so dramatically in the last decade that the assumptions and "norms" of centuries no longer hold. These "tipping points," all of which have arrived in just the past few years, suggest that the future of our oldest and most basic institution is truly in doubt:

1. We are very close to the point where there will be more US adults who are single than who are married. In 2011, for the first time, fewer than 50 percent of US households were made up of married couples, and only one-quarter of twenty- to twenty-nine-year-olds are married compared with 70 percent in 1960.[1]

2. In several Western countries, very nearly as many children are now born out of wedlock as in.[2]

3. More US marriages now end in divorce than stay together.[3]

4. In many major world cities, there are now more households that are occupied by one single individual than households inhabited by any kind of family.[4]

5. In England, a majority of women of childbearing age say they would rather buy a house than have a child, and one-third say they do not ever want children. In some Asian countries, there are now more women between twenty and forty who say they do not want children than who say they do.[5]

6. In the United States and Europe, among couples that move in together, far more now choose cohabitation than marriage.[6]

7. More than half of Hispanic children in the United States are now raised in fatherless homes. (Among African-American families, seven in ten kids are raised without a dad.)[7]

8. Throughout the world, higher percentages now seem to believe that "the family should support the career" than believe that "the career should support the family."[8]

9. Women now constitute more than half the American workforce, and women are now the primary breadwinners in 40 percent of families. The labor force participation for women aged twenty-five to fifty-four has increased from 37 to 75 percent between 1950 and 2010. [9]

10. In 2014, for the first time, more than one-half of the nations on the planet (116 of the earth's 224 recognized sovereign states and countries) have birthrates below the replacement rate of 2.1 children per woman and now must either encourage more births or count on in-migration to maintain their work forces.[10]

The frightening thing about these tipping points is how fast they are coming upon us. As the Pew Research Center has observed, "Social institutions that have been around for thousands of years generally change slowly, when they change at all, but that's not the way things have been playing out with marriage and family since the middle of the twentieth century. Some scholars argue that, in the past five decades, the basic architecture of these age-old institutions has changed as rapidly as at any time in human history."[11]

The bottom line is that the "silent majority" is quickly becoming a silent minority—partly *because* we are silent! Those who still believe in natural or traditional marriage and family, and those who recognize the crisis and the curse that comes without them, need to make some noise about it and need to do something about it.

> *The bottom line is that the "silent majority" is quickly becoming a silent minority— partly because we are silent!*

THE BASIC FUNDAMENTALS

Is there anything more fundamental than where our hearts are turned?

Is there any unit more basic than the family?

Is there any macro aspect of our world of which the family is not the essential micro?

Is there any large institution that is not made up of and dependent on the most basic institution? Our economy? Our culture? Our political infrastructure? Our whole society? Don't they all ultimately depend, for their survival on households, on families?

Is it any wonder that wrong-turned hearts could dam our happiness and "curse" or "waste" our world?

CRISIS

Western society as we know it is not sustainable for very long within the ever more threatening construct of increasing divorce, cohabitation without marriage, fatherless homes, births to single women, rising abortions, and falling birth rates. Each of these trends, even by itself, threatens the very roots of our society.

Statistics abound showing the negative impact of divorce on childhood socioeconomic status and eventual wealth attainment; on quality of parent-child relationships; and on children's academic achievement, education attainment, communication skills, social connections, perceived social support from others, and anxiety in personal relationships. In short, nearly everything takes a hit.

Cohabitation, Fatherless Homes, Fertility Rate, and Childless by Choice

In virtually all developed countries, cohabitation, gay marriage, and intentional single parenthood are expanding rapidly as traditional marriages and birthrates decline.[12]

Cohabitation without marriage produces disastrous statistical results. Cohabiting relationships tend to be fragile and relatively short in duration; less than half of cohabiting relationships last five or more years, and the divorce rates of women who cohabit are nearly 80 percent higher than those who do not. And for low income and low education groups, cohabitating unions are less likely to end in marriage than in dissolution.[13]

Long-term, committed marriage is something that many young people have never seen.

The major problem with cohabitation is that it is a tentative arrangement that lacks stability; no one can depend upon the relationship—not the partners, not the children, not the community, not the society. Yet in Europe, eight in ten people say they approve of unmarried cohabitation. In Scandinavia, 82 percent of firstborn children are born outside marriage.[14] Long-term, committed marriage is something that many young people have never seen.

At Trader Joe's one day, a cute, chatty, check-out girl in her early twenties asked me, while she was ringing up my groceries, if I was going to do anything fun that night. Richard and I were celebrating our wedding anniversary by going out to dinner and a concert and, since she asked, I shared that with her.

"How many years?" she asked.

When I replied "Forty-five" she opened her mouth and looked totally astonished.

"Did you mean to be married that long?" she asked in total amazement. I assured her that when I got married I was in for the long haul. Totally committed! She was incredulous.

I realized again that many in her generation assume that when you enter into a relationship, it is on a casual, trial basis. If it doesn't work out, no big deal; just go on to something different, especially if there are no children involved. She had no idea she was part of a crisis!

For children growing up without both parents, the trends are equally dramatic. In the United States, the proportion of children being raised by a single parent has more than doubled in the last four decades, and a record 40 percent of all households with children under the age of eighteen now include mothers who are either the sole or primary source of income for the family. Women make up almost half (47 percent) of the US labor force today, and the employment rate of married mothers with children has increased from 37 percent in 1968 to 65 percent in 2011. Adolescents raised in intact, married homes are significantly more likely to succeed educationally and financially. The benefits are greatest for less-privileged homes—that is, where their mother did not have a college degree. Men and women who hail from intact families are about 40 percent less likely to father or bear a child outside of wedlock.[15]

While we have enormous admiration for single parents, many of whom are true heroes, there is no question that children who grow up in single-parent and fatherless homes have a much greater risk of major challenges in life than those who grow up with a father at home. Again, the statistics are alarming: Young men who grow up in homes without fathers are twice as likely to end up in jail as those who come from two-parent families. 71 percent of all high school dropouts, 85 percent of all children that exhibit behavioral disorders, 70 percent of juveniles in state-operated institutions, and 63 percent of youth suicides are from fatherless homes. Across the board, children raised by a single parent are at greater risk.[16]

Los Angeles Times columnist Kay S. Hymowitz, writing about a recent study by the Brookings Institution that tracked five thousand urban, primarily minority children, says:

> What these kids lack most of all is stable families. . . . Children living with single mothers have more behavioral and academic problems, which worsen with each new relationship and breakup. . . . the arrival of a new partner is "salt in their wounds." Dads visit less . . . and give less financial support "when a new man is in the house." . . . Worst of all, children growing up with a boyfriend or stepdad in the house are at greater risk of abuse. These are realities that aid programs, jobs, or money can't fix.[17]

And then there is the compounding problem of demographics. The US population (and that of most developed countries) is aging at the same time the fertility rate is dropping. This drags down (some would say "dooms") the global economy. As fertility rates remain below replacement levels, there are fewer children and more seniors as a percentage of the population.

Japan is an extreme example because with one of the lowest fertility rates in the world, it also has one of the longest longevity rates. Japanese culture expects women to stay home with babies, but employers often refuse to allow this, and well-educated women feel that having a child forces them to give up their careers, their independence, and the use of their educational degrees—and most are just not willing to do it. The low birth rate and high longevity rate is creating a perfect storm. As Sarah Eberspacher wrote in a 2014 story in *The Week*, "By 2060, the government estimates, there will be just 87 million people in Japan; nearly half of them will be over sixty-five. Without a dramatic change in either the birthrate or its restrictive immigration policies, Japan simply won't have enough workers to support its retirees, and will enter a demographic death spiral. Yet the babies aren't coming."[18]

Another penalty of falling birthrates throughout the developed world is that entrepreneurialism—which is highly concentrated among young people—declines, causing societies to lose their dynamism culturally, economically, and technologically.

> *On recent trips to Beijing and Shanghai, we have been intrigued with the common sight of six adults—two parents and four grand-parents—indulgently hovering over one child as though the boy were a little king. Indeed, the name given to the single children by the press is "Little Emperor." The kids are spoiled and entitled, but the bigger disaster is that the workforce is not and cannot be sustained with the One-Child policy that has been in effect since 1979. It is in contrast to the previous China policy of institutionalizing children in massive commune kindergartens where they were given no attention at all and perceived as spokes in a wheel.*
>
> *Now, of course, like many parts of the world, the Chinese government is incentivizing parents, particularly well-educated parents, to have a second or even a third child. But the family culture has been undermined, perhaps irreparably.*

The trend away from families is now going even beyond divorce and cohabitation and few or no children—the ultimate extension of the deterioration is the elimination not only of families but also of all forms of commitment and even of sharing a home. In Stockholm today, 60 percent of the households or places of domicile are now occupied by a single resident. Several other European cities have similar figures.[19]

The whole sequence begins to look like a death spiral for families: First, the divorce rates increase, then fewer get married at all and more cohabitate, and then, finally, people just live alone and give up on any form of living with anyone else.

Basic Assumptions Now Under Fire

A generation ago, no one would have questioned the premise that the family is the basic unit of society. Today, it is questioned from many sides. In his ominously titled, landmark work *The Rise of Post Familialism: Humanity's Future*, demographer Joel Kotkin says, "Today, in the high-income world and even in some developing countries, there is a shift to a new social model. Increasingly, family no longer serves as the central, organizing feature of society . . . [and] as Austrian demographer Wolfgang Lutz has pointed out, the shift to an increasingly childless society creates 'self-reinforcing mechanisms' that make childlessness, singleness, or one-child families increasingly prominent."

Kotkin goes on to point out the ramifications of this shift, some of them political: "A society that is increasingly single and childless is likely to be more concerned with serving current needs than addressing the future-oriented requirements of children. Since older people vote more than younger ones, and children have no say at all, political power could shift toward non-childbearing people."[20]

David Brooks, of the *New York Times*, adds, "In a 2011 survey, a majority of Taiwanese women under fifty said they did not want children. Fertility rates in Brazil have dropped from 4.3 babies per woman thirty-five years ago to 1.9 babies today. These are all stunningly fast cultural and demographic shifts. The world is moving in the same basic direction, from societies oriented around the two-parent family to cafeteria societies with many options."[21]

Ryan Streeter, a policy analyst, puts it this way "Family—getting married, and then having kids—used to be woven together with other threads of the American Dream. Not so anymore."[22]

It is this societal shift that should motivate right-thinking people everywhere to fight even harder to re-enshrine marriage and to promote the "natural family" way of life. Even for those who do not equate marriage with morality, there are adequate economic and emotional reasons to fight hard against continuing family decline. Perhaps the most obvious of these is the simple fact that societies with declining birthrates that fail to adequately replace one generation with another inevitably face a skewed "dependency ratio" where ever fewer active workers support more and more retirees. The result is an inverted pyramid of aging people supported by a dwindling number of younger people.

Governments that once worried about population control are now panicked by their less-than-replacement birthrates, and countries ranging from Russia to France to Singapore now offer cash premiums for babies, even bonuses that jump substantially upward for the third and fourth child.

The whole sequence begins to look like a death spiral for families: First, the divorce rates increase, then fewer get married at all and more cohabitate, and then, finally, people just live alone and give up on any form of living with anyone else.

In the United States, while people over sixty-five represented 9 percent of the total population in 1960, it is 16 percent today and will reach 25 percent in 2030, corresponding with a steep decline in the number of younger workers. And people over sixty-five receive seven times more in federal spending than children under eighteen.[23]

Anyone hoping for a strong economy must pay attention to studies which consistently show that married adults with children do better in terms of their incomes, their savings, and their preparation for retirement than their single counterparts. After all, the term *economics* is taken from the Greek *oikos* for "home," and *nomia* for "management." As economist Nick Schulz says in his aptly titled *Home Economics*, "The collapse of the intact family is one of the most significant economic facts of our time."[24]

The bottom line is that the economic numbers add up much better in a society where marriage and families are strong than in those where they are not. Declining birthrates, marriage rates, and increasing singlehood and childlessness are ominous signs.

The decline, demise, and disappearance of functioning families is, simply put, the biggest crisis facing the developed world today.

And if the economic arguments aren't enough, the emotional statistics ought to be.

The National Marriage Project from the University of Virginia offers evidence that married people, with or without children, have significantly less depression than singles; and 57 percent of married women with children felt their life had an important purpose, while only 40 percent of women without children felt the same.

The decline, demise, and disappearance of functioning families is, simply put, the biggest crisis facing the developed world today.

Perhaps the greatest social service that can be rendered by anybody to this country and to mankind is to bring up a family.

—GEORGE BERNARD SHAW

CHAPTER THREE

THE CURSE

"Social Problems"

That Are Crushing Society

---

curse *noun* \ˈkərs\

   1. evil or misfortune that comes as if in response to deeds
      or as retribution

*The malignancy and terror of what we benignly call "social
problems" is torturing individuals and blackmailing society.
It is an economic, political, moral, and personal curse—truly
a scourge. And it comes in response to wrong-turned hearts.*

GOING DOWNHILL FAST

We were doing a seminar with a large group of teachers and parents
from several elementary and secondary schools in Mexico City, and
in the pre-conference briefing session, the teachers were telling us
how dramatically the seriousness and consequence of student prob-
lems had increased in recent years. One teacher said, in essence,
"Too many of our students can rap but can't read. Too many know
everything about drugs but can't pass chemistry. Too many have sex
but have no love."

This experience reminded us of a comparison we made in one of our earlier books. A generation ago, a survey revealed the seven biggest problems in one high school to be:

1. Talking out of turn
2. Chewing gum
3. Being disruptive, making noise
4. Cutting in line
5. Running in the halls
6. Dress code violations
7. Littering

A more recent survey at the same school provided stark contrast. The seven biggest problems were:

1. Alcohol abuse
2. Drug abuse
3. Robbery
4. Teen pregnancy

5. Assault

6. Rape

7. Suicide

Social problems have placed much of the developed world on the literal brink of demise. And as mentioned earlier, "social problems" is far too tame a word. It's too academic, too theoretical, too political to encompass what has come to pass in much of the world today. What we need is a word that suggests how dramatic and deep the dangers are. We don't have to look far. The scriptural prophecy of Malachi has already given it to us. What is happening in our homes, our schools, and our streets is a curse—a freedom-threatening, economy-threatening, life-threatening curse.

A Nation at Risk

In the 1980s, two personal acquaintances of ours, Education Secretary Terrell Bell and University President David Gardner, led a task force that produced a landmark document called "A Nation at Risk." The study pointed out the serious declines in American public education and made disturbing connections between those declines and America's decreasing ability to compete and prosper in the global economy. Many of the education reforms that we are currently trying and struggling with were catalyzed by the study and its dire conclusions.

But our educational deficiencies do not threaten the very existence of our society. Our social problems do!

The mushrooming violence, addictions, absence of personal responsibility, lawlessness, and poverty across the globe put most cultures of our current world in jeopardy. In the United States, because of our social problems, we are, more than at any time in our more than two hundred years, a nation at risk.

In fact, our much-discussed declining educational achievement is the direct result of the social and family problems that beset us.

In his book *How Children Succeed*, Paul Tough tells the compelling story of Fenger High School, a school in Chicago's south side that had been in crisis for twenty years in a neighborhood riddled with poverty, unemployment, crime, gangs, and drug abuse. The high school had a record of dismally low test scores, discipline problems, and high drop-out rates.

Starting in 1995, some of the most celebrated educational leaders in the country tackled the enormous problems at Fenger High School, thinking that they could solve the problem with better administrators, professional coaching for teachers, an almost completely new teaching staff, well-financed technology, and science labs with millions of dollars being spent on the latest state-of-the art equipment. But despite all of the expense and effort, nothing much changed—in fact, violence escalated. Apparently, the lack of good teachers, equipment, and technology had not been the problem.

Rather, says Tough, it was "a deeper set of problems, born out of students' troubled and often traumatic home lives."[1] The bottom line seemed to be that until they could find a way to change the student's family and neighborhood situation, added help from schools or teachers or technology would do little good.

Part of the problem (and part of the reason that most of us don't fully realize the risk) is that there is such a terrifying amount of economic and social diversity in today's world. Those who live in safe zip codes don't realize what is going on in dangerous ones. We are less and less integrated in today's developed countries—the well-off don't cross paths with the less well-off. In many of the world's most prosperous countries are pockets

Those who live in safe zip codes don't realize what is going on in dangerous ones. We are less and less integrated in today's developed countries—the well-off don't cross paths with the less well-off.

of the planet's most dangerous and devastated neighborhoods. The gap between rich and poor continues to widen. The majesty of macro prosperity is matched by the mercilessness of our micro poverty. Often, those who are most prosperous and most safe are more aware of overseas violence and Third World poverty than they are of the violence and poverty that exist closer to home, sometimes just blocks away from their offices.

The anger that seethes in its most violent forms in the jobless hopelessness of inner cities and in some whole regions of the world is just a deeper concentration of the same frustrations, dangers, and mushrooming social problems that spread throughout suburbia and cross over all socioeconomic divisions.

And in the parts of our demography that are prospering, parents are giving their children entitlement attitudes that rob them of initiative and motivation and ensures that they will become part of the problem rather than part of the solution.

We are a nation at risk—a world at risk. Everything that has made western societies great (and *safe* and *prosperous*) is at risk. *All* of us are at risk because the artificial membranes that now separate rich and poor, safe and violent, stable and volatile are stretched thin and cannot, on our present course, hold together for very long.

Startling Statistics

Numbers and trends can be presented as proof of both the tragic seriousness of our symptoms and the steepness of their recent increase. For our purposes, even a few statistics from half a dozen sample categories are enough to underscore the huge pain and overwhelming danger—particularly to those who are young.

VIOLENCE[2]

- 125 school shootings occurred between 2006 and 2012 in the United States alone. From 2013 to March 8, 2014, fifty-seven more US school shootings have occurred.

- In 2008, 2,947 children and teens died from guns in the United States, and 2,793 died in 2009, for a total of 5,740—that's one child or teen every three hours, eight every day, fifty-five every week for two years.

- In 2011, more than 700,000 young people in the United States, aged ten to twenty-four years, were treated in emergency departments for nonfatal injuries sustained from assaults.

- Almost sixteen million US teens have witnessed some form of violent assault.

TEEN PREGNANCY/PROMISCUITY[3]

- 47 percent of high school students in the United States report having had sexual intercourse.

- About sixteen million girls aged fifteen to nineteen years and two million girls under the age of fifteen give birth every year worldwide.

- Worldwide, one in five girls has given birth by the age of eighteen. In the poorest regions of the world, this figure rises to over one in three girls.

- An estimated three million unsafe abortions occur globally every year among girls aged fifteen to nineteen years.

- In low- and middle-income countries, complications from pregnancy and childbirth are the leading cause of death among girls aged fifteen to nineteen years.

- In 2012 in the United States, there were 305,420 babies born to females between the ages of fifteen and nineteen. Nearly 89 percent of these births occurred outside of marriage.

- An estimated forty million Americans visit a porn site at least once a month, and 25 percent of all search engine requests in the United States are for porn.

- In 2007, studies found that 21 percent of all college students said they watch porn "every day or almost every day."

- There are an estimated 420 million adult web pages online.

SUBSTANCE ABUSE[4]

- In the United States, the average age of first marijuana use is fourteen, and alcohol use starts earlier. And in 2013, 15 percent of high school seniors reported using a prescription drug non-medically in the past year.

- 33 percent of eighth graders have tried alcohol, and in the United States, 47 percent of those who began drinking before age fifteen experienced alcohol dependence at some point in their life

- In the United States, over five thousand people under age twenty-one die each year from alcohol-related car crashes, homicides, suicides, alcohol poisoning, and other injuries such as falls, burns, and drowning.

- The average minimum legal drinking age (MLDA) is very low. In a study of 138 countries:
  - 27 have no MLDA
  - 12 have an MLDA of sixteen to seventeen
  - 85 have an MLDA of eighteen to nineteen
  - 3 have an MLDA of twenty
  - 6 have an MLDA of twenty-one

- 1,168 German teenagers between the ages of fourteen and twenty had been admitted to hospital in the past three years for alcohol poisoning, and one in five binge drinkers started consuming alcohol before the age of twelve.

- 10.8 percent of eighth graders in the United States have used inhalants, which is nothing compared to Nairobi, Kenya, where an estimated sixty thousand children live on the streets and almost all are addicted to some sort of inhalant. In the Pakistani city of Karachi, there are an estimated fourteen thousand street kids, of whom 80 to 90 percent sniff glue or solvents.

DEPRESSION/SUICIDE[5]

- In the United States, approximately 20 percent of youth ages thirteen to eighteen experience severe mental disorders in a given year. More than 90 percent of those who die by suicide had one or more mental disorders. Suicide is the third leading cause of death for fifteen- to twenty-four-year-olds, and the sixth leading cause of death for five- to fourteen-year-olds.
- Cyberbullying increased in Malaysia by 55.6 percent in one year, from 2013 to 2014.

SCHOLASTIC DECLINE[6]

- In 2013, about one in five US students did not graduate high school with their peers.
- Among students who do graduate, 20 percent need remedial courses in college.
- The average American teen spends more than 7.5 hours a day consuming media—watching TV, listening to music, surfing the Web, social networking, and playing video games. By the time of high school graduation, they will have spent more time watching television than they have in the classroom.
- The College Board, sponsor of the SAT, says that roughly six in ten college-bound high school students who took the test were

so lacking in their reading, writing, and math skills, they were unprepared for college-level work.

EATING DISORDERS[7]

- In the United States, as many as ten in one hundred young women suffer from an eating disorder. Two psychiatric eating disorders—anorexia nervosa and bulimia—are on the increase among teenage girls and young women and often run in families.

- Great Ormond Street, the famous children's hospital in central London, has a special unit for treating young children with eating disorders. Girls as young as seven or eight have been treated there.

POVERTY/HOMELESSNESS[8]

- The National Runaway Switchboard estimates that, on any given night, there are approximately 1.3 million homeless youth in the United States living unsupervised on the streets, in abandoned buildings, with friends, or with strangers.

- "Street children" are found across Brazil. In São Paulo alone, the capital, there are more than 1.2 million homeless children, and most are addicted to cocaine.

- An estimated half million children in the African country of Burundi are orphaned and living on the streets. A study found that nearly 60 percent of the children under five were malnourished.

- It is estimated that five thousand unaccompanied (homeless) youth die each year in the United States alone as a result of assault, illness, or suicide.

- In Ethiopia, there are nearly 600 thousand children living on the streets. This has led to a rise in child work exploitation, with nearly 40 percent of children starting to work thirty-hour weeks before the age of six.

- One in seven US young people between the ages of ten and eighteen will run away from home.
- 75 percent of homeless or runaway youth in the United States have dropped out or will drop out of school.
- More than sixteen million children in the United States—22 percent of all children—live in families with incomes below the federal poverty level.

Our growing social problems, our erratic economy, and our increasingly amoral society cannot be fixed by big, sweeping political or national policies or legislation. The borrow-and-spend, debt-laden fiscal and monetary policies of so many of today's governments are essentially a reflection of the irresponsibility of parents and families who live on instant gratification and credit card debt and pass on an entitlement attitude to their children.

The simple truth is that macro problems can often be solved only with micro solutions. The way we will save our society is one family at a time. The way we will save our economy is one household at a time.

Political or governmental macro solutions for any of our economic or political woes do not work very well. Consensus is virtually impossible, and even when various factions agree on a broad direction to meet a recognized need, implementation becomes incredibly complex and expensive. The simple truth is that macro problems can often be solved only with micro solutions. The way we will save our society is one family at a time. The way we will save our economy is one household at a time.

The "curse" foretold in scripture centers on the poverty, the violence, the drug abuse, the promiscuity and pornography, the scholastic decline, and the depression and suicide that are so linked with family decline. But there are other parts to the curse as well, such as the steady and oppressive growth of government and public sectors in their efforts to assume the functions that families are abdicating.

THE FAITH AND FAMILY FACTOR

One clear lesson of history is that politics and the public sector, if not balanced and held in check, will expand and grow at the expense of individual freedom and independence.

The only things strong enough to accomplish this balance and restrain government are faith and family. The greatest institution (the sovereignty of God) and the most basic institution (the family) are the only elements powerful enough to keep public institutions from growing and spending excessively and from sucking away individual agency.

Faith and family, if healthy and vigorous, can squeeze government down to size. If faith and families are not strong, the process works in reverse.

Faith is the force from the heavens above, the belief that God's word is more important than man's. Family is a force from the grassroots below, the belief that the fundamental unit of society is what makes up and controls all larger institutions.

When faith and family weaken, the middle institution of government swells—partly because of its inherent thirst for power, and partly because it is trying to do the social jobs that family and religion are failing to do.

The problem, of course, is that government, when compared to family or to faith, is horribly costly and inefficient at handling social problems of welfare and justice and moral training. And the more it grows, the more it oppresses and removes our powers of choice.

When faith and family weaken, the middle institution of government swells—partly because of its inherent thirst for power, and partly because it is trying to do the social jobs that family and religion are failing to do.

From the Roman Empire to modern day China, the decline of family solidarity and of religious faith has precipitated not only growing decadence but expanding government and the steady loss of individual freedom; and as government grows, it tends to become protective of its powers and creates programs and policies that are increasingly secular and either immoral or amoral—either anti-family or without regard for family.

This is why communist and socialist governments and all totalitarian regimes try to eliminate religion and undermine families. Churches and synagogues are marginalized or eventually banned, and families are unfairly taxed or depleted by laws about how many children they can have. The norms and personal priorities in such societies begin to shift from commitment and family-focus to materialism and self-focus, and people begin to abandon parenthood and family ideals in favor of more personal comfort and government programs.

We heard a stark example of this being carried to the extreme when we were in Hong Kong several years ago. After we finished a two-hour family seminar with successful young executives, we were approached by a man in his mid-thirties. He explained that he had never been married and had no children. He was the only seminar attendee who was from mainland China, and he had overcome some visa problems and traveled a long way to be there.

We wondered why he had gone to so much trouble and expense to attend because he knew it was a seminar on raising responsible children, and he had no kids. His story was fascinating. He grew up during the Cultural Revolution, and since his parents were academics, they had been sent away to be "re-educated" (which usually meant hard labor on a farm far away in the country with meager food and shelter). At the age of four, he had been sent to be raised by the government in a commune along with hundreds of other young kids whose well-educated parents had been sent to work camps.

At age twelve, he was transferred to a large factory that produced envelopes, and for many years he dutifully worked as an envelope maker. When he was in his late teens, the government began giving all the children across the country IQ tests. China was desperately in need of scientists and businessmen, and when he scored very high, he was immediately given a scholarship and sent away to be educated in the United States. Although he had no formal education to that point, he was an exceptional student, and when he finished his studies, he went back and become a hugely successful businessman, bringing millions of dollars to the communist Chinese economy.

"And that's the reason I'm here," he said. "I do want to marry and have a family, but I have no idea what a family is or how a family functions. I need all the information I can get in order to create the happy family I never had, which is my fondest dream."

In suppressive, collectivist nations, government seeks to control people's entire lives, and communes replace families and nationalism replaces faith. In "free" countries, the secular, materialistic abandonment of faith and family creates a "cult of the individual" where selfish options are valued more than commitment and sacrifice—and where we hear much about individual rights and individual freedom and being true to yourself and little about family rights and religious freedom.

Sometimes even one of the two critical institutions (faith and family) is enough to save a society, or at least stave off disaster. Mexico, over the last three or four decades, may be an example. Enduring almost every conceivable social and economic problem—from run-away inflation to political

corruption to drug and crime cartels to natural disasters, and experiencing
a steady decline in faith and religion—the extended family structure of most
Mexicans stayed strong; while still mired in problems and poverty on many
levels, the country is surviving and becoming more stable and prosperous.

> *During a dinner with a brilliant eighty-year-old man and his wife,
> who were the founders of several fine private schools in Mexico
> City, along with their son, who was now the CEO of the schools,
> we learned something interesting about Mexican families. Already
> impressed with what we had observed about the rich family culture
> that still abides in Mexico and throughout Central America, large-
> ly due to the charitable traditions of their Catholic faith, we were
> taught a valuable lesson that evening.*
>
> *This man had lived through corrupt government after corrupt
> government, cartel after cartel, but he taught us that a country can
> be strong even in the face of government corruption and rampant
> crime if the basic unit of society, the family, is strong—strong in
> their faith and their determination to do what is right.*
>
> *He said that after the massive earthquake of 1995, the center
> of Mexico City, one of the biggest cities in the world, was ruined
> beyond recognition, but the government didn't show up to help.
> Families banded together and went to the rescue. Thousands of
> faithful families, men, women, and children showed up day after
> day with shovels and helping hands and worked tirelessly "in the
> trenches" to provide the miracle that was needed to put homes and
> lives back together.*

In the United States and most of Europe and Asia, we seem to have a lot
of things backwards. We think that poverty and crime and drugs and bad
public policy are destroying families. We even hear that a natural, traditional
family is now a luxury that only the rich or highly educated can afford.

In fact, it is the opposite. The decline of families and of faith is creating poverty and crime and abuse and addiction and bad politics and thus destroying cultures and countries. Solid family life, far from being a luxury, is the only way to flourish and the only meaningful and lasting way to help society survive.

To put the world in order, we must first put the nation in order; to put the nation in order, we must first put the family in order; to put the family in order, we must first cultivate our personal life; we must first set our hearts right.

—CONFUCIUS

CHAPTER FOUR

THE CONNECTION

Deteriorating Families Are the Cause—Everything Else Is the Effect

---

con·nec·tion *noun* \kə-ˈnek-shən\

1. causal or logical relation or sequence
2. the link or tie between two things

The connection between family and society is one of cause and effect, wherein the smaller part brings about the bigger part.

Some connections are temporary and fluid. But the one between the well-being of families and the health of society is permanent and irrevocable.

QUESTIONS OF CAUSE AND EFFECT

It is commonplace to equate poverty and debt and crime and various other social problems with divorce, single-parent households, fatherless homes, cohabitation, or with dysfunctional families and inadequacy of parental supervision. And indeed, the connecting statistics are very persuasive:

The Connection between Family Decline and Social Problems

- Children from divorced families are twice as likely to drop out of high school.[1]

- More than 56 percent of children living in poverty are being raised by a single mother.[2]

- 25 percent of adolescents who have experienced the divorce of their parents became disengaged from their families.[3]

- 16 to 20 percent of Australian fathers work fifty-five or more hours per week, and so are more likely to have young sons with a higher level of aggressive behavior, compared with boys whose dads worked fewer hours.[4]

- Children whose parents divorce experience difficulties as adults. Men from divorced families had more than three times the odds of suicidal ideation in comparison to men whose parents had not divorced. Adult daughters of divorce had 83 percent higher odds of suicidal ideation than their female peers who had not experienced parental divorce.[5]

- Among all children living only with their mother, nearly half— or 45 percent—live below the poverty line.[6]

- The percentage of children with serious behavioral and emotional difficulties is twice as high among those from single-mother families as among those from two-parent families.[7]

- At the family level, adolescent girls with mothers who (a) gave birth as teens and/or (b) have only a high school degree are more likely to have a baby before age twenty than are teens whose mothers were older at their birth or who attended at least some college.[8]

- When children are left home alone, about 51 percent are doing poorly in school. Most teachers believe that being alone at home is the number one cause of school failure.[9]

- Afternoon hours are the peak time for juvenile crime. In the last eleven years, juvenile crime has increased 48 percent.[10]

- Eighth graders who are alone eleven hours a week are twice as likely to abuse drugs as adolescents who are busy after school.[11]

The *New York Times* reported a major study showing that the children of single parents have less upward economic mobility than the children of two parents have. In this day of heightened concern with economic equality, it turns out that the marital status of a child's parents is the single biggest predictor of that child's economic mobility.[12]

The clear connection between the decline of families and the world's social problems cannot be ignored. The trick is figuring out which is the cause and which is the effect. Most economists and politicians blame both social ills and family instabilities on poverty. Our thesis is that the cause and effect works both ways and that poverty, instability, and social problems are often the direct result of declining or poorly functioning families.

A strong case can be made for family (or lack of family) as the cause and everything else as the effect or the result. After all, everything, including each of us, originates with families, with homes, with parents; and how those homes function largely determines the economic, moral, and character results that come out of them.

Analysis Paralysis

Today, because our viewpoints and our perspectives are so oriented to money and economics, it's natural to look for an economic scapegoat—to say "poverty is the cause." After all, violence happens more in the poor inner cities—as does educational decline, as do drugs and gangs and teen pregnancy. But that only leads to the next question, which is, "What causes the poverty?" and then we find ourselves mired in a debate about government policies or urban design, and we circle back into recommending and funding expensive Band-Aids that only treat the symptoms.

The clear connection between the decline of families and the world's social problems cannot be ignored. The trick is figuring out which is the cause and which is the effect.

What we commonly refer to as "social problems" are really the *symptoms* of something bigger—a disease that can ravage society if left unchecked. The prescriptions don't work because we've misdiagnosed the disease. We've debated and talked ourselves into a corner and ended up at a dead end. We try to extract ourselves by saying, "Maybe we've got it backwards; maybe it's the drugs or the crime or the teen pregnancy that causes the poverty." We find ourselves deep in analysis paralysis, debating whether the stress causes the pain or the pain causes the stress. But, we still haven't addressed the real issue. Where and what is the root cause of our worsening social problems?

It's only recently that sophisticated academic statistical analysis has begun to take us toward where common sense has pointed all along: one of the key *causes* of our worsening social problems and our sadly shifting paradigms is the breakdown of our most basic social institution—the family.

Treating the Symptoms Versus Finding a Cure

The social problems that are overwhelming our world must be cured. But the medicine we're using isn't working. We're treating the symptoms. We're taking painkillers while we ignore the source of the pain, and we don't seek ways to stop the pain at its source. It is a little like taking an aspirin to treat a broken leg. Only, in this case, the medicine is incredibly expensive and seems to have negative long-term effects—actually making the problems worse. Our welfare system and tax laws all over the developed world, even as they threaten to bankrupt us, actually destroy initiative and encourage people not to work. Our expensive criminal justice system doesn't rehabilitate, doesn't deter, and actually creates a culture of crime (especially in our prisons, which are a training ground for living outside the law).

> *Our youngest daughter, who spent eighteen months doing mission-*
> *ary and humanitarian work in some of the poorest parts of London,*
> *told us of her encounters with young teenage girls who had decided*
> *to find someone to get them pregnant so they could have a baby*
> *and get the childbirth bonus and extra welfare money that it would*
> *bring.*

"Forget the old notion of the class system," says Janet Street Porter, a columnist in *Britain's Daily Mail*. "There are just two classes in modern Britain: those who want to work and those who 'can't see the point in getting off their backsides.' The latter group is getting bigger all the time. There are 250 thousand households in Britain in which no adult has ever held a job. The children in these homes have been raised on the dole. They have no role models and 'no incentive to do any better than Mum and, if there is one around, Dad.' It's a lost generation."[13]

Seeing the Real Problem

Typically, the reason we look for *causes* is to permit the intelligent search for cures. In sports or in business, or in a whole society, just as in medicine, if something is wrong, we have to isolate the cause before we can find a cure.

As mentioned, it's common (and popular) to blame problems on poverty or on the growing gap between rich and poor. But to say that economic conditions cause the social problems may be a little like saying that the rash and the fever cause the illness. Economic conditions are a result rather than a cause far more often than popular thinking (and popular media) suggest. All of the social problems presented in the last chapter have economic costs and financial consequences.

But whether economic problems cause social problems or social problems cause economic problems (or whether the two repeatedly cause and exacerbate each other in a cause-and-effect spiral) the bigger questions are these: What are the underlying causes? What brings to pass the social and economic curse? What is the deeper spiritual crisis?

> *I had a wonderful old sage of a professor at the Harvard Business School whose motto was, "Understanding the real problem is what's hard. When you do, the solution is usually obvious." He also liked medical metaphors: "The symptoms are so easy to see, the virus and bacteria are so hard."*

Treating symptoms can be so frustrating. How many headlines have you read about "solutions" through gun control, drug testing, more prisons, rehab centers, crisis day care, v-chips, safe sex, gang elimination, mandatory sentencing, or welfare reform? *The problem is that they're all treating symptoms*, and they're treating them at the wrong level. Problems of uncertain values, poor communication, and lack of direction and discipline spill out of our most basic institutions—home and families—into the large institutions of government, of justice and welfare systems, *transforming* themselves into life-threatening violence, irresponsibility, and dysfunction. When problems spill over and grow in this way, they become impossibly expensive, incredibly complex, and disturbingly self-perpetuating. The answers to societal problems will be found not in the Houses of Congress, not in the White House, but in *your* house.

That last sentence is a paraphrase of Barbara Bush, speaking at the
1990 graduation ceremony of Wellesley College, the alma matter
of three of our daughters. Her exact words were: "Our success as a
society depends not on what happens inside the White House, but
on what happens inside your house."[14]

The solutions lie not in new laws or public intervention, but in new hearts and private introspection; not in political policy or institutional mandates, but in personal commitments and individual morality. No one needs simple cookie-cutter "answers." Rather, we need a clearer understanding of what's gone wrong and how *far* wrong it has gone. The solutions lie not in changing our minds but also in turning our hearts.

The core of the curse is the poverty and desperation and alienation and addiction that ravages ever more of our citizens. And the cause of the curse is that our hearts are not turned enough to our families.

The Connection between Social Problems and the Decline of Family and Values

It is a mistake to oversimplify or to claim that all social problems are directly created by inadequate families. Our social ills have many causes, but the "cause" of the most far-reaching and devastating "effects," a.k.a. "social ills"—and the one we are finally on the verge of understanding—is the decline and breakdown of the family and the accompanying deterioration of basic personal values.

There has been no shortage of comment and speculation about "family decline" and "values deterioration" in recent years, but two things have been wrong, or at least inadequate, in most of what has been written and spoken.

First, most of the dialogue is too theoretical and academic. The statistics about divorce, latchkey children, decreasing parent-child communication, and time spent together are academic parts of sociology courses. Increases in violence, gangs, substance abuse, bullying, teen promiscuity and pregnancy, crime, teen suicide, gang violence, school dropout rate, and AIDS are daily headlines, nightly news, and the subjects of all kinds of popular discussion and the targets of all kinds of proposed "solutions." But these are rarely *connected* clearly to their most predictable cause—the breakdown of the families and values. Common sense tells us of the connection, of the cause and effect, yet we keep talking about, worrying about, and working on the effects and ignoring the cause.

The fundamental question that always arises is, "Are social problems ravaging our families, or are failing marriages and troubled families making social problems inevitable?"

The real answer, of course, is, "Both."

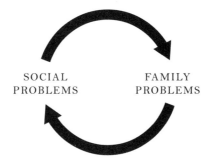

SOCIAL PROBLEMS   FAMILY PROBLEMS

In a classic vicious cycle, more of one breeds more of the other, and more of the other breeds more of the one.

But chicken-and-egg dilemmas are not entirely imponderable or unsolvable. In fact, the metaphor is perfect for this discussion. Viewing social problems as the chicken and ineffective, uncommitted dysfunctional families as the egg should make it clear that we must focus our efforts on the micro if we want to impact the macro. The "chicken" is running around, hard to catch, hard to effectively examine or fully diagnose, as well as being expensive and complicated to deal with. Social problems are as elusive as a wild, erratic chicken. We try to deal with them with more money, more police, more jails, and more public education. More often than not, we seem to make them worse. Eventually, we bankrupt ourselves and exhaust our well-intentioned idea. Once the "chicken" is hatched—out of the "egg" and into our court system, our welfare system, our legislative system—it becomes impossibly expensive. It is estimated that, in the United States, we spend over twenty billion dollars annually dealing with the "chicken" of teen pregnancy (the preventive programs, the educational decline, the abortions, the huge welfare payments to unwed mothers and poverty-stricken children . . . the list doesn't stop). Similar "run amuck" scenarios exist with drugs, violence, abuse, gangs, and with *every* social problem.

Once the "chicken" is hatched—out of the "egg" and into our court system, our welfare system, our legislative system— it becomes impossibly expensive.

The egg, on the other hand, is small, stationary, right under our noses, and can be positively impacted by our solutions. We have to reach the *egg*. Solutions to most social problems lie in the home. The home-egg must be valued, prioritized, strengthened so that it produces solutions rather than problems, contributors rather than abusers, builders rather than destroyers.

THE VALUES AND FAMILIES CONNECTION

Turning from the examination of a connection between negatives to a connection between positives, we need to ask, "Do basic values strengthen and preserve families, or do strong families teach and proliferate basic values?"

Once again, the answer is "Both."

But this time a positive and powerful synergy exists—an ascending spiral of beneficial, mutual dependency. Strong families are based on and built on values of commitment, fidelity, dependability, honesty, loyalty, discipline, courage, love, self-reliance, respect, unselfishness, justice, and mercy. And strong families also become the stewards, the safeguards, the preservers, and the bequeath-ers of those values. Strong families cannot exist without values. Values cannot endure without strong families. They are each other's lifeline.

Lately, in our society, the coupling of the two words—family and values—has given us the political football of "family values." It is important to push that stereotype aside and concentrate on each word separately and on their overriding individual importance. Strong families and strong values are separate, absolute necessities, but each requires the other to thrive. In order to revalue the family and put it at the center of our lives, and to draw on it as the source of our values, we must:

1. Personally re-prioritize and re-*value* our children, our parents, and our siblings, re-enshrining our own families in our minds and in our commitments.

2. Place ultimate *value* on families societally—in our laws, our courts, and our whole national, regional, and community outlook.

3. Support families in the same sense that we fuel a car to keep it running well by putting basic *values* more prominently back into our home, our commitments, our beliefs, and our every-day lives.

4. Provide parents with good information and materials for *values* training.

Family and Society

Our economic stability hinges on some very basic individual and societal values like honesty and respect and self-reliance. We all need to become more conscious of (and more committed to) certain simple behavioral principles as the antidote for our social ills. And values come principally from and through families.

Can we teach saving, enduring values in our society at large—character education in our schools, virtues in our literature, morality in our business and governmental institutions?

We can. But there are always disconnects and debates and bureaucratic dilutions when large institutions try to do the job of the most basic institution—the family. Values are personal and intimate and powerfully influential. They must be taught first and foremost in the most personal and intimate setting and the most powerfully influential relationship that is the home and the parents.

If we take the rate of increase in our serious social problems and project it over the next decade or two, an already rushing river turns into a torrent, then into a flood, then into a waterfall. We are a society adrift, approaching Niagara Falls without rudder or oar, tiller or engine, without even a compass. Trying to solve these torrential social problems through our welfare programs or justice system is like trying to reverse the flow of water—trying to turn the current upstream—away from the falls.

We must learn that the worry is not the water; the worry is the boat and the *people* in it. The boat is the *family*. Give a family the engine of priority and commitment, and the tiller of values, and we can escape the current.

Having used the terms *symptoms, illness,* and *cure* earlier in this chapter, the medical metaphor should be completed as a final summary of these connections. The world's severe social problems are painful, life-threatening symptoms. Family breakdown is the loss of health and resistance that makes us susceptible to the germs of negative values and the immune deficiency problems of declining values and false paradigms.

We are a society adrift, approaching Niagara Falls without rudder or oar, tiller or engine, without even a compass.

We can recover and reverse our symptoms by rebuilding the strength, immunity, resistance, and health of our families and by attacking the family-destroying germs with the antibodies of recommitment and values.

The cure begins as we understand the cause.

What's Right Versus What's Practical

Increasingly in our world, idealism is labeled unrealistic and characterized as theory rather than as actuality. We create a conceptual chasm between what is *right, best, moral, ideal*, and *true* on the one hand and what is *practical, realistic, possible*, and *workable* on the other. We also tend to separate what we perceive as difficult and depressing from what we see as pleasant and pleasurable.

In fact, more often than not, and certainly in the area of families, there is a perfect match between what is right and what is practical and between what is hard and what is happy. Prioritizing commitment and living and teaching values in homes is not only the correct path; it is the only practical and workable path in a world that tears apart families that do not have these priorities. As hard as it may be to put family first, it is the single most happiness-enhancing habit any person can practice. Marriages with fidelity are the safest, the healthiest, and the most sexually fulfilling relationships that exist on this planet, and parents who love and prioritize their children are the happiest, most loving, and most loved persons who populate it.

A RETURN TO THE FAMILY

Governments and other institutions keep trying to find external solutions to social problems, but the only solution is to turn our hearts—and efforts—back to the family. When (and where) families are valued and prioritized, societies have stability and safety, and the larger institutions of the private, public, and voluntary sectors have vitality and values. These larger institutions may be linked by common interests, politics, economics, or even noble purpose, but families are linked by genetics and by physical and spiritual unions and commitments.

When (and where) families are valued and prioritized, societies have stability and safety, and the larger institutions of the private, public, and voluntary sectors have vitality and values.

Too often today, these unions and commitments are wearing thin. If we define *decline* as diminishing in priority, commitment, and values, then the family has declined more steeply over the past three or four decades than at any other time in history. Fortunately, there are signs of family resurgence—and just in time, because the family is the world's last, best hope. We are beginning to recognize the social and personal prices we pay when families fail. We are waking up to the reality that the happiness we all seek is dependent on family relationships more than on any other factor.

Never has there been a time with richer potential for the flourishing of strong families. We are, today, capable of choosing the priorities and the places where we will focus our efforts and our energy. Yet the paradigms propagated by materialism, media, and mixed messages blow us off course and spin us into currents of missed opportunities and ultimately meaningless ambitions and accomplishments.

Surviving and Thriving

We can save our culture and our society, but only if we do it one family at a time! The "macro" of cultural survival is not the chief motivation for reprioritizing the family; rather, the goal is the "micro" of personal joy. Joy is best defined not simply as happiness, but as the deepest experiences and feelings of life—as the very purpose of mortality—having as much to do with pain as with pleasure. Families are the epicenter of emotional experience, proving and allowing higher, more selfless levels of love and deeper, more teaching levels of pain. We need our children as much as they need us. We are completed by them. They are our most lasting source of joy. They should be our most welcome burden.

This earth, and our lives upon it, is *about* families. In being children and parents, as well as brothers and sisters, we learn life's most valuable lessons, feel life's deepest emotions, and are given life's richest joys.

Today's core challenge is not to make the family more like the world; it is to make the world more like a family. If we don't make these changes, there will be a continuing escalation of every conceivable "social problem"—those things that scripture calls the *curse*.

Other things may change us, but we
start and end with the family.

—ANTHONY BRANDT

CHAPTER FIVE

THE CAUSE

Media, Technology, Entitlement,

Materialism, and "Bigness"

cause *noun* \ˈkȯz\

1. something or someone that produces an effect, result, or condition
2. the person or thing responsible for something

Concluding that the curse of society's problems results from the crisis of broken and dysfunctional families leaves us with one remaining, crucial question: what is causing the decline of families?

WHY ARE FAMILIES IN DECLINE?

As we were on a long flight returning from a parenting seminar in South Africa, we were reflecting on all the ills that Apartheid had led to and wondering about the cause. What were the forces that led to Apartheid? At the time, we were putting together an early draft of this book and had decided to call the world's escalating social problems a "curse" and the decline of families a "crisis." As we tried to explain the causal relationship between the crisis and the curse, it became obvious that we would have to go a step further and understand the cause of the crisis that leads to the curse.

If A can be fixed by repairing B, then we need to look further into what causes B. If our social problems can be fixed by repairing the family, we need to ask: what is causing family decline? If the "curse" is caused by the "crisis," then what is causing the crisis?

Human beings are wired to have and to want families. It is natural to want commitment and security and even responsibility. Why, then, are we seeing fewer new families formed and more established families breaking up?

Before we search out the culprits, it is important to look at what the causes are *not*. Let's eliminate some of the obvious possibilities. Are families breaking up and deteriorating because we don't care about them anymore? A resounding *no*. Polls continue to tell us, as they always have, that we value our families above all else. Are families declining because we think them unnecessary? Again, a resounding *no*. Polls show that large

> *Human beings are wired to have and to want families. It is natural to want commitment and security and even responsibility. Why, then, are we seeing fewer new families formed and more established families breaking up?*

majorities think they are the most important and needed thing in the world.

And the cause is not that parents are less interested in their kids or not trying to find parenting answers.

> *We were giving a keynote address at a regional conference of teachers and school administrators in Cartagena, Columbia, where an articulate school principal made a point that led to a question. "What I see," he said, "are parents who, in some ways, are thinking harder and working harder at their parenting than ever before. The students at our school come from good homes and from parents who want them and who read parenting books and who try very hard. But they are all over-committed, and they don't have time to really do right by their kids; and they are so busy competing economically and being sure they have all the advantages and all the options that their children just don't see enough of them."*

The Second "Why?"

Children have an innate need to know. We can learn a lot about the question "Why?" from them. The first "why?" kids ask usually isn't so hard. It's the second, and follow up, "why" that is usually harder and more challenging to answer.

Question: "Why do I have to go to school?"

Answer: It's the law.

Second Question: "Why is it the law?"

It's the same with the issue we've been dealing with here.

Question: "Why are America's social problems so profound (and so escalating)?"

Answer: Because of the breakdown of families.

Second Question: "Why are families breaking down?"

The second "why" forces us to seek out the real cause for the situation. In finding a solution, we can follow this sequence: cataloging symptoms leads to defining the illness which, in turn, can lead to determining the cause and then the cure.

In the case of society:

- Symptoms are social problems.
- Illness is the breakdown of family.
- The virus of cause is complex but must be isolated.

The cure can't come until we comprehensively know the cause. Diagnosing the illness is important—but that gets easy after a while and doesn't lead to a deeper understanding of where the illness comes from. Years ago, every doctor could easily recognize the symptoms and diagnose polio or yellow fever. But until the microbe *cause* for these illnesses was determined, real cures could not be developed.

Virtually every sociologist, statistician, spiritual or secular observer would answer the question, "Why are the world's social problems so profound and escalating?" with a response that acknowledges some connection with family decline. But the germs that cause the illness of family decline are hard to define and harder to find. In this case, though, it's not the microscopic nature of the causes that make them hard to isolate—it's their *bigness*. They are so big we can't see the whole thing—they are too wide for our field of vision to take them in. They are so "normal" and so pervasive that we don't recognize them for what they are. And there is not one big cause, but four, all interrelated:

1. An over-emphasis on individual rights and freedoms at the expense of family commitments. This shift is so strong that we call it "The Cult of the Individual"—which comes partly from . . .

2. A migration to cities—an urbanization and escalating sense of entitlement that breaks up family cultures and orients young

people toward media and materialism and away from family ties—which results partially from . . .

3. Larger institutions taking over the functions of the family— which contributes to . . .

4. Inaccurate perceptions, perspectives, and paradigms about what is important and what is not.

1. THE CULT OF THE INDIVIDUAL OR "ME" VS. "WE"

The Oxford Dictionary chooses a "word of the year" each year—determined by a vote of independent linguists; this is the word that, by its common and popular use, best defines where our culture is going. The word of the year for 2013 was "selfie." And it means more than the photos we take of ourselves with our smart phones and post on social media. It symbolizes, at least in our minds, a society that is overemphasizing the importance of the individual self and undervaluing the importance of the family and the community.

Most free societies are built around individual rights and personal freedoms, and it sounds almost revolutionary to want to limit them. Perhaps what is needed is not limits, but balance. Because it is not the individual that is the basic unit of society; it is the family. There are and always will be tradeoffs between the "freedoms" and options of the individual and the commitment, sacrifice, and responsibility of having a family.

What we must realize is that it is the latter, not the former, that creates a strong society and molds individual character. David Brooks of the *New York Times* put it this way: "People are not better off when they are given maximum personal freedom to do what they want. They're better off when they are enshrouded in commitments that transcend personal choice—commitments to family, God, craft and country."[1]

The idea of not wanting to give up personal options and happiness by making commitments or taking on the responsibilities and sacrifices of marriage and children is a completely misplaced notion. Because, in fact, it is those very sacrifices and commitments that lead to the deepest kind of happiness.

Still, we live in a world that literally worships the cult of the individual. Everyone wants to be "their own man" or "their own independent woman," and we are sold the bill of goods that therein lies fulfillment.

In actuality, a constant quest for unfettered freedom and avoiding being "tied down" grows increasingly hollow and ever less fulfilling, while commitment and loyalty to people who we love more than ourselves (spouse and children) deepens both how we feel and who we are.

People are not better off when they are given maximum personal freedom to do what they want. They're better off when they are enshrouded in commitments that transcend personal choice—commitments to family, God, craft and country.

People who have had a bad family experience or who have not had good family examples, become part of the demise of family simply by choosing not to participate in a family life of their own. They decide, based on the "false advertising" of the culture of the individual, to simply abdicate on family—to either not have one or to not be fully committed to whatever family they have.

A friend of ours and a noted family law expert named Bruce Hafen poses this question: "The liberation and equality movements are gaining such a head of steam—do you think the very idea of individual rights will ever develop so much momentum that it could overpower the principles that should be balanced against it?" He quotes Harvard Law School Dean Roscoe Pound, who defined "the social interests" in family law as "society's interest in maintaining marriage as a stable social institution in which parents protect, nurture, and teach their children the qualities of character that maintain a stable future society."

Hafen goes on to say that now, "In a nutshell, advocates have begun using the constitutionally charged language of individual rights to challenge laws that were intended to support the interests of children and society in stable family structures." He cites no-fault divorce as one example where we no longer "look at marriage . . . as a [social] institution. Rather, no-fault sees marriage as an essentially private relationship between adults, terminable at the will of either. . . . Thus, when marriage commitments intrude on personal preferences, people are more likely to walk away."

And Hafen certainly views it as more than a US problem. He says "And these developments have international implications. A Japanese family law scholar told me that the influence of American legal ideas about individual rights—along with American movies and TV—is a major cause of the recent destabilization of Japanese attitudes about kinship and family."[2]

2. THE FAMILY-DEVOURING FORCES OF URBANIZATION, MATERIALISM, MEDIA, AND ENTITLEMENT

> *We were in Vietnam to give a speech to a group of CEOs and business leaders and asked our host if he could explain the steep decline of marriage and birthrate in their cities over the past few years. His limited English made his answer very direct and to the point: "We wanted less children born, but not this less. . . . Our youth moves to city for a job, gets bit of money, goes to clubs, sees glitzy life, decides no children wanted, loses touch with home and village."*

The bottom line is that virtually wherever you go, as technology and jobs and media cluster more people into urban areas, both the lifestyles and the societal norms shift away from families and attachment and more toward comfort and consumerism. But it comes back to bite you.

We reflected on how interesting it is that developing countries around the globe seem to unintentionally go through a particular sequence with regard to how they think about families. It's hard to generalize, but the sequence often looks something like this:

Phase 1: An effort is made to lower birthrate and limit population based on the belief that too many people will decrease the quality of life.

Phase 2: Migration accelerates from countryside and rural areas to cities where more money can be earned but where the concept of family is limited or eliminated for many young people and where more abortions occur and more kids are born out of wedlock and with no family ties.

Phase 3: More government intervention and programs are developed to take care of the increasing homelessness, orphans, drugs, and crime that come as a result of less family structure.

Phase 4: Dramatically declining birthrates and a dwindling workforce cause the government to try to reverse Phases 1 and 2 and to offer incentives to have one child, or for additional children. (While in Singapore recently, we learned that parents now receive a $20,000.00 benefit per child born in their family.)

Phase 5: Government recognizes that even if it persuades people to have children, the parents need to be motivated and taught how to raise kids, because their own exposure to family and parenting has been limited. So public sector ministries or agencies are set up to encourage family and community development.

Countries like Singapore have been through all five phases, and are finding that it is not easy to recover or rekindle a family-centric culture once it has largely slipped away in the face of materialism, urbanization, government intervention, and amoral cohabitation or childless by choice.

Europe is on exactly the same path. The United States, although our size and diversity slows down the process, is steadily progressing through the same sequence.

Wouldn't it be wonderful if we could short-circuit the process and jump from Phases 2 and 3, where we are now, directly to an expanded version of Phase 5, where not only the public sector of government but the private sector of business and the voluntary sector of churches and communities recognize the supreme importance of families and give parents more support, more encouragement, and more credit for the huge contribution they make to the broader society.

We end up with a generation of selfish, entitlement attitudes where kids imagine that they deserve whatever they want, and whatever their friends have, right now, without working and without waiting. Parents foster these attitudes by giving kids things instead of time.

Many developed countries are far enough into the sequence and into Phase 3 to know that the "treatments, medications, and surgeries" we try to perform on the ills and social problems of society are vastly more expensive and far less efficient than the "preventative medicine" of doing all we can to help families survive and thrive and turn their children into responsible citizens.

The migration to urbanization and limited or eliminated families is pushed and fueled by media and internet messages of materialism, and we end up with a generation of selfish, entitlement attitudes where kids imagine that they deserve whatever they want, and whatever their friends have, right now, without working and without waiting. Parents foster these attitudes by giving kids things instead of time.

Throughout the developed world, but particularly in our recent travels through Asia (China, Japan, and Korea) as well as Southeast Asia (Indonesia, Malaysia, and Singapore) we continue to be amazed at the sometimes perceived and sometimes real need for both parents to work multiple jobs and endlessly pursue greater upward economic mobility, even as they leave their children for long hours with nannies, helpers, maids, and babysitters. And when work takes a huge quantity of time away from family life, the almost inevitable end result is parents who make up for time lost with the kids with gifts like smart phones and tablets.

The resulting entitlement attitude of the kids becomes a trap that robs them of initiative and motivation and gratitude. We called our last book *The Entitlement Trap* because once children are caught by that attitude, it rarely lets them go. Entitlement ranges all across the economic spectrum, from poor kids on welfare who come to expect that government programs will give them everything to über-rich kids who don't even think they should have to wash or feed themselves.

A principal at an expensive International School in South America told us this story: "We have a child in our school whom we suspected was having a problem with entitlement. He showed no initiative and took no responsibility whatsoever at school. He was not turning in homework and didn't seem to care about his grades. If his pencil dropped to the floor, he expected someone else to pick it up for him. When I called the parents into my office for consultation, the problem became apparent. I asked them what they thought they could do to help give the boy a little more responsibility at home. The mother thoughtfully reflected, "I guess we could have him wash himself in the shower instead of having the maid clean him. Usually he just holds out his arms and she washes him."

The father had a good idea, too. "Perhaps we should insist that he stop playing on the computer so he can have dinner with us in the evening instead of having a maid feed him while he stares at the screen and works the keyboard. He loves computer games and hates to be interrupted, but maybe we could talk him into joining us and feeding himself."

3. THE SAD PARADOX OF LARGE INSTITUTIONS REPLACING SMALL ONES

If families are strong, valued, and important—if they truly are the most basic institution of society—what, besides personal abdication, can break them? Only one thing: *bigger institutions.* The huge private institutions that have grown up over the last eighty to one hundred years—from media systems to merchandising giants, public education to ever-expanding government— have had a profound effect on families. They have changed our lifestyles and priorities, created anti-family perspectives and paradigms, and in many cases, have built or perpetrated themselves either by *substituting* for families or by *undermining* families for their own preservation and growth.

None of these larger institutions were established with the intent to destroy families. On the contrary, all came about to serve families. But, like a robot that develops the ability to serve itself and turns to threaten its master, many of the large institutions we have created over the last century now threaten the very families they intended to serve. And the basic, and ancient, institution of family, instead of asserting itself and reminding itself of its primacy and priority, has let the massive new adolescent institutions crowd it out and con it into servitude.

While the family has been society's smallest, most basic, and most essential institution since the beginning of time, our present larger institutions are a much more recent phenomenon, having been with us only during the last hundred years or so. Until the industrial age, the principal larger institutions were churches, tribes, kingdoms, countries, and other political entities that, outside of war, had a limited effect on basic family life. With the industrial age came urbanization and a whole host of larger institutions—financial, industrial, educational, social, entertainment, informational, wholesale, and retail—which changed the very patterns of society and created a separation between people's work lives and family lives. In an agrarian society, work was usually *with* family and was always perceived as *for* family. Now, work competes with the family for time and attention, and we often have to choose between the needs and demands of larger institutions and the needs and demands of family.

Our larger institutions have become preoccupied with preserving and nourishing themselves rather than preserving and nourishing families.

In addition, our public and private institutions, while serving us well in so many ways, have gained frightening lives of their own and, motivated by self-preservation and growth, have begun to squeeze and supplant and substitute for the very entity that they were intended to strengthen, support, and supplement. They have taken over some of the functions that should belong to families and fostered the impression that families are losing relevance to the point of becoming redundant.

Also, sometimes wittingly and sometimes unwittingly, larger institutions have created and fostered some false paradigms that have duped families into accepting bad priorities and weakening their internal commitments. The paradigms that undermine family include viewing work as our main identity, material possessions as our credibility, or corporate or political allegiance as our primary loyalty.

In short, our larger institutions have become preoccupied with preserving and nourishing themselves rather than preserving and nourishing families. This kind of phenomenon is not hard to understand if we use some parallel examples and comparisons:

- A large company, bent on its own growth, begins to view small companies as competitors and seeks either to undermine or destroy them, or to swallow them up by acquisition and taking over their functions.

- The federal and state governments take over functions of local government and pass laws that supersede those of towns and cities.

- A big country overwhelms a smaller one—using psychological warfare to weaken and then using its military or financial might to take over.

- An immune system is destroyed, allowing the larger force of bacteria to take over a small organism.

The family is analogous to the little company, the basic local government, the tiny country, the small organism. Declining values and false paradigms are the psychological warfare or broken immune systems. Big private and public institutions are the dominators, the destroyers, the "underminers,"— in short, the "culprits." We will look more closely at each of these culprits in the next chapter.

4. THE FALSE PARADIGMS THAT BLIND US TO WHAT REALLY MATTERS

Despite these first three causes, families should be able to survive and to ward off and resist their destructive influences, or at least put up a better fight. After all, the natural bonds and self-preservation instincts of families are strong, and parents ought to be capable of having more control over their family's destiny from the inside than larger institutions or cultural influences have from the outside. Unfortunately, it doesn't seem to be the case.

So why don't families have more resistance against the perils inflicted on them by outside forces? Why can't the "bull's-eye" of family shield itself and wall itself off from the negative influences coming from the outside? Why can't we at least filter out some of the factors that try to undermine or weaken our families?

Because we don't fully *see* the danger! We're aware enough of some of the threats to give them names: "materialism," "misplaced loyalties," "amorality," "entitlement," "wrong priorities," but we don't see our new world and its family-destructive forces *accurately*. Our perspectives, our world-views, our *paradigms* have been altered by the messages we receive from the very large institutions that threaten us.

If a paradigm—or the *way* we see something—is off or skewed (or blurred), then we have a false perception of reality, and we can fail to recognize a danger or fail to realize that we have the power or ability to solve a problem or resist a threat. For example, if media convinces us that all teenage kids get involved in early, recreational sex, we may give up on trying to help our own kids avoid it. Or, if advertising convinces us of the paradigm that we need a bigger house or newer car more than we need time with our kids, we may spend our time and effort on the wrong things.

If media convinces us that all teenage kids get involved in early, recreational sex, we may give up on trying to help our own kids avoid it.

Summary of the Four Causes

The first two causes ("Individual over Family" and "Migration toward Materialism and Entitlement") are largely of our own making, and the simple way out of them is to understand that they are harming us and to move ourselves in the opposite direction. We must make personal and conscious choices of the responsibility and sacrifice of family commitment and priority over the false freedom of endlessly serving our own comfort and options.

And we must deliberately decide to stay rooted in our families and to create cultures in our own homes that are stronger than the media, internet, entitlement, materialism, and peer cultures that swirl around us. We simply have to fight the mentality that makes family and marriage and children the supporters of work and "things" rather than the other way around.

The third and fourth causes ("Larger Institutions" and "False Paradigms") are less of our own making and more the fault of forces and entities much larger than ourselves. They each deserve a chapter of their own, (Chapters 6 and 7) because they can be changed only by a movement, only by a culture war, only by using people power to persuade these entities to change. In the meantime, the better we understand these larger institutions and false paradigms, the more we can do to rescue our own individual families from them.

The only rock I know that stays steady,
the only institution I know that works, is
the family.

—LEE IACOCCA

CHAPTER SIX

THE CULPRITS

Large "New" Institutions Are

Substituting for Small "Old" Families

---

cul·prit *noun* \ˈkəl-prət, -ˌprit\

1. the source or cause of a problem
2. one guilty of a fault or deserving blame for an unhappy condition

Unintentionally and largely unconsciously, our newest, largest institutions are destroying the oldest, smallest institution of family.

These culprits were all established to support, sustain, and supplement the family. But in their instinct for self-preservation and growth, they now supplant and substitute for the family while (wittingly and unwittingly) attacking its roots.

PLACING THE BLAME

Not long ago, as we were speaking to an audience of parents at a national convention in the United States, we walked them through the curse of social problems and the crisis of family breakup and asked them who the culprits were. They all tended to blame themselves.

"Not spending enough time with my kids."

"Working too much."

"Not knowing their friends well enough or their caregivers, or what they watch on TV or what they do online."

We probed further. "Do you really blame yourselves? How many of you think of your family as your highest priority?" Ninety-five percent of the audience raised their hands. "Then why do you let these things happen?

With that question, the tone of the audience's responses changed. Hands went up all over the auditorium.

"We don't let *them happen!"*

"We don't choose how long we work . . . or what is put on the Internet . . . or the attitudes our kids pick up from their friends or their school."

"We're the victims of it—it happens to us.*"*

"Well, then," we rephrased the earlier question, "who do we blame—who are the culprits?" Now the audience was releasing themselves from parental guilt, realizing there were relatively new, larger forces causing many of their family problems and undermining their efforts to be good parents to their children. We got answers from the personal to the sweeping.

"It's my employer."

"It's greedy corporate America."

"It's the Internet."

"It's advertising and instant gratification."

"It's all the easy credit and debt."

"It's the schools—what they're teaching and what they're not teaching."

"It's the movies and the rap music and the violence and the pornography."

We made a long list of "culprits" on a big white board (it matched pretty closely the list of "larger institutions" coming up in this chapter), and we asked the next question. "What do we do about it?"

"Boycott them."

"Write our Congressman!"

"Sue them!"

But the answers rang a little hollow. We were all feeling our smallness and inadequacy as parents to fight such big and powerful "culprits." Then, from a young mother at the back of the hall, came the key answer, "It seems to me that we can blame a lot of these bigger forces, but I doubt we're going to change them. Maybe if we just see and understand what all these things in our society are doing to our families, we can talk to our kids about them and work out how to use more of the good and avoid more of the bad."

We agreed with that young mother then, and we agree with her now! The first step to making change is understanding how we got to where we are now.

How Families Are Changing and Who Is Changing Them

Changes happen gradually, and it's sometimes hard to realize how different families are today and how different the world is in which they exist.

Prior to the twentieth century, most households were farm and rural families. Work/family tradeoffs didn't exist because farm families worked together, and family communication happened in connection with that work time spent together. The specialized roles of husband and wife, mother and father were accepted and recognized, so expectations were more clear and results more manageable. Children learned responsibility by necessity and learned to work by having to work. When chores didn't get done on a farm, the penalties or negative results were immediate and obvious. Delayed gratification was a way of life because no other way existed.

> *I remember reading my grandfather's journal. As a young father, he faced unbelievable hardships, working twelve hours a day as a farmer and carpenter, trying to make ends meet. Yet the further I read, the less sorry I felt for him. In fact, I began to envy his life. He worked with his wife and children. They had fun as they worked to-gether—and they communicated and trusted each other. Their life had simplicity and a quality almost impossible to find today.*

During the first half of the twentieth century, as families urbanized and suburbanized, most households took on an adjusted and updated version of the rural lifestyle. Parents still had fairly clear roles according to gender, kids were expected to do household chores instead of farm chores, and both divorce and living together before marriage were shunned to the point of social stigma. Families were still expected, both by themselves and by society, to perform the seven essential functions laid out in Chapter 1, and to embody the four essential elements.

All these "norms" began to change in the sixties, and the acceleration of these changes increased as the last decades of the century played out, finally reaching the stages of crisis and "curse" as we advanced into the new millennium.

The engines of change—the huge, seemingly irresistible forces that pushed the changes into effect—were the new, large institutions of the public and private sectors. Their growth, their instinct for self-preservation, and their agenda for profit have simply overwhelmed the family.

Outer Sector Pressures

In terms of our diagram, the outer rings of the public and private sector have swelled and thickened dramatically:

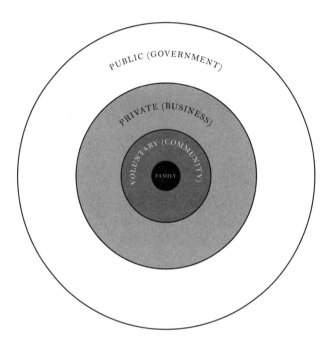

The public sector, comprised of all levels and branches of government and all agencies, bureaus, and systems, has expanded and mutated so rapidly during the twentieth century, and even more so in the twenty-first, that its effect on and relationship to the family is completely different than it was a hundred or even fifty years ago.

Every element of this outer ring, from our courts and our welfare systems to our public education and our tax structure, was originally conceived and set up to protect and serve our families. But it now looks less and less like a protective shield and more and more like an ever tightening vice that squeezes us and makes it ever harder to raise, support, and have control over our own families. Government tax policy in most developed countries puts economic penalties on being married and having kids. Legal precedent and court policy makes it easier to abandon and run from family responsibility and commitment than to face it and resolve it. Public schools often seem to undermine family values and parental authority. Welfare regulations reward families when the father leaves. And government as a whole seems determined to take over every traditional function of the family until parents essentially become redundant.

The business or private sector grew up to meet and serve the needs of families—from employment to providing the goods and services that households needed and wanted. But the emergence of massive corporations, fueled by executive greed and stockholders' demands, has led to these corporations abandoning any loyalty or responsibility they once felt for families. Big companies demand more time and loyalty from workers than ever before, and pay less for it. They want our loyalty and wish to be our prime identity—often at the expense of our families.

Within the corporate world, certain sectors pose even more specific threats to families. Media entities undermine values and portray traditional families as outdated and irrelevant. Financial institutions encourage instant gratification and over-extended credit. Merchandising companies use advertising to promote materialism and con us into measuring ourselves by what we own within the economy rather than by who we are within our families.

> Sometimes half an hour is long enough to make a parent realize what he's up against from the private sector. One parent said it this way: 'I sat down to watch a sitcom with two of my children, but it was filled with sexual innuendo and it portrayed promiscuity and disrespect as appealing and as the norm. During the program, there were three car advertisements and two clothing advertisements, prompting one of the kids to say, 'Dad, we really need a new car,' and the other to say, 'My phone is like a dinosaur—I'm embarrassed to even use it at school.'"

Even the nonprofit voluntary and community sector—traditionally an extension of family, the "village" that it takes to raise a child—has become, in many ways, more an enemy than a friend. Our recreational and cultural complexes, from sports to the arts, have become so big and institutionalized that they divide families—some family members go here, some there, each with different loyalties and time-drains. Evenings and weekends and other traditional family times are sucked away. Churches, community centers, and clubs, instead of being the family's strongest advocates and supporters, seem to be trying to substitute for the family. And a whole new institution of pop psychology and "self-help" puts such emphasis on *individual* fulfillment and personal freedom that it undermines family commitment and responsibility.

Essentially, all three of the "outer rings" of our target—which in previous eras have acted almost as a uterus by protecting, supporting, nourishing, and supplying the family—have now mutated into oppressive forces that imprison, choke, and suck the essential elements out of families.

Essentially, all three of the "outer rings" of our target—which in previous eras have acted almost as a uterus by protecting, supporting, nourishing, and supplying the family—have now mutated into oppressive forces that imprison, choke, and suck the essential elements out of families.

In the still-early stages of the twenty-first century, the three outer sectors do damage to families in four particular ways:

1. *By substituting for families*—taking over too many of their functions and replacing too many of their roles.

2. *By "sins of omission"*—failing to do some of the things they should do for families.

3. *By "sins of commission"*—doing certain things that undermine families and tear down the values that hold families up.

4. *By creating negative perspectives and false paradigms*—making families think they're okay when they really are not.

The Faux Family

Back in the early 1980s, I went to China. It was a period when very few Americans were getting in, and I spent time in the countryside as well as the cities. What I observed was a country deliberately and consciously trying to make the large institutions of the state more important and more functional than the small institution of the family—essentially trying to render the family redundant in the social scheme of things. While both parents worked in commune industry or agriculture, children lived in the commune care facility where they were fed, educated, and collectively cared for. Some of the children still slept in their parents' apartment, but it was the larger commune that had the responsibility, the authority, the loyalty, the identity, the resources, and the vitality.

Today, in America and the West, responsibility and priority is also transferring from smaller institutions to larger ones. Though it may not be by design or conscious intent, it is happening—slowly and steadily and seemingly irreversibly. Most of our larger institutions were established to serve families rather than substitute for them, but the *results*—in terms of what is actually *happening* to families—are as dangerous and as chilling as what I observed in China. The family, and its basic purposes and functions, is being swallowed up, undermined, and rendered irrelevant by our larger institutions. The family is the victim, and the larger institutions, whether purposefully or innocently, are the culprits.

In our private sector, company identity and corporate loyalty have too often replaced family identity and loyalty. We're more likely to tell new acquaintances "what we do" or where we work than tell them about our family. We're so worried about meeting quotas or impressing our boss that we don't have the time or energy to worry as constructively as we should about our kids.

Some companies, often motivated by their bottom line more than by genuine concern for our families, hold out "solutions" like maternity leave, on-site childcare, job sharing, flex time, work-at-home, and "mommy tracks," but these are usually aimed more at the goal of not letting families hurt the job rather than not letting the job hurt families.

So they (the companies we work for) try to provide day care, and other private entities (a whole, huge new industry) offer childcare in all of its varieties. But these efforts substitute for families rather than supporting them, and, just as in sports, the substitute is never as good as the first-string player.

As parent loyalty and identity shifts to career and company, other parts of the private sector are hard at work winning the loyalty of kids to various brands, styles, sports teams, or TV and music personalities and life styles. The media as a whole substitutes for families in the entertainment and social/cultural education of our children, and it cons parents into thinking they can make up for the *time* they don't give to their children by giving them more *things*.

The outer ring—the public sector—substitutes for and replaces families in even more obvious ways. Public schools attempt to take ever-increasing responsibility, not only for the intellectual education of children, but also for their character and values education, for their social behavior, and for their after-school care. While it is, in many ways, admirable that teachers and schools accept more responsibility, it is a poor substitute for the full accountability and involvement of parents.

The courts, the legal systems, the legislatures, and all conceivable kinds of agencies or bureaus also increasingly substitute themselves into the traditional roles and functions of families. Courts are so preoccupied with individual rights that they ignore and undervalue family rights and responsibility. Children can sue their parents. Child protective services can take kids from their parents on the hearsay of neighbors. Custody rulings seem designed to pull families apart. Adoption procedures take forever. Legislatures continue to try to fix social problems by enacting new laws.

In their attempts to assist children, government social services and welfare too often circumvent and disregard the basic purpose and position of families. While there are family situations where the greatest need is to protect a child from a parents, there are far more family situations where the real need (and the real solution) is to help parents to take care of their own kids.

> *About the same time that I went to China, way back in the 80s, I was named by President Reagan to direct the "White House Conference on Children." My first move was to try to change the name of the conference to the "White House Conference on Children and Parents"—so the emphasis would shift from social agency solutions to parental and family solutions. The name change met with substantial resistance from many welfare social service entities who seemed to view parents as the primary problem rather than the solution.*

Even the community and voluntary sector, the churches and clubs and other neighborhood entities that should be closest and most nourishing to families often seem bent on making the family redundant. Plenty of activities and involvements are offered, but kids are encouraged to do things individually and with their peers far more than to do things with their parents and families.

More and more stressed and busy parents seem to be following the "general contractor" model for parenting—a general contractor hires sub-contractors to do all the work.

More and more stressed and busy parents seem to be following the "general contractor" model for parenting—a general contractor hires sub-contractors to do all the work, from the electrician and the plumber to the carpenter and the painter. As long as parents get their kids to school, scouts, music and dance lessons, sports and summer camps, after-school programs, etiquette classes and tutors, and college test prep coaches, the "subcontractors" will do all the work and everything will be fine. Just get the kids to where they need to go and let the institutions of the public, private, and community sector raise them.

The biggest problem with this general contractor approach is that it doesn't work. What children need is the unconditional love that only a parent can provide. They need the time and attention that is only fully meaningful when it comes from a parent.

The bottom line is that no other element or agency or institution can provide the unconditional, even *irrational* love that children need to grow up emotionally healthy and happy. Other entities can give help and support for raising children, but none are adequate substitutes for parents and families in the seven essential functions or the four essential elements (see pages 5–9).

> *Our two oldest daughters each interrupted their university studies to spend eighteen months doing humanitarian service and missionary work—and assisting in orphanages—in Romania and Bulgaria. From their letters and from the two visits we made while they were there, we saw that the basic physical care the orphans received was minimally adequate. Yet their dark, hollow eyes and empty emotions spoke volumes about what they didn't get—personal, individual, unconditional love. We were reminded of the studies done with baby monkeys who were offered a wire-mesh "mother" or a soft, furry, stuffed animal "mother" in place of the real thing. Although they were given plenty of nourishment and a "fake" mother (almost all chose the soft furry one), none of the infant monkeys lived to maturity. They died from a lack of parental love.*

The starting point in looking for real solutions is the acknowledgment that nothing can adequately substitute for real family.

Sins of Omission
(How Each Sector Has Failed Families)

While the public, private, and community sectors often assume too much responsibility for kids and substitute too much for parents, they often do far too little in terms of supporting and supplementing parents in their difficult job.

Let's start with the next-to-the-family voluntary or community sector. Where have churches and synagogues been during the last fifty years in defending and upholding the family? Certainly family commitment and fidelity are a part of the tradition and stated belief of virtually all religions, but too often faith communities have tried too hard to accommodate and be tolerant of anti-family social change rather than standing up to it and challenging it.

The starting point in looking for real solutions is the acknowledgment that nothing can adequately substitute for real family.

Community and voluntary groups, too, while undertaking all kinds of creative and compassionate activities for downtrodden and unfortunate *individuals*, have done too little to help in-need families as units. With all the big-brother, big-sister and other mentoring programs, where are programs that mentor parents or that link a relatively functional family with a dysfunctional one in a one-family-to-one-family supportive relationship?

Even in the best religious and community organizations, with all their good intent, whole family and parent involvement and improvement solutions are too often just not on the radar screen. By trying to help children without involving parents, we commit the classic mistake of giving a fish without teaching anyone how to fish.

The private sector is *full* of "sins of omission" when it comes to families. In their emergence as huge new institutions, corporations have viewed families as *competitors* for the time and allegiance of their workers and thus failed to offer very much, if any, meaningful help to families or even to consider family needs as they formulate policies and work expectations. By becoming far more loyal to their stockholders than to their workers, corporations lay off and downsize without regard to families and deprive workers of the kind of flexibility and selective time off that could make huge differences in their ability to be effective parents.

Although there are some bright exceptions, it seems almost as though corporate boards and decision-makers all across the United States sat down and said, "Now, what can we do to make it as hard as possible for our employees to have strong families and a fulfilling home life." This didn't actually happen, of course. What did happen was *nothing*—no agenda where the family and home needs of workers were discussed. It constitutes a classic "sin of omission."

> We frequently address corporate or association groups on topics of "Lifebalance" and prioritized time management. Generally speaking, as long as we tie everything to the goal of improving the company's bottom line, we are well received by top management. But when we deal bluntly with what is best for the family and fail to tie it directly to some benefit for the company, most corporate leaders listen politely but fail to invite us back.

The public sector's omissions relate most to government's failure to recognize the social and economic value of the raising of children into productive citizens. Down through history, most societies have given recognition to the importance of parents by giving fathers and mothers a certain status and often a certain economic acknowledgment. While there is a tax exemption for dependent children in most countries' tax codes, the amount is declining as a percentage of income, and is not nearly equal to the actual costs of raising and taking care of children. Over the last thirty years, it has become dramatically more expensive to feed, clothe, house, and educate a child, yet our tax structure has given parents dramatically less help in covering those costs.

Beyond economically abdicating and ignoring parenting value and needs, government has put far too little social and political focus on parents and families. Because children have no vote and parents with children have no more voting power than adults without children, the needs and problems of families and parents go unnoticed and are too often ignored by politicians and by public policy.

The real tragedy of these sins of omission by the three outer sectors is that they are poisoning *themselves* as they fail to nourish and protect families. Every family failure and every child who doesn't get what he needs at home puts an incremental burden on the larger public and private institutions of society and robs those same institutions of a potential productive, helpful addition. Once the problems of a child spill out of the family into the welfare system, the justice system, the corporate structure, the community and neighborhood, the problem becomes impossibly complex and expensive, making all of our institutions pay directly or indirectly for their earlier omissions.

The broadest failure or omission is that our larger institutions do not recognize, value, or reward the responsibility of parenthood or family. Not enough credit or credibility or accommodation is given either to parents or to families.

Sins of Commission
(How Each Sector Has Weakened Families)

If families had only been neglected and omitted from the concerns and priorities of larger institutions, they might still survive and prosper through their own instinctive strengths and resilience. But our newer, larger institutions have not only failed to help and support families, they have, in many ways (sometimes deliberately and sometimes inadvertently) taken actions that undermine and weaken families directly and indirectly.

The private sector may be the biggest culprit when it comes to sins of commission. Entertainment, the Internet, and media institutions bombard children and parents with an amoral mix of games, movies, television, and music that glamorizes recreational sex and random violence and that belittles and ridicules traditional family life. Financial institutions have promoted easy and unwise credit and have effectively bankrupted countless families. The Internet clobbers kids with sex and violence, and these days it seems that parents and kids are better at communicating with a keyboard than with each other. Merchandising and advertising fosters a mentality of materialism whereby we measure ourselves by our possessions and our accomplishments rather than by our family relationships. Technology and its gadgets and devices push family and relationships to the side simply by absorbing enormous quantities of time from parents and from kids.

The broadest failure or omission is that our larger institutions do not recognize, value, or reward the responsibility of parenthood or family.

The public sector sins against family by imposing a "marriage tax," where two married people pay more income tax than the total of what the two would pay as unmarried individuals and by making it more profitable for many people to live on welfare than to work. The courts make divorce ever easier and less stigmatic. And child protective services have the right to take away any child from any parent.

One social worker we know puts it this way:

> "Is it any wonder that more and more fathers, especially poor fathers, are leaving their marriages and their families—often for *economic* reasons as much as for personal or emotional reasons. Is it any wonder that less than one-third of black children live with their fathers? Imagine for a moment that you are a black father, struggling economically, living with your family near the poverty line. First, you feel less and less responsibility for your

family because various welfare and special agencies are assuming that responsibility. Second, your kids and wife get less welfare and subsidy money if you live with them than if you move out. Third, both you and your wife will pay fewer taxes if you don't stay on as part of the family. And fourth, as you watch TV, you are constantly assured that broken, split-apart families are the norm anyway. Why stay at home?"

The above scenario becomes even more disturbing when we realize that a child who does live with both parents is less than *half* as likely to drop out of school, to get arrested, to use drugs, or to commit suicide. Typically fathers ("dead-beat dads") are blamed for leaving, but we need to put the blame where it belongs—on public policy that provides an incentive against keeping family together by giving a woman more aid for the care of her children if she does not have a partner living in the home.

Even the community and voluntary sectors commit "sins" against the family. Games, concerts, and recreation are scheduled profusely on Sundays and evenings, eliminating the only times parents who work long hours can be with their kids. Self-help books and seminars convince us that we need to "look out for number one" and to be more concerned with our individual comfort, looks, and status, even if it's at the expense of family responsibility.

Misery Loves Company

The syndrome of larger institutions competing with and destroying the family is fueled by people who have largely lost their own family focus and fulfillment and turned from parenting as a priority. It's a corollary on the old axiom that misery loves company. Those who have a different set of priorities subconsciously want us to adopt theirs as our own. Someone once said, "We are all trying to convert each other." Those who have expended the time and effort to be in a position to *run* other larger public and private institutions have usually sacrificed a lot of family time and family focus to get where they are. Subconsciously, they seem to want us to join them and to become their customers, their cohorts, or common sympathizers with their choice of lifestyle and priorities.

The past half-century has witnessed a "sea change" in what our larger institutions are and in what they do to us and to our families. They capture our loyalty and identity. They take over our parental functions—for profit or out of misplaced altruism. They take our responsibility and offer us redundancy. They fail to support and sustain and supplement us in the ways we need most, even as they undermine and weaken the values and societal norms that could protect us.

> *The past half-century has witnessed a "sea change" in what our larger institutions are and in what they do to us and to our families. They capture our loyalty and identity. They take over our parental functions— for profit or out of misplaced altruism.*

MIXED BLESSINGS

We have often tried to spend our vacations away from society as we know it. One summer, we took a six-week vacation, with all the children, high into the Blue Mountains of Eastern Oregon and attempted to better understand our pioneer roots by building a log cabin. We were an hour's drive away from electricity and a world away from the kids' peer groups and from life as usual. We had no electronics, no connectivity, and no electricity. First we slept in a tepee and then moved into the one-room log cabin when the walls were part way up.

The whole experience was the perfect illustration of the friend/ foe nature of modern society and of the love/hate relationship most parents develop with technology and with large institutions. On the one hand, there were so many things we missed from "regular life."

We missed the convenience, the entertainment, the information, the communication, the readily available goods and services. But we loved the simplicity, the togetherness, and the unity we felt as a family. We worked together; we talked together without being interrupted by the phone; we ate together; we played simple board games and card games together; we hiked and swam in a mountain lake together. We were each other's best friends and best helpers. Our family was the only institution for miles. It was both the hardest and the greatest six weeks of our lives.

In pointing a finger at "large institutions," in blaming them for the undermining and sometimes willful destruction of the smallest institution, we should be aware that we are making culprits out of our biggest benefactors.

So let's think first about who and what these larger institutions are—and about what we owe them. Let's consider what they do *for* us as well as what they do *to* us.

Our financial and industrial and business institutions have made a quantity and quality of goods and services available that could not have even been comprehended a century ago. Our legal institutions have protected us; our medical institutions have lengthened and improved the quality of our lives; our media/entertainment, informational, and educational institutions have opened the world to us and delivered enjoyment as well as enlightenment. Our government institutions have preserved our freedom and provided a safety net for people unable to care for themselves. All combined, the emergence in the twentieth century of stable, sustained larger institutions have dramatically increased our wealth, our access, our freedom, our awareness, our health, and have enhanced our tolerance and our capacities to understand each other. They have changed the world, made daily living less harsh and less punishing, and given us convenience and opportunity that our great-grandparents could not have imagined.

So why call these institutions culprits? Simply because, despite all the good they may provide, they are endangering and undermining families.

They do this by expanding and enriching themselves at the expense of families and by ignoring the values that are necessary to preserve families. They are thus the classic, macro example of a mixed blessing.

The question, then, is not how we can set the clock back or how we can eliminate these large institutions. Who would want to? The question is how families can successfully coexist with them. How can families take and benefit from what larger institutions offer them and yet not be swallowed up, or made redundant, or lose their sanctity or their priority in our minds?

How can families take and benefit from what larger institutions offer them and yet not be swallowed up, or made redundant, or lose their sanctity or their priority in our minds?

Because most of these larger institutions did not even exist until the twentieth century, these are relatively new questions. How can we, as individuals, revalue our families, accepting all the good that can come to us from larger institutions, while sidestepping or skirting or shielding ourselves from the bullets of family irrelevance or abdication that they shoot in our direction?

And how can these larger institutions themselves be persuaded to re-examine their policies and practices in light of their effects on families. How can they be reminded that they were created to serve families and that they themselves can only survive over the long term if families survive?

EMERGENCE OF FAMILY COMPETITORS

I was flying home from a trip to a rural, backwoods part of Mexico, traveling with my six-year-old daughter. We'd become acquainted with a very poor family there and had been in their tiny, dirt-floored home. I turned to my daughter in the next seat and said,

"Saydi, they sure live in a different world, don't they?" She gave me a blank look.

As we talked, I realized she hadn't really noticed the differences as much as the similarities. She knew that they were a family like us—that they loved each other and did things together. She was too young to focus on the materialistic.

Some things never change: the innocence of children; our own innate, intuitive, inherent love of children and family; and the natural emotional tendency to prioritize spouse and kids. These feelings, these priorities have not changed from the beginning of time. And they are the same within all families, regardless of where they live and where they are on the socio-economic scale.

But while the essence of families doesn't change, other things change completely with the emergence of larger institutions—economic, social, governmental, and informational—that are so driven toward self-preservation and growth that they sweep aside and swallow up the very families (or smaller institutions) they were intended to serve.

For the most part, these larger institutions are not philosophically anti-family. On the contrary, they reach out to families; they frequently cater to families and sell themselves or their services or their goods to families; they often pose themselves as the servers, the suppliers, even the slaves of families. But there are ways in which they are *practically* and in *practice* anti-family. What they *are* and much of what they *do* and big parts of the paradigms they *create* work against the cohesiveness, the commitment, and the continuity of families.

Categorizing Larger Institutions

There are nine broad categories or types of larger institutions that belong on the culprit list. Although some overlap, four are essentially from the private sector, three from the public, and two from the community or voluntary arenas.

1. Business/work/professional institutions

2. Financial and merchandising institutions

3. Entertainment and media institutions

4. Internet, information, and communication institutions

5. Political and governmental institutions

6. Educational institutions

7. Courts and legal institutions

8. Community recreation and social/cultural institutions

9. Religious, psychological, and self-help institutions

Let's take a look at each one through the lens of what it does for and against families:

1. BUSINESS/WORK/PROFESSIONAL INSTITUTIONS— "LIVING TO WORK"

There is nothing families need more than employment and income. Yet, ironically, more and more of the institutions that provide these things, in their own efforts for self-preservation and growth, have become a destructive force operating against the best interests of families.

Today, employers are more than a source of income and support. They are sources of identity and of image, and they exert more and more control over where people live as well as how people live.

C. S. Lewis said, "The home is the ultimate career. All other careers exist for one purpose and that is to support the ultimate career."

Today, it seems the opposite is often the case. The family seems to exist to support the career, or at least to play second fiddle to it. If the employment institution wants to transfer us to another location, we go, without very much serious thought about what the move will do to our family. If a promotion is available, we take it, without much consideration of how the new responsibility or new hours will affect family. We've become a society that lives to work rather than working to live.

Also, in their obsession for self-preservation and profit, many work in-stitutions of today are downsizing, making cutbacks, and forcing reductions and compensation restructuring which have everything to do with the bot-tom line but nothing to do with responsibility to the families of employees. Second incomes and longer hours become "necessities" to families who are trying to live the American dream created by merchandising and financial institutions (which we'll get to next). The whirl of money, things, position, status, appearance, and promotion is what we read about, think about, talk about, and worry about, and in the process, the big institutions win and the little institution—the family—loses.

Let's be specific about how this happens: Private sector business, partic-ularly large corporate structures, employ most parents and supply families with all essential goods and services. Yet in supreme irony, corporate America is ravaging families in all sorts of unprecedented ways. The damage is being done on four primary fronts:

- Wages, in real terms, are declining for blue collar and non-man-agement workers.
- Insecurity reached an all-time high in 2008, and downsizing and layoffs continue to loom as a constant threat.
- Workdays and workweeks are getting longer.
- Corporations are not doing nearly enough to assist and ac-commodate parents and to address work/life issues.

The growing chasm between the ever-increasing wealth and prosperity of US corporate management (particularly top management) and the common employees and workers in those same corporations is shocking and truly dangerous. The top executive in a typical mid- to large-size US corpora-tion makes nearly three hundred times as much as the lowest paid full-time worker in that same company. Top executives' pay goes up dramatically even as companies downsize. The CEO-to-worker compensation ratio was 20.1-to-1 in 1965 and 29.0-to-1 in 1978. It grew to 122.6-to-1 in 1995, peaked at 383.4-to-1 in 2000, and was 300.5-to-1 in 2014.[1]

It used to be that as economies grew, entire populations prospered accordingly; but in more recent times "the rich get richer and the poor get poorer" with bigger percentages of economic gain going to smaller percentages at the top.

With all the talk we hear about a kinder corporate America offering flexible work schedules and other stress-busting programs, most companies still go by the old rules. Family-friendly programs such as job-sharing, shorter workweeks, elder care help, and on-site childcare are hardly universal.

Managers' minds are on profit margins, competitive edge, mergers and acquisitions, and the bottom line, *not* on the human, personal, and family needs of their employees.

The top executive in a typical mid- to large-size US corporation makes nearly three hundred times as much as the lowest paid full-time worker in that same company.

With the ever-present culture of downsizing and layoffs, employees are understandably hesitant to ask either for better wages or for more family-friendly benefits. A significant number of downsized workers fail to find new jobs, and many of those who do end up with a lower-paying job.

To many, it seems that even as workers get lower wages and poorer job security, they are working longer hours, and in more and more cases, both parents feel that they have to work full-time, sometimes in multiple jobs. As is so often the case in economic hardship, the children are the real losers.

These troublesome trends in wages, job security, hours, and other work/life issues are evident throughout the private sector. And within several sub-categories of business—particularly the financial, merchandising, media, and information institutions—additional factors are at work that undermine and threaten families.

2A. FINANCIAL INSTITUTIONS—"THE DEBT CULTURE"

Ever since there has been money, there have been bankers or their equivalent—people who borrow and lend money. But it is only recently that financial institutions have become so huge and so influential that they exert major control over many aspects of our personal and our societal lives. They have, in essence, created a credit society and a debt culture in which families spend before they earn and in which we are oriented to instant gratification at almost every level.

> *Pre-approved credit cards arrive in the mail—even to college freshmen and eighteen-year-olds who have no clue how to use credit. We heard about this issue first-hand when our daughter left for her freshman year at Wellesley College in Boston and actually asked me for advice on what to do when a credit card arrived in the mail! I told her to get a good pair of scissors and to cut in half every unsolicited credit card she received. She told me later that she used those scissors more than a dozen times. Her roommate, I found out, never borrowed the scissors and presented her parents with a $5,000.00 credit card bill when she went home for Christmas during her freshman year.*

People buy everything from cars to Christmas presents based on the amount of the monthly payment rather than on the total price. Often they do not even know the full ticket cost, let alone the total amount they will ultimately pay including interest.

Parents, in an effort to "keep up with the Joneses" and to give their children all they need, become debt ridden and, in the process, teach dangerous financial principles to their kids, even as they spend less and less time with their families because they work longer and longer hours to pay their bills.

It has been observed that you can tell a lot about a society by which of its sectors is building the biggest or most magnificent edifices. For centuries, churches and cathedrals and synagogues and temples were the most impressive structures. Then there was a span of years when government buildings seemed to be the biggest and most opulent. They were soon dwarfed by skyscrapers, plants, and corporate headquarters of major industrial corporations. Today, many would argue that the most opulent and pretentious new buildings house banks and other financial institutions. The competition between them and their push for growth and stockholder profit has been their incentive to create a debt and credit mentality that is hugely destructive to families—and, in turn, our economy.

> *People buy everything from cars to Christmas presents based on the amount of the monthly payment rather than on the total price.*

2B. MERCHANDISING INSTITUTIONS—"SHOP 'TIL YOU DROP"

There have always been salesmen. The very essence of commerce and economy at any level is the promotion and marketing of goods and services. And certainly a desire for things—materialism in some form or other—has existed since the beginning of time.

What has changed everything, however, is the emergence of huge and influential marketing and advertising institutions whose single goal or reason for existence is to sell more product without regard to the true needs or buying capacities of the consumer.

> *A close friend of ours, chairman of a worldwide ad agency, is uncommonly objective and frank about his profession. "The basic goal of advertising," he says, "is to make people think they need*

what they really only want." Think about the implications of that. Hundreds of advertising impressions (from billboards and radio to Internet pop-ups and TV spots) come at us every day, each carefully designed to make us dissatisfied with what we have, how we look, where we are, what we do, and how we live.

Because of the messages of advertising, people tend to measure themselves (and others) by what they have rather than by what they are. Appearances supersede substance. Things become more important than people. Acquisition and achievements are given more time and more effort than relationships and family.

Occasionally, an ad plays on warm family images, but most often glitz, social status, materialism, and "freedom" from burden or obligation is the portrayed ideal. Our own work-a-day family responsibilities look boring and mundane next to advertising images.

Thus, parents and families take a double hit:

- They are prompted to be dissatisfied with simple, family-oriented lifestyles.
- They are enticed to spend more on things that compete with family needs.

And it's not just advertising. The huge American merchandising machine includes everything from infomercials and shopping channels to wholesale clubs, rebates, and high-powered retail promotions. And the biggest push and volume of all—online marketing, merchandising, and purchasing. It is incredibly easy to buy things and to pay for them with credit. On the one hand, all of these serve our consumer needs and can make life more convenient; but on the other hand, they fill our lives with complexity, with unmet "needs," and with debt—robbing us of family time and family awareness and priority in the process.

In marketing parlance, there is a distinction made between "demand pull" and "product push." Sometimes a real need or demand "pulls" or creates a product and a distribution system. Other times, a product "pushes" or creates its own interest and market. Before the twentieth century, most of our economy operated primarily by demand-pull. But with the emergence of today's huge merchandising/advertising institutions, there is a massive shift to product-push—and the "products" range from unlimited *things* to

And it's not just money they extract— it's time and attention and priorities.

styles to *programming* to *attitudes.* And very few of them enhance the family—in fact, most compete with and deprioritize family and neighborhood relationships.

Merchandising institutions, from agencies to the marketing arms of retail and industrial giants to internet merchandisers of all kinds, measure themselves on how much product they can sell and how much money they can extract from people—from families. And it's not just money they extract— it's time and attention and priorities, much of which might otherwise go to children and to maintaining and strengthening family relationships.

Naturally, this "merchandising institution culprit" is linked to the "financial institution culprit." The wants that are cultivated and encouraged by the merchandisers lead to the need for the easy credit that is extended by the financials. The one-two punch works particularly well on families. Children are often the prime target of advertisers, and parents overextend their credit to give their children things to make up for the very time and attention they are putting elsewhere.

3. ENTERTAINMENT, NEWS, AND MEDIA INSTITUTIONS—"LET ME ENTERTAIN YOU"

Entertainment has existed as long as people have, and the messages of song and dance, theater, the visual arts, and even of sports have always been varied and diverse. Various ways of reporting on events or "news" have also existed forever.

But it is only recently that entertainment and news have combined with electronic media and internet technology and become an institution so vast, so powerful, and so centralized that its messages could threaten and undermine families and the values that sustain families on a wide, even global scale.

On the positive side, in theory at least, entertainment media, from movies and TV to music and even some video games, can bring families together, give them a shared experience, help them communicate, and at times even uplift and inspire them. News media keeps us informed and up-to-date like never before.

Yet, at the same time, our media today is so pervasive and so addictive that it takes time away from families and substitutes for communication within families even as it douses us with content that desensitizes us to violence, to dangerous, casual sex, and to other destroyers of family. We are raising a whole generation of kids who communicate better with their thumbs than with their voices. Albert Einstein may have foreseen this when he said, "I fear the day that technology will surpass our human interaction. The world will have a generation of idiots."

When innocuous movies, soap operas, and sitcoms portray promiscuous teenage sex as the norm, it becomes the norm. When movies or TV dramas or reality shows portray indiscriminate violence as commonplace, it becomes commonplace. When rap songs depict hatred and bizarre acts as the thing to feel and the things to do, they become exactly that for millions. When news covers

When innocuous movies, soap operas, and sitcoms portray promiscuous teenage sex as the norm, it becomes the norm. When movies or TV dramas or reality shows portray indiscriminate violence as commonplace, it becomes commonplace.

only the sensational or the violent, we think that's how the world is. And when irresponsible or valueless behavior is presented without any reference or connection to *consequences*, young people (and older ones for that matter) begin to believe they can get away with anything.

> *In a television debate we watched not long ago on who should take responsibility for a horrendous high school murder and suicide tragedy, a producer/director-type was insisting that it was unfair to blame media or video games. Where then, questioned his opponent, did the shooters get their graphic images of dark gun violence, spurting blood, and exploding bodies? Did they get those images from their parents? From their school? From their church?*

We know how susceptible the human mind, especially the *young* mind, is to visual and audio suggestion. It's why companies are willing to pay millions for a thirty-second impression during the Super Bowl. Yet we continue to allow violent, anti-social images to flow at our children almost constantly.

Teen pregnancy and sexually transmitted diseases are at epidemic proportions in many parts of the world as kids watch movies and reality shows where people jump into bed on the first date and sex is generally treated as a form of recreation. Divorce, single parenting, and various alternative lifestyles get far more play than stable marriages and families, so much so that someone really committed to his marriage and family might tune in for an evening of standard fare TV and conclude that he was a dinosaur—hopelessly old-fashioned and out of touch.

Daytime TV talk shows and every variety of reality show, in their quest for ratings, compete against each other in terms of which can find and present the most irresponsible and bizarre behavior. In the process, they "lower the bar" in terms of what is acceptable and undermine the values and behaviors that are necessary to preserve and protect families.

> *An astonishing example of this came a friend who had just produced*

a terrific movie called Nowhere Safe *about the devastating effects of cyberbullying on a young high school girl and her creative ability to handle the situation. In an effort to get this important message to a wide audience, he went to Los Angeles and pitched it to a top executive at ABC Family, which seemed like a great fit.*

He sent us the following note about his meeting:

We had a cordial visit and discussed the role of positive media and then discussed the anti-bullying message of Nowhere Safe. She agreed that bullying and cyberbullying are perhaps the biggest issues facing young people today. So I asked her, why not show it on ABC Family, even one time, and we'll give her the movie for FREE for a one-time showing (just to get a positive message out to the young people). She then turned around and pointed to the posters on the wall behind her and said, "We need more shows like this." What posters did she point to? The Fosters, a new show that follows the life of an interracial lesbian couple raising children together; and Pretty Little Liars, a show that follows the lives of four teenage girls who are in a clique. (Just the opposite message of Nowhere Safe.) As I left I noticed their new moniker: "ABC Family—A New Kind of Family."

We appreciate all kinds of families, but would welcome a little more positive attention to traditional families.

Here's another way to look at it: We used to look through our rectangular glass windows and see our neighbors and feel connected to them and share their same values. We still do that today, but our rectangular glass windows turn on and off with the click of a remote or when we open or close our laptop or switch on our smart phone or tablet. Our view through these windows is of fictional neighbors whose behavior carries no consequence, who get their problems resolved by the end of the half hour, who seem to effortlessly have everything we want without paying for it, and who make us think we're old-fashioned because we don't live or think like they do. With our electronic windows, if things don't go as we want them to, we just restart the game, change the channel, or move to the next Internet site.

It's not only the entertainment media that sucks away our time and influences our values; it's the news media as well. "Staying informed" takes up big chunks of our day, and, far from being "values neutral," much of the data that reaches us is slanted or "spun" to make most everything else seem more important than family.

Never before have we been so in touch, so well informed, so up-to-date on so much of what is going on in the world. But in addition to not being very practically useful, much of the information of our informative age is anti-family in various ways.

It is a generally accepted fact that the press and news media, taken in aggregate, is more liberal, in both its ideology and its lifestyle, than the average American. And the most visible conservatives in the media are often so strident and self-righteous in their style that they become hard to identify with. Thus, anti-family lifestyles are treated as legitimate lifestyle alternatives, and traditional, measurably functional families are portrayed as outdated, old-fashioned, or more and more often, as nonexistent.

We used to look through our rectangular glass windows and see our neighbors and feel connected to them and share their same values. We still do that today, but our rectangular glass windows turn on and off with the click of a remote or when we open or close our laptop or switch on our smart phone or tablet.

Even "reputable" news shows seem compelled to present what shocks us rather than what helps us.

Several years ago, the TV show

20/20 called us to ask if we'd help them with a show on values. We were excited to do so in light of some work we were doing with inner-city kids based on our book, Teaching Your Children Values. *They came and filmed for two days and got some very touching footage of disadvantaged kids who were really turning their lives around by understanding and implementing values. In one particular segment on having the courage to stand up for what you believe, a beautiful but victimized eight-year-old was responding to "scenarios" in a color-coded teaching game. "Someone offers you drugs:" Yellow—"You take them." Orange—"You say no." Red— "You turn in the kid that offered them." None of the scenarios were hypothetical to this little girl—she'd faced them all. At the end of the game, I asked her what she thought she was—yellow, orange, or red. With a tear in her eye, she said, "I've been mostly yellow, but I'm trying to hang out with more reds so I think I'm kind of orange now." It was a beautiful, positive moment, and the film crew recorded dozens more like it. But when the show was produced and aired, the upbeat, hopeful stuff was all cut. They used footage of hard, defiant kids who made shocking statements about their lack of values. Completely unbalanced, the show implied that all kids are basically monsters.*

Why is disproportionate news coverage given to violence and cruelty? Why do reality shows and magazine shows and news features seem so preoccupied with deviance and dysfunctionality? The answer, of course, has to do with profit. News ratings, just like entertainment ratings, go up in proportion to the sex and violence they cover.

The omni-present Internet and news and entertainment media bring things into our homes that have never been admitted before: violence in online computer games and on the evening news, pornography on the Internet and cable, divorce statistics that are skewed to make it appear that no marriage survives, celebrities who are negative role models for our children, and a general impression that people with money and power are the ones to emulate, not the people with families.

One part of parenting that has always been assumed, if not guaranteed, is the responsibility and the opportunity of deciding *what* children should learn or be exposed to or become familiar with, *when* they should receive it, and *how* they should view it or prioritize it or think about it. Parents, in other words, were essentially in charge of how their children would initially see the world. They were thus able to mold and shape children's paradigms and early values, giving them a foundation on which to build their own beliefs and perspectives, their own lives.

The massive news and information institutions of today have seized that function—snatching it away from parents by their very pervasiveness. Short of living somewhere on a primitive island, families have no way of shielding children or screening what they see and hear.

4. INTERNET, INFORMATION, AND COMMUNICATION TECHNOLOGY—"EVERYTHING AT MY FINGERTIPS"

A generation ago, parents complained about TV—the programs and how much time it took out of our lives. But the TV was usually in the living room or family room, and it was possible to sit down *with* the kids and watch it. Today, the Internet poses a far more difficult challenge. Kids can go online from almost anywhere and view raw and explicit sex and violence. And much of what they can find is interactive, and rather than passively watching, they are engaged with the material, thus giving it more impact on their attitudes and behaviors.

With a few strokes on a keyboard or on a smart phone, by typing in the most violent and sexual words they know, kids can be in direct (and interactive) touch with hard-core pornography, with violent blood-gushing "games," with online pedophiles, or with detailed instructions for how to construct a bomb.

Few would want to do without the marvels of our information age and our social media. Our data and communication systems serve us magnificently.

They keep us in touch with each other and with the world. They put limitless information and knowledge at our fingertips. They tend to increase our tolerance and understanding—to break down barriers of ignorance and prejudice. Communication and information institutions, from utilities to Internet companies to computer networks and systems, literally make the world work; and they make our own individual worlds so much bigger.

If a parental vote could be taken, it's likely that the Internet would win out as the most-feared large institution of all.

Nevertheless, these institutions are definite culprits in the destruction of our families. Their methods of destruction range from the benign to the malignant, from the domination and consumption of our time to the intentional pollution and perversion of our children's perspectives, morality, and standards. It's not just a question of how much interaction and family time a child is missing by spending five hours a day in front of a tablet or a laptop or a smartphone; it is a question of how much filth and misinformation he or she is ingesting from these sources.

If a parental vote could be taken, it's likely that the Internet would win out as the most-feared large institution of all.

5. PUBLIC/POLITICAL INSTITUTIONS—"BIG BROTHER GETTING BIGGER"

There have always been governments—from tribal councils to despot kings—and they have always had the power and potential to be destructive to family life. But it is only in the last several decades that the public sector, our governmental structures, have become big enough and institutionalized enough to systematically take over many of the functions of families and to monitor and tax families to the extent of threatening their viability.

The size of government today, and its scope of "services," taxes families to the point of threatening their economic survival, and then it makes families seem redundant by attempting to supply, via its larger institutions, the services, the welfare, the child and elderly care, and a host of other elements that families used to provide for themselves.

Unfortunately, government on virtually every level, has strayed from and gone beyond that ideal, passing and implementing all kinds of obtrusive and intrusive tax and regulatory laws that undermine the inner sectors in numerous ways and that particularly threaten the bull's-eye of the family. Legislative, executive, and judicial branches of federal and state governments, often in well-intentioned efforts to protect individual rights, have failed to consider family rights or parental responsibilities.

"Protect" is the operative word, and the concept around which debate must center. *The goal must be to protect individual rights without jeopardizing families.* A tax law that makes married individuals pay more than they would if they were single does not pass that test. Nor do laws that make it easier (and cheaper) to find daycare for a newborn than to have maternity leave and nurture the child. Nor do laws that are so overzealous in protecting children that they undermine a parent's right to discipline a child, or to take him to church, or to make decisions about his education.

Our elected governments, like every large institution–culprit we've identified, gravitate to their own survival and expansion, and in the process, they overwhelm families even as they fail to protect them.

6. EDUCATIONAL INSTITUTIONS—"WITH THEM, WHO NEEDS US?"

Ideally, schools and parents become partners in the intellectual and character education of children. In earlier days, schools were run by communities. They broadened kids' horizons and, in some cases, their levels of diversity and tolerance. Parents, if not in charge, at least had meaningful input and saw the schools as

Ideally, schools and parents become partners in the intellectual and character education of children.

extensions of themselves and as "helpers" in bringing up their children.

Today, the massive institutions of state school systems, federal education departments, and national teachers' unions often work around parents rather than through them, assuming much of the responsibility that should stay with parents and substituting (inadequately) for the family in many areas.

> *When I lost my gubernatorial campaign in our state a few years ago, many friends told me they thought it was directly due to my opposition by the Teacher's Union. I had proposed a voucher system for parental school choice that apparently threatened the power and the job security of the union's leadership, and they worked tirelessly against my election. Despite the generally conservative nature of our state and the usual popularity of free-market approaches, vouchers, more charter schools, and more parental choice were all demonized, and the campaign turned out to be a victory for voices that wanted to protect and maximize teacher and bureaucratic power and minimize parental power and involvement.*

Filled with well-meaning teachers and administrators, school systems accomplish all kinds of good things and would never identify themselves as being family-destructive in any way. Yet their *size* and *reach* weaken families in at least four primary ways:

1. Schools assume responsibility for sex education, character education, behavior monitoring, career counseling, after-school care, and other activities that parents should be more involved in. Parents feel relieved and absolved of those responsibilities and can become more removed and less communicative with their kids.

2. Schools create a school culture and a peer culture that often supersedes the family culture. Kids' time, loyalty, activity, leisure, and work are all more involved with school and with various

types of sports, music, dance, and other "lessons" than they are with family. Parents can begin to think of themselves merely as the taxi service that gets kids from one thing to the other, or as the "general contractor" who watches the subcontractors of schools, clubs, teachers, scouting, and sports teams do all of the actual work with kids.

3. Schools sometimes teach anti-family or family-irrelevant views of the world. Overriding emphasis on the scientific, the economic, and the political worlds can (in the minds of children) seem to supersede the religious world or the family world.

4. Daycare, preschool, and after-school programs, while providing services that many families need, can become substitutes for parents and for family time, creating situations where parents spend less and less time with children and feel less and less responsibility for them.

The challenge for parents, of course, is to value and appreciate all that schools can do for children without letting the school culture or the peer culture supersede the family culture.

7. COURTS AND LEGAL INSTITUTIONS—"WHO REPRESENTS FAMILIES?"

There have always been conflicts and a need for facilitators to resolve conflicts. But large legal institutions, for whatever worthwhile purposes they serve, are inherently interested in their own preservation and growth, and thus they tend to foster and even to create the very kinds of conflict that support them and keep them viable. (Illustrated by the old joke about the only lawyer in town who was starving until a second lawyer moved in, and then they both got rich.)

There are laws designed to enhance the commitment of marriage and the responsibility to children, but lawyers and legal institutions today seem to have more to do with the dissolving or undoing of commitment and the dividing of families.

Most laws are designed for the protection of the *individual,* not of the family. Therefore, when two individuals try to use the law to protect their personal *rights*—their individual entitlement—they often proceed by pulling families apart. There are a lot more divorce lawyers than marriage-preservation counselors, more custody battles than successful parent-parent-child reconciliations, more probate lawyers than simple wealth transfers, more litigators than arbitrators, more losses than wins for families.

There is no question that we need lawyers and legal institutions. But in families, we have to rely more on love and commitment than on individual rights, more than giving what is needed than getting what we need, and more on being there for someone than in having an attorney be there for you.

Our courts and public justice system also undermine families by putting the rights of individuals so far above the needs and nature of family units. Courts and legal interpretations end up supporting kids who sue their parents or child protection agencies who take kids away from parents with hearsay "evidence." No-fault divorce laws dramatically increase the numbers of divorces.

Family Law expert Bruce Hafen (quoted earlier on page 64) offers clarity on the intent and the effects of no-fault divorce:

> No-fault divorce was first adopted in California in 1968 and then, with some variations, over the next twenty years it became the law in every state. No-fault significantly changed the way people thought about marriage. Under the old divorce laws, married people couldn't just choose to end their marriage; rather, they had to prove spousal misconduct—like adultery or mental cruelty. In those days, people perceived the state as a party to the marriage—remember

the "social interests" in family law. Therefore, only a judge representing society's interests could determine when a divorce was justified.

As originally conceived, no-fault divorce had worthy goals. It added irretrievable marriage breakdown, regardless of personal fault, as an additional basis for divorce—which simplified divorce actions and reduced messy personal litigation. No-fault also improved how the law saw the economic interests of women. And, in theory, only a judge, who represented society's interests, could decide whether a marriage was indeed beyond repair. But in practice, family court judges began to defer to the personal preference of a couple; and eventually they deferred to whichever partner wanted to end the marriage.

So, as one Canadian lawyer put it, no-fault divorce no longer "looked at marriage . . . as a [social] institution." Rather, no-fault saw marriage as "an essentially private relationship between adults terminable at the will of either," without regard to the consequences for children, let alone the effect of divorce on society. Before long, judges' doubts about society's right to enforce wedding vows gave married couples the false impression that their personal promises held no great social or moral value.

As these new legal assumptions have blended with larger cultural swings, most Americans no longer see marriage as a relatively permanent social institution; rather, they see it as a temporary, private source of personal fulfillment. So when marriage commitments intrude on personal preferences, people are more likely to walk away. Thus today is the age of what someone called the "non-binding commitment," whatever that oxymoron means.[2]

Family dangers imposed by our courts continue to proliferate. It's hard to imagine (and hard to overstate) the power the judicial branch of government wields through its interpretation of laws. When a court or a judge writes an opinion, he is taking a law and telling us not only how to interpret it but how to enforce it. Thus, someone with an anti-family or family-weakening idea doesn't have to get elected to implement a destructive policy—doesn't even have to influence the elective process or the legislature or city hall. All he or it (the person or the idea) has to do is to directly or indirectly influence an opinion written by a judge.

> *Friends of ours attended a conference on families in Budapest, where unbinding, theoretical resolutions are passed that point in the direction of easier divorce laws, less restrictive abortion policies, and overblown concern about population control. The delegates to this conference are not elected or even appointed. They are just self-selected people who have various political agendas. No effort has been made to balance the conference or make it representative. The resolutions are not laws or even proposals for legislation. But they go out, under a United Nations letterhead, and begin to influence judges and legislators.*

Our private litigation system is also to blame. Litigation, in general and in most of its forms, is harmful to families. Typically, the only family one could argue it helps is the family of the lawyer who collects the fees. And when litigation (or custody or any other legal controversy) is between family members, it almost always tears apart and destroys relationships. It is rarely win-win. It is sometimes win-lose. It is usually lose-lose.

The adversarial mentality of the divorce court and litigation institution spills over into families, where spouses threaten separation or divorce rather than communicating and compromising, or where family members "fight it out" as prequels to court battles rather than hashing things out in good faith and in private.

This is an area where we can learn much from the Asian mindset. Most Asian countries have less than ten percent of the number of lawyers (and amount of litigation) per capita as the United States and many other Western countries. There are bright spots, though. Canada's litigation rate is very low, and there are countries that have more registered "arbitrators" or "conciliators" than they do litigating or divorce lawyers. We need to move closer to that pattern rather than away from it.

8. RECREATIONAL AND SOCIAL/CULTURAL INSTITUTIONS—"WHO NEEDS THE HOME?"

Recreation and social activities used to happen within and among families. Now, they often occur independent of and at the expense of families within larger sports, music, cultural, social, and leisure institutions.

A list of the social, cultural, and recreational institutions that have come into being over the last hundred years includes everything from sports leagues to summer camps, from concert and theater guilds to fraternities, from spas and gyms to fast-food restaurants. Great and useful as they are, they sometimes take the place of family time, and many create competition rather than cooperation among and between family members.

Americans no longer see marriage as a relatively permanent social institution; rather, they see it as a temporary, private source of personal fulfillment.

Furthermore, many of these teams, clubs, guilds, camps, and societies become the identity or self-image or pride of individuals, more than their own families, and pull our allegiance and our attention from our families as well as our time.

Many recreational, social, and cultural events are scheduled during hours that traditionally have been family time. Evenings, Sunday afternoons, and summer vacations—the time blocks that families used to spend together—are now increasingly devoted to other activities and other groups. Instead of rushing from work to home, we rush from work to tennis lessons or to the spa or to the concert or to the book club. Instead of a family dinner, we refuel on the run at McDonald's. Instead of church and a family gathering on Sunday, we do the soccer league and the flute class and then watch the big game—the big games are always on Sunday.

Many parents consider the games, camps, and clubs as their family time. They are with their kids, taking them places, watching them. But these can be poor substitutes for traditional kinds of family time. There is little interaction among family members. Attention is focused on competition and comparison rather than on cooperation and communication. The logistics and expenses of getting to everything, outfitting for everything, paying for everything creates its share of stress and family tension.

Few of us would like to do away with the recreational and social opportunities that these elements of society give us, but most parents recognize the need to limit and govern and think about their families' involvement and the tradeoffs and sacrifices that are involved.

9. RELIGIOUS, PSYCHOLOGICAL, AND SELF-HELP INSTITUTIONS—NON-PROFIT AND VOLUNTARY ORGANIZATIONS

Voluntary and non-profit humanitarian sectors are much more developed and wide-spread in the United States than in other Western countries. There needs to be more international synergy and more recognition that a family focus makes all interventions and initiatives more sustainable.

One of the more subtle and yet dangerously powerful transitions of the last century is the substitution of psychological and self-help approaches for religious institutions and approaches of faith. They encourage and support relying on the practical and psychological rather than the spiritual.

Most Americans and strong pluralities in most developed countries still go to church, at least occasionally, and profess belief, but they are inclined,

more and more, to turn to prescription drugs and to self-help and psychological help in dealing with their fears and problems, as well as their hopes
and dreams. Even the word "spiritual" has come to have more connection
to self than to God. Words like "spirit," "soul," and "faith"—once the domain
of the church—are trendy and popular now to mean *my* spirit, *my* soul, *my*
inner consciousness, *my* faith in *my* self. As such, they create dependence
on and reverence for self that can work against a reverence for God and a
dependency on His will and power. With self-orientation and self-help can
come a kind of selfishness that detracts from family commitments and family-oriented priorities and solutions.

The books that line the large self-help sections of bookstores typically deal
with three themes—gaining more control, ownership, and independence.
While all three qualities are important and desirable in certain contexts,
each one, carried to extremes or pursued too vigorously or too exclusively,
can rob us of joy and faith and can seriously undermine our families. Think
a little deeper about how contrary they are to spiritual faith:

- Gaining more *control*. Most people of faith would give *control*
  to God and would not place their own importance or control
  above that of another person. They would be more interested in *guidance* (seeing and conforming to God's will) than in
  control (making things happen according to their own will). A
  guidance mentality makes parents more nurturing and observant and less overbearing and demanding.

- Obtaining more *ownership*. People of faith would acknowledge
  God's ownership of all things and perceive themselves as *stewards* over what God had entrusted to them. Thus they would
  be less materialistic and less inclined to spend all their time
  chasing possessions and position. In this stewardship mode,
  children, spouse, and family become our respected responsibilities rather than our possessions.

- Becoming more *independent*. People of faith realize their *dependence* on God and are more inclined to be humble and to work *with* others, understanding that everyone is linked and that we thus all need each other. Such persons make better— and more committed—spouses and parents than those who perceive themselves as independent islands who need and are responsible for no one but themselves.

As the institutions of self-help have grown and as the *curses* of selfishness have multiplied (teen pregnancy, violence, substance abuse), most religious institutions have been silent, or too insular, or too cautious in taking strong stands and making a stronger case for family priorities and family-prioritized life styles. There are too many politically correct churches and too many religious leaders and religious teachers who emphasize tolerance at the expense of all other values and teach us that how you live doesn't matter much as long as you accept how every other person has chosen to live. As G. K. Chesterton said, "Tolerance is the favored virtue of those who believe in nothing."

The challenge for parents is to realize how dependent they really are, how far their own skills and insights fall short, and how much they need God's help to raise God's children.

GRAPHIC REVIEW

Each of these nine sets of large institutions was born (or developed, and matured) in the last century to serve and sustain and make life more comfortable and convenient for individuals and families; but they have evolved and mutated in ways that seriously threaten the ongoing viability of families. The effects, good and bad, and the false paradigms and errors of these friend/enemies, these servants/enslavers, can be charted:

1. WORK/PROFESSIONAL INSTITUTIONS	
Who	The Private Sector, Employers, Corporate America
Good Side (Family-Beneficial)	They provide our income, our employment, and our professional identity.
Bad Side (Family-Destructive)	They demand more and more time. They cause disruptive relocations and sometimes cause kids to be raised by institutions other than family.
What/How (The Essence of the Problem)	Our jobs have become our identity more than our family. Too much mental energy, as well as too much time, is spent on work, too little on family. Being at work is easier (and gives us more status) than being at home.
False Paradigms (Lies, False Impressions, and Self-Justification)	"You are your work." Two incomes are almost always required to support family. There is more recognition and reward for work than for family.
Errors	**Key misused words:** • "Status" (meaning "job title and income") • "Freedom" (meaning "bondage now so that *someday* money will give you more options") **Lifestyle mistakes:** • Prioritizing work over family • Greed **Bad tradeoffs** • Things for time • Work position for family position • Job/company loyalty for family loyalty

2A. FINANCIAL INSTITUTIONS	
Who	Banks, Credit Unions, Mortgage Companies, Credit Cards, Investment Brokers
Good Side (Family-Beneficial)	They allow us to buy homes, earn on savings, etc. They facilitate our physical care of families.
Bad Side (Family-Destructive)	They make credit and credit problems too easy to come by. Debt creates stress and takes away parents' time with kids. Stress breaks up marriages.
What/How (The Essence of the Problem)	Easy credit spoils the work ethic. Families live beyond their means and prioritize things above relationships.
False Paradigms (Lies, False Impressions, and Self-Justification)	"You deserve it—before you've earned it" (instant gratification) You need to "have it all." "All I want is the land next to mine." (greed)
Errors	**Key misused words** • "Fulfillment" (meaning "instant gratification") **Lifestyle mistakes** • Living beyond income • Excess spending; insufficient saving **Bad tradeoffs** • Excess for balance • Instant gratification for delayed gratification

2B. MERCHANDISING INSTITUTIONS	
Who	Retail, Advertising, Marketing
Good Side (Family-Beneficial)	They deliver needed goods and services to families.
Bad Side (Family-Destructive)	They take both time and money away from family. They foster materialism.
What/How (The Essence of the Problem)	There is too much out there—and advertising and merchandising are the fine art of making us think we need what we actually only want. Things get prioritized above relationships.
False Paradigms (Lies, False Impressions, and Self-Justification)	"More is better." I deserve instant gratification. You are what you own. He who dies with the most toys wins.
Errors	**Key misused words** • "Needs" (meaning "wants") • "Wealth" (meaning "money" and "things") **Lifestyle mistakes** • Misuse of credit **Bad tradeoffs** • Work for family • Money for time • Gifts of things over gifts of time

3. ENTERTAINMENT AND MEDIA INSTITUTIONS	
Who	Movies, Music, TV, Radio
Good Side (Family-Beneficial)	They bring families together for a shared experience. They entertain us, "broaden" us, inform us, and help us communicate. They can uplift, motivate, and inspire.
Bad Side (Family-Destructive)	They take time away from families. They desensitize us to violence, extramarital sex, and divorce. They create false paradigms and surface value systems.
What/How (The Essence of the Problem)	A small "cultural elite" of producers, directors, and writers control virtually all of what we see and hear in media. Their hugely disproportionate influence allows this generally non-family-oriented minority to masquerade as a majority.
False Paradigms (Lies, False Impressions, and Self-Justification)	"Everyone does it." "There are no consequences." "Media just reflects and reports values and attitudes; it doesn't create or influence them." Tolerance is the chief (perhaps the only) virtue. Traditional values and traditional families are old-fashioned and unenlightened.

Errors	**Key misused words** • "Love" (meaning "lust") • "Adventure" (meaning "violence") • "Tolerance" (meaning "license") • "Wealth" (meaning "money") • "News" (meaning the "spectacular" and the "negative") **Lifestyle mistakes** • Intimacy and cohabitation prior to marriage • Violent, win-lose conflict resolution **Bad tradeoffs** • Thrill for commitment • Self for family

4. INTERNET, INFORMATION, AND TECHNOLOGY INSTITUTIONS	
Who	The Internet, Telecommunication Systems, Data Banks, and Access
Good Side (Family-Beneficial)	Information sources are accessible in the home 24/7 (which allows more work to be done, and more time to be spent, at home).
Bad Side (Family-Destructive)	It takes huge chunks of our time (from family interaction). Pornography and violence are only a click away.
What/How (The Essence of the Problem)	There is too much exposure to violence and all varieties of immoral and amoral behavior, too much time wasted with superfluous information, and too much virtual interaction with destructive ideas and practices.
False Paradigms (Lies, False Impressions, and Self-Justification)	"You're in touch." Sex and violence are recreational. Virtual reality is reality.
Errors	**Key misused words** • "In touch" (meaning "online" or "informed" but not connecting with people) • "Important" (most of it isn't) • "Connections" (not *personal* ones) • "Knowledge" (meaning "information") **Lifestyle mistakes** • Sitting, observing, not doing **Bad tradeoffs** • Cyberspace for real space • Information for wisdom • Information for common sense

5. POLITICAL/GOVERNMENTAL INSTITUTIONS	
Who	Government at all levels, Executive and Legislative
Good Side (Family-Beneficial)	It protects us from outside aggression and from each other. It provides essential services and a safety net for those who can't help themselves.
Bad Side (Family-Destructive)	"Marriage penalty" tax codes. Filled with oppressive bureaucracies. Welfare system destroys initiative/responsibility.
What/How (The Essence of the Problem)	The "Big Brothers" of government can never substitute for the parents of families. Regulation, taxation, and welfare have all become "family unfriendly."
False Paradigms (Lies, False Impressions, and Self-Justification)	"Bigger is better." Poverty causes values destruction (instead of the other way around). "My private life only affects me." "Nice guys finish last." Public is better than private.
Errors	**Key misused words** • "Equality" (meaning "bringing everyone down to a common level") • "Opportunity" (meaning "conformity") • "Benevolence" (meaning "the destruction of initiative") **Lifestyle mistakes** • Depending on government rather than on ourselves and our families. **Bad tradeoffs** • Security for agency • Dependence for independence

6. EDUCATIONAL INSTITUTIONS	
Who	Preschools, Primary and Secondary Schools, Universities
Good Side (Family-Beneficial)	They expand our horizons and improve perspective. They inspire and motivate us. They help develop children's social and emotional capacities.
Bad Side (Family-Destructive)	They don't teach values/character/discipline/responsibility (and parents think they do). They take over too much of child-rearing, allowing parental abdication. They sometimes cause early-age separation of children and parents (boarding schools).
What/How (The Essence of the Problem)	Schools sometimes become substitutes for families rather than supports, trying to do things independently for children (from teaching about sex to caring for them in after-school programs) that parents should be involved in.
False Paradigms (Lies, False Impressions, and Self-Justification)	You must have "professional expertise" to teach kids. Nurseries and preschools can handle kids better than parents. We can understand and explain everything "scientifically."

Errors	**Key misused words** • "Values neutral" (meaning "no values at all") • "Education" (meaning "imparting information") **Lifestyle mistakes** • Trying to know more and more about less and less • Turning over a child's present and future to the schools • No teaching of social or emotional intelligence which could thwart bullying **Bad tradeoffs** • "Tolerance" for absolutes • Their responsibility for ours

7. COURTS AND LEGAL INSTITUTIONS	
Who	Courts, Judges, Legal Firms, Lobbyists, Litigators
Good Side (Family-Beneficial)	They protect our rights, assets, and persons. They provide a "way out" for truly irreconcilable differences.
Bad Side (Family-Destructive)	Anti-family interpretation of law is common. Probate battles, custody battles, and divorce battles are hard on families and children. "Rights" become selfish demands that alienate family members from each other.
What/How (The Essence of the Problem)	Legal "rights" and legal battles pit individual needs and wants above family commitments and pit family members against each other, pulling families apart. Judges prioritize individual rights above family commitments and obligations.
False Paradigms (Lies, False Impressions, and Self-Justification)	The state knows more about what's good for children than parents. It's better to escape problems than to resolve them. If a marriage isn't good, admit your mistake, divorce, and move on. If you are unhappy, sue. Kids are always better off with parents separating than staying together in conflict.

Errors	**Key misused words** • "Prenuptial agreement" (meaning "tentative, conditional commitment"). • "Custody" (meaning "win-lose"). **Lifestyle mistakes** • Measuring success materially rather than matrimonially **Bad tradeoffs** • Proving you're right for saving kids • My needs for family needs • "Freedom" for responsibility • Money for relationships • Individual rights for family commitments

8. RECREATION AND SOCIAL/CULTURAL INSTITUTIONS	
Who	Sports, Arts, Clubs, Leagues, Fast Food, Summer Camps, and some aspects of Medical Care
Good Side (Family-Beneficial)	Most can be participated in by families. Many were created to assist and support families. Some aid and maintain family health.
Bad Side (Family-Destructive)	Parents don't teach kids directly. They substitute for family, take the place of family, and make family seem less necessary. They can take the allegiance that should go to family. They take prime family time (Sundays, holidays, etc.). Grandparents become less involved. Families don't eat together or talk together.
What/How (The Essence of the Problem)	Social and cultural institutions substitute for families, and recreational institutions soak up family time.
False Paradigms (Lies, False Impressions, and Self-Justification)	"No time for kids . . . or for more kids." "You owe yourself." (selfishness) "If it feels good, do it." (hedonism)

Errors	**Key misused words** • "Time saving" (meaning "time wasted") • "Happiness" (meaning "stretched too thin") • "The good life" (meaning "over-scheduled") • "Freedom" (meaning "no commitment or responsibility") • "Accomplishment" (meaning "I won, he lost") **Lifestyle mistakes** • "Subcontractor" approach to parenting ("Others will take care of the specifics of teaching my kids.") **Bad tradeoffs** • Friends for children • Physical for spiritual • Group traditions for family traditions

9. NON-PROFIT VOLUNTARY SECTOR AND RELIGIOUS INSTITUTIONS, SELF-HELP/PSYCHIATRIC HELP	
Who	NGOs, Churches, Synagogues, Mosques (in decline); Analysts, Seminars, Infomercials, Gurus (on the rise)
Good Side (Family-Beneficial)	They do humanitarian and family rescue work. They can promote faith and values. They instruct, help, and support families.
Bad Side (Family-Destructive)	Too much humanitarian focus on individuals, not enough on family. Too many religious institutions not taking strong stands on what is *right*. Churches are not giving people enough chances to serve. There is widespread loss of worship and faith. It is being replaced by self-help. Medications are overprescribed.
What/How (The Essence of the Problem)	Too many NGOs, voluntary organizations, and churches have been irrelevant bystanders in the decline of values and the disintegration of families. Instead of faith, we've begun to rely on popular self-help ideas to bring us happiness and fulfillment.
False Paradigms (Lies, False Impressions, and Self-Justification)	Charitable work is sustainable without families. Morality is "situational" and values are "customizable." Religion is self-righteous and self-serving. The wrong people (off-putting, far-right spokespeople) are saying the right things, thus discrediting them. "I'm number one."

Errors	**Key misused words** • "Control" (meaning there should be "no surprises") • "Independence" (meaning "needing no one") • "Crutch" (meaning you are weak if you can't handle everything yourself) **Lifestyle mistakes** • Nothing sacred (God's name, God's laws, God's day, etc.) **Bad Tradeoffs** • "Tolerance" for absolutes • Self-confidence for faith • Short-term for long-term • Easier quick-fix happiness for harder long-term joy

In Summary

Our largest, newest institutions are disrupting and destroying our smallest, oldest institution.

They are doing it constantly and steadily—by replacement, by false paradigms, and by "sins of omission and commission." They are doing it with and without thought, purposefully and accidentally. Parents need to be on vigilant watch for the mechanisms these large institutions use to supplant the primacy of the family.

As Sylvia Ann Hewlett and Cornel West wrote in, *The War Against Parents*:

> This [erosion of the parental role] is happening not because parents are less devoted than they used to be. They do not love their children less. The truth is, the whole world is pitted against them. One of the best-kept secrets of the last thirty years is that big business, government, and the wider culture have waged a silent war

against parents, undermining the work that they do. Some of the hostility has been inadvertent, and some of it has been deliberate. But whatever forces are responsible for the war against parents, one thing is for sure: parents have been left twisting in the wind by a society intent on other agendas.[3]

Before we can curtail, counter, or challenge what our welfare and larger institutions are doing to our families, we must know—really know—who and what these institutions are. We must identify and understand the false paradigms and the overt and covert messages broadcast by those who are responsible for the decline of the family and for all of the problems spawned by that decline.

You can kiss your family and friends
good-bye and put miles between you,
but at the same time you carry them
with you in your heart, your mind, your
stomach, because you do not just live in a
world but a world lives in you.

—FREDERICK BUECHNER

CHAPTER SEVEN

THE CONUNDRUM

Parents' Perspectives Are Distorted by False Paradigms

---

co·nun·drum *noun* \kə-ˈnən-drəm\

   1. a confusing or difficult problem

   2. a problematic question

par-a-digm *noun* \par-ˈa-dime\

   1. a viewpoint or world view

It's hard to solve a problem when we can't see it because of the clouded, distorted lens we see through—a lens of anti-family paradigms.

Social problems are the symptoms. Broken families are the illness. Larger institutions are the bacteria or "germs." Eroding values and false paradigms are the deficiency in our immune system.

PARADIGM PROBLEMS (HOW WHAT
WE SEE BECOMES WHAT WE GET)

Paradigms are more than perceptions. A paradigm is like a framework, a formula, an equation. When it changes, conclusions change, circumstances change, consciousness changes. *Paradigm* is a heavy word. It sounds ponderous, and it is. A paradigm shift is like an earthquake. A crust of earth slips, the old crumbles, and everything is altered. A paradigm is like a filter on a lens; it colors and alters everything we see. Another way to think of it is that a paradigm is like the map of a territory. If the map is inaccurate, no amount of energy or tenacity can get us to where we want to go.

False paradigms create the conundrum of understanding that families are at risk but not being able to find the means or the motivation to do anything about it.

If we think of the destabilizing forces of large institutions as the bacteria that cause the *illness* of family breakdown, which, in turn, brings the pain and *symptoms* of serious social problems, then false paradigms could be thought of as an *immune system deficiency* that renders families unable to fight off family destruction and disintegration. This creates the medical conundrum of seeing the symptoms and identifying the bacteria but still not having the resistance to get over the illness.

Paradigm shifts

A near-sighted child puts on glasses for the first time and sees a whole new world. A hologram shifts in the light and reveals a completely different picture. An Australian aborigine returns from a walkabout, and, unaware of his wife's appendicitis and need for surgery, assumes evil intent from the recently arrived medical missionary who he finds cutting his wife with a knife. The American public cheers the exposure of communist sympathizers until The McCarthy Hearings were exposed as a witch hunt. The United States ignores the Nazi party as an insignificant new German movement until we see Hitler's goal of world domination and his massacre of Jews.

When new light or insight suddenly reveals recently obscure reality, the world can suddenly look very different. Light can become dark, bad can change to good, whole world-views or paradigms can shift.

People are not as careful with their paradigms as they should be. We let our worldviews be manipulated by media's masquerade of majority. We allow advertising to persuade us that we need what we really only want. We permit spin-doctors to influence how we perceive what someone said, or meant, or did.

Paradigms are powerful (and dangerous) because they are starting points. If they are unclear or inaccurate, our conclusions, our decisions, even our convictions that we derive from them will also be inaccurate.

Paradigms are powerful (and dangerous) because they are starting points. If they are unclear or inaccurate, our conclusions, our decisions, even our convictions that we derive from them will also be inaccurate. Incorrect and potentially dangerous paradigms are sometimes born of simple ignorance or incomplete, lazy thinking. But they are sometimes skillfully implanted in us by those pursuing profit and power.

Procuring, perfecting, and proclaiming proper paradigms is a little like planting a new lawn. First, we have to root out the weeds, wherever they lie, completely removing them from the earth. We can clearly identify the weeds when we hold them alongside the good grass we have just acquired. Then, we plant the new and nurture the good, genuine green grass of things as they really are.

Paradigms as Starting Points

The biblical metaphor for a paradigm was old bottles that exploded when filled with new wine. If we have "old bottle" paradigms, if we see the world and ourselves inaccurately, we can't handle new information well; we're less confident and sure of our convictions and our abilities; and there is stress, desperation, and fear of "mental explosion" as we try to cope with it all.

For example, think about the old medical practice of bloodletting. Because the problem (or the *cause* of people's health problems) was thought to be bad blood, bleeding or bloodletting was the widely accepted "cure" for a multitude of illnesses.

Imagine applying a modern approach to fixing something that is institutionalized but isn't working. What happens when bloodletting doesn't work, but the false paradigm is still in place and is not challenged or replaced? Well, better *techniques* would be proposed—faster, better methods of bloodletting, or methods of drawing off *more* blood—and would be put into practice. Perhaps there would be better-trained "bloodletters" or better preparation and education of patients or more money spent on bloodletting facilities. Maybe bloodletting would be re-engineered or restructured. Imagine positive mental attitude training for bloodletters so they could radiate positive energy or team-building or total quality management practices in the field of bloodletting.

Until the incorrect paradigms are isolated, identified, exposed, and expunged, they will grip at us, influence us, deceive us, and undermine most any intentions we have that run contrary to their gravity.

Of course, nothing would help to "improve" bloodletting, because the paradigm was wrong in the first place. In the meantime, there were clues suggesting some error in the prevailing medical cause-and-effect thinking between bad blood and illness and disease. In war, more men were dying behind the lines in clinics than at the battle front itself. Infant mortality was better when midwives delivered than when doctors did because midwives were cleaner.

When Anton van Leeuwenhoek discovered "germs," (the Dutchman called them the "wee beasties") the paradigm about illness and disease changed, and with it, causes, effects, and prevention shifted. Progress became possible. The problem wasn't with the blood, and the core solution wasn't even in the hospitals. The solution could be found in people's personal lives—in the cleanliness of homes and in the personal habits of doctors treating patients.

When we look at "social problems," the problem, as the name implies, is thought to be *society*. So we try to eliminate bad society with tougher laws or more police or bigger jails, or we try to fix society with more education or more welfare. We use all kinds of techniques and behavioral methods.

However, until the causes—the "germ" of breaking families and negative values—are identified at the source and the home and family are recognized as the place where cleaning and revaluing must occur, we will be fighting windmills, wasting money, and spinning our wheels.

Paradigms, Attitudes, and Actions

Paradigms are incredibly important because the way we see things, and the framework within which we interpret or understand them, determines what we think and how we think. It creates our attitudes; it causes our actions!

Think how easily mistakes are made when we believe the wrong people or follow the wrong examples. We go wrong when we make false assumptions or follow false paradigms. All of these paradigm problems are deceptions based on inaccurate and negative-consequence-producing paradigms:

- A parent's effort to discourage aggression in a young teenager would be undermined if the teen (or the parent) perceived, based on TV and movies, that nearly everyone resolves differences with violence.

- A person trying to improve the important relationships in his life might be distracted and lose focus as the world around him emphasizes material accumulation and accomplishment over less measurable things like the well-being of friendships or family bonds.

- We might discount any idea or message that we need to hear because its spokesperson or presenter didn't look right or sound politically correct.

- We might conclude that today's world is too complex and frantic to allow for real peace and balance in life.

- We might become persuaded, or allow ourselves to rationalize, that other people—or preschools or professionals—can do a better job of training our children than we can.

- We might become convinced that good marriages and intact families really don't exist anymore, that nearly everyone has sex outside of marriage, or that children are too massive an economic and emotional burden, and thus lose both hope and effort in building committed marriages and stable homes and raising good children.

- We might believe that humans are inherently base or bad and that our natural instincts are dark and selfish—and we might become what we believe we are.

- We might conclude that we can truly *own* things and that accumulation is the measure of happiness.

- We might be conned into thinking that a positive attitude can solve everything and that it is possible to plan and control all parts of our lives.

- We might conclude that there are no absolute evils, that ethics are conditional.

- We might believe that all teenagers are sexually active and decide that all we can do is give them condoms.

Until the incorrect paradigms are isolated, identified, exposed, and expunged, they will grip at us, influence us, deceive us, and undermine most any intentions we have that run contrary to their gravity.

On a visit to Saudi Arabia, we met with a group of outstanding parents who had produced delightful, responsible, respectful, and moral children. The day after our speech, we were invited to lunch with several of the families with teenage children for some follow-up questions. One of the moms suggested that we divide the group during dessert and have the moms and daughters sit at a separate table.

During our conversation with the bright-faced, abaya-shrouded women and teenagers at our table, one courageous sixteen-year-old asked, "Is it true that American teenagers usually have sex after a first date?" Given the Muslim's strict rules about saving sex until marriage, most often an "arranged marriage," this concept was totally mystifying to them, and the curiosity was palpable.

I was astonished at their assumption, and I assured them that my religion also discourages sex before marriage, and that many American parents were teaching their children that principle. They were not only incredulous but also unconvinced.

"No, no. I have read your magazines and seen your movies, and I don't think that there are any American teenagers who believe that is possible," the little teenager responded. I doubt that there was any way I could change her mind about that false paradigm. The media had done its job!

Four Paradigms that Negatively Impact Families

There are four huge family-affecting paradigm problems at large in our society today. And each is far more sinister than it initially appears. We are used to them, you see. They are all around us and everyone seems to believe them, or at least allow them. They are also subtle and gradual; they seem to have grown up with us. They are familiar and comfortable. But, in fact, they are traitors, they are lies, and they carry with them huge power for real destruction. This deception perception was created—directly and indirectly, sometimes on purpose and sometimes inadvertently—by larger institutions bent on their own preservation, growth, and profit.

- Media minority masquerading as a majority
- Materialism
- Recreational sex, hedonism, and instant gratification
- Conditional or situational ethics

Media Minority Masquerading as a Majority

We consume an enormous amount of media. Entertainment media, from music to movies to television, and particularly data from the Internet, fill several hours each day for most people living in developed countries. We are exposed to hundreds of advertising impressions each day. And we soak in news and information constantly online and from radio, TV, and print. Media literally surrounds us and permeates our thoughts and actions.

Most entertainment media *represents* itself as the *reflection* of typical or majority lifestyles, values, and conduct. And news media poses as the reporter and revealer of events, trends, and opinions.

In fact, however, media is more and more in the business of creating trends, suggesting lifestyles, and remaking values and moral codes.

In fact, however, media is more and more in the business of creating trends, suggesting lifestyles, and remaking values and moral codes.

Media gives a tiny and grossly non-representative minority an enormously disproportionate influence over the rest of us. In entertainment, a few hundred individuals (media executives, producers, directors, moguls) influence virtually every movie or TV show we see. Similar disproportionate influence exists in the music we hear. And this tiny "cultural elite" is widely removed from the mainstream. Most are far less oriented to family and considerably less likely to be married, to attend church, or profess belief in God. They have far more money than typical, average people. Most live materialistic jet-set lives, and often disdain and belittle traditional values. Yet they *portray* what they produce as typical, as average, as mainstream. And they do it *convincingly* enough that:

- A southern housewife watches the soaps and decides—at least subconsciously—that her life is incredibly drab and unexciting and that she must be the only woman in America who stays home with young children.

- A California teenager listens to rap, goes to movies, plays computer games, and feels increasingly uncomfortable and out-of-step in being a virgin and not using drugs or alcohol. The paradigm problem is also a blockade for her parents, who give her condoms and begin to see their hopes for her continuing abstinence from drugs, alcohol, and promiscuous sex as naive and unrealistic.

- A single, unemployed twenty-five-year-old in England has moved back in with his parents, spends most of his time playing video games, and finds himself more comfortable and at home in virtual reality than in real reality—and increasingly comfortable with violence and sexual exploitation.

- A South Korean professional man doesn't want to be out-of-step or behind the trends, so he buys cars and clothes he can't afford to meet the expectations put on him by advertising.

- A grandmother in France becomes both increasingly scared of and increasingly desensitized to the violence that media shows her to be the norm nearly everywhere. There don't seem to be many quiet, peace-loving people like herself anymore.

In reality these people—the average, value-holding people—are the majority. Though that majority is declining, most of us still prioritize family and relationships, have faith in God and traditional values, believe in and practice fidelity in marriage, avoid drugs, try to live within our means, and abhor violence and gangs. We even believe in and try to practice discipline, self-reliance, and delayed gratification and avoid excessive materialism and self-gratification. We might choose, if it were available, to see a movie or watch a reality show about loyalty, dedication, or a well-resolved moral dilemma rather than one about violence, debauchery, or evil.

Whenever a minority masquerades as a majority, the real majority is made to feel like a minority. Too many of us today have been made to feel awkward and defensive about our lifestyles, about our values, and about our morality. It is not only the *entertainment* media that is involved in this deceptive masquerade. Predominantly liberal (not only politically liberal but morally liberal) decision-makers dominate our news media. Too often, amoral beliefs and behavior are reported and depicted as mainstream or "normal," and moral, conservative, values-driven beliefs and behavior is treated as fringe.

> *Whenever a minority masquerades as a majority, the real majority is made to feel like a minority. Too many of us today have been made to feel awkward and defensive about our lifestyles, about our values, and about our morality.*

When we try to find a more conservative voice, we end up with the shrill, extreme, self-righteous positions of the far right, which repel us back toward the middle—and yet the middle doesn't seem to exist anymore. Gone are the moderate centrist voices that used to create good compromise and bring the right and left together on important legislation and policy.

Statistics are constantly interpreted by much of our media as evidence of a "new morality," and the message is a subtle justification of irresponsible and amoral personal behavior.

Nowhere is this more prominent than in the family-undermining dooms-day statistics we read, which suggest that (1) having children contributes to the rampant overpopulation that will doom the world, (2) a majority of marriages are doomed to failure and divorce, and (3) the financial costs and obligations associated with having and raising a child are astronomical and impossible for average people to bear.

Increasing population will create shortages for all, we read; more than half of all marriages end in divorce; and it will cost at least half a million dollars to raise and educate a child. And we're reminded daily of the ever-increasing numbers of children who have serious troubles with drugs, gangs, teen pregnancy, dropping out of school, and suicide. We read it and hear it and watch it broadcast until it seems to some that the only safe course, the only logical decision, is to steer clear of the land mines of marriage, family, and children altogether.

In fact, most of the doomsday statistics commentaries we hear are huge misinterpretations of the facts. The truth is that:

1. Birthrates in most third-world countries are plunging, and in most developed countries, the birthrates are below re-placement levels. As mentioned earlier, 116 of the world's 224 nation-states actually have declining populations, except for in-migration—and their problem is not too many people but not enough people to maintain their workforces.

2. There have been years in which there were half as many di-vorces in America as there were marriages, but there are far more married adults than single. So the numbers do not mean that half of the marriages are ending in divorce. In fact, over 80 percent of first marriages survive until death, and nearly 80 percent of married people are still married to their original marriage partner. It's the high divorce rates in second and third marriages that push us toward the 50 percent overall number

that we hear so often. And the real problem is the paradigm that suggests that there is no need or real benefit to getting married in the first place.[1]

3. Statistics actually show that adults with children do better financially than those without. Of course, children cost money, but they can also help and earn and eventually become independent. While it is hard to raise kids today, and many families are in trouble, it is, of course, still possible to create strong families and raise successful children.[2]

What a tragedy it is when a false paradigm keeps many people from life's most joy-providing experiences and roles and stewardships—those of marriage, commitments, children, and family.

As though it weren't enough to have such a small and atypical minority holding such huge influence through the mainstream media, the paradigm problem is further exacerbated by the fact that many of the things most of us do believe in are being championed in media by people who seem either so self-righteous or so little like us that we have a hard time identifying with them.

Why is it that the conservative, values-oriented, family-centered, God-acknowledging message which most of us agree with is so often delivered or represented by people with personalities that polarize, by people with whom many can't identify—the intolerant egocentrics, extremists, and bigots? Why, on the other hand, are so many of the liberal, politically correct, and often anti-family-and-values messages presented so appealingly by such appealing people?

The bottom-line danger of this first false paradigm is this: when we perceive things around us to be worse, less moral, and less hopeful than they really are, we tend to give up, to cave in, and to think, "If you can't beat them, join them." It's the old adman gimmick of "Everyone's doing it, so why not you." The false paradigm grows far beyond a simple misperception. We laugh and join in and think we must be on the right train because everyone else is there. But we're headed for a cliff.

DANGEROUS NOTIONS STEMMING FROM MEDIA'S MESSAGES:

- "Marriage is pointless or doomed. It's expensive and selfish to have kids, and it's heroic and resource-saving not to."
- "Everybody does it." (Especially casual, recreational sex.)
- "Violence is just part of the landscape and shouldn't shock or disturb us that much."
- "Tolerance is the prime virtue—anything that anyone does is okay."
- "Traditional values and traditional families are out of date and old-fashioned."
- "There are no consequences. If it doesn't hurt anyone, it's not a problem."
- "You're in touch, and therefore, in tune."
- "We don't create society's values; we just reflect them."

Materialism and Entitlement (Putting Achievements above Relationships and Looking for External Security rather Than Internal Security)

Most people would say they would choose time with their families over more time spent at work. However, most of our regrets and our guilt come from inadequate efforts that we put into our relationships—spending too little time with family. We acknowledge that relationships are more important than achievements, but our actions are not congruent with our beliefs.

This second false paradigm problem is related to the first. The masquerading minority promotes materialism, encourages us to measure and judge ourselves and others by wealth, position, comfort, social status, and owner-ship. But it's more than that. We live in a world where profit is the bottom line, where everything is explained in an economic model. (Pundits will say that "poverty causes anti-social values" when actually it's the other way around.) When we meet someone, the first question we ask is about their job. Money, instead of being the *means* to worthy *ends* like education, family, experience, and service to others, becomes an end in itself.

This paradigm problem also seems to have convinced us that our world is too complex and demanding to allow real balance between work and fam-ily, between ambition and relaxation, between quantity and quality.

We acknowledge that relationships are more important than achievements, but our actions are not congruent with our beliefs.

The truth is that we gravitate to achievements because they are *easier* than relationships—easier to obtain, to preserve, and to measure. They are also less risky; they take less emo-tional energy than relationships. Deep down, most of us know that the very concept of *own-ership*, which drives most of our "achieving," is flawed. We really don't *own* anything. Things pass through us. We are temporary *stewards* over everything from our cars and houses to our children. An ownership mentality always produces greed, envy, and jealousy on one hand and pride, conceit, and condescension on the other. Yet we all seem locked into the idea of wanting more.

Another aspect of this paradigm problem is thinking that our sense of inadequate safety is caused by guns, gangs, violence, and by too little polit-ical intervention, protection, and police—and that it can be solved by more of them. "Crime" is often the most frequent answer to the public opinion survey question, "What is the biggest problem in America today?" Most Americans feel terribly insecure and vulnerable. It is the same or worse in most developed countries. The buffer of law and order that used to separate good, respectable citizens from the elements of violence and fear has been breached. So, we campaign for external solutions—more police enforcing more increasingly complex laws, bigger prisons, and tougher drug penalties. We make our kids overly paranoid about strangers, and we arm ourselves with guns and mace, and still we can't recover the feeling of safety.

In fact, the only real security and the only real solutions comes from within—within ourselves and within our homes. The crime problem is caused by the breakdown of families and will be solved only by the revaluing of families and the inner recommitment to values. Kids join gangs because they need a larger-than-self identity and security that they don't find in their dysfunctional and inadequate homes. People use drugs to escape the reality of crumbling or non-existent relationships. And violence erupts out of the frustration of wrong expectations and failure at the things that really matter. The error of worldly paradigms looking to external achievements, wealth, or security is always exposed in personal life as individuals achieve these external things and still find no inner peace or deep satisfaction. But we need to acknowledge it before we spend a lifetime figuring it out. We need to reject it early rather than later, while our lives (and the real joys) are still ahead of us.

DANGEROUS NOTIONS STEMMING FROM MATERIALISM:

- "You are your work."
- "He who dies with the most toys wins."
- "Image is everything."
- "All I want is the land next to mine."
- "It takes at least two full-time incomes to raise a family."
- "You deserve it before you earn it." (instant gratification)
- "Have it all."
- "More is better."
- "It's impossibly expensive to raise a child today."

- "Money is the goal. Work is the purpose. Economics is the explanation."

Recreational Sex, Hedonism, and Instant Gratification

Our society somehow manages to glorify and debase sex at the same time—both falsely. Sex is portrayed and perceived as the ultimate easy pleasure, the ultimate test of manhood or womanhood, the almost-instant result (and gratification) of any remotely romantic encounter. Alternatively, it is portrayed and perceived as cheap, casual, or violent.

This false paradigm tells us that fidelity is rare in marriage and that chastity is almost nonexistent prior to marriage. ("Chastity" has become a quaint, archaic word.)

This paradigm implies that singles and swingers have more sex, and enjoy it more, than people who are monogamous and married. Furthermore, the paradigm implies that marriage is boring, spells the end of romance, and causes people to take each other for granted.

In reality (in the true paradigm) things are very different. More than 75 percent of married women and nearly as high a percentage of married men have never had an extramarital affair. More than half of female high school graduates are virgins. Married adults report more and better sex than unmarried "swingers" (more quantity and quality).[3] Marriage, when it is worked at and committed to, brings the peace and security most people long for, and can produce a miraculous kind of synergy where two people become more than the sum of their parts. And romance of the mind and spirit—courtship that saves the physical union until the time of commitment and marriage—still exists, still works, and still *thrives*. And the point is, it

Romance of the mind and spirit—courtship that saves the physical union until the time of commitment and marriage—still exists, still works, and still thrives.

would thrive *more* and produce more joy for us all if we could rid ourselves of the false paradigm.

A connected paradigm problem is that of personal discipline and conservative values being perceived as constraining and freedom-inhibiting.

> *A former business partner of mine used to say, "If it feels good, do it." He prided himself in living for the moment, having it now, and having no inhibitions. Because of my association with him, I was particularly aware of how often his philosophy was reinforced by media and by the prevailing attitudes around him. I noticed how often ministers or preachers were portrayed on TV or in the movies as out-of-touch, uptight fuddy-duddies, or as hypocrites—how often our heroes were wild rebels, liberal carousers, or big-hearted whores.*

In this false paradigm, nice guys often finish last or are not even in the race; people live or behave irresponsibly without consequences; and standards, from religious commandments to committed personal values, are seen as chains that bind people and take away their freedom to act, to express themselves, to fully live.

Actually, of course, the precise opposite is true. Irresponsibility and instant gratification always have consequences, and immoral and amoral behavior always hurts people and ultimately hurts the practitioner. The consequences and the hurts are what rob people of the freedom to fully live and to find their best selves; and take away their ability to find themselves by fully embracing and being embraced by family.

Much of this false paradigm is driven by pornography, which is both the fastest growing and most profitable business in many developed countries.

> *We have a good friend who, in his somewhat wealthy semi-retirement, went looking for a cause on which to spend some of his money and his energy. Concerned about various types of addiction,*

he discovered that porn may be the most widespread addiction of all. "On the surface," he says, "cocaine and porn don't seem to have a lot in common. One is purchased in seedy alleyways; the other is free to download. One habit can get expensive pretty fast, while the other is about the price of a high speed Internet connection . . . but studies are showing that viewing pornography tricks your brain into releasing the same pleasure chemicals that drugs do." His conclusions were that "porn is a lie that kills love, ruins your sex life, hurts your partner, and leaves you lonely." He also says that, "to viewers, pornography can appear a fantasy world of pleasure and thrills. To those who create and participate in making porn, however, their experiences are often flooded with drugs, disease, slavery, trafficking, rape, and abuse." He decided that the best thing he could do for families was to fight pornography, and he created the website and movement called "Fight the New Drug."

The fundamental problem with the false paradigm of hedonism, as with each of the others, is that it is a lie. Hedonism actually takes away the very freedom that it promises to give us. And the joys of delayed gratification—the magic and romance of waiting and the power of putting commitment before consummation—are never experienced.

Perhaps the essential difference between humans and animals is that animals achieve their purpose and potential by following and being controlled by their instincts and appetites. People, on the other hand, achieve their full purpose and highest potential by controlling and governing their appetites. Whether the appetite is for food, sex, power, wealth, or achievement, happiness comes through control and discipline.

Spiritually, inwardly, most know that this is true, yet it is so much easier to let our appetites win. In the false paradigm, appetite is tied to excitement and fulfillment, while values, which are essentially appetite controls, are thought of as boring and old-fashioned.

DANGEROUS NOTIONS STEMMING FROM RECREATIONAL SEX, HEDONISM, AND INSTANT GRATIFICATION:

- "What I do in my private life only affects me."
- "If it feels good, do it."
- "Nice guys finish last."
- "Affairs are the norm; teen sex is the norm."
- "Sex is recreation."
- "You owe yourself."

Conditional or Situational Ethics and the Oxymoron of "Self-Help" (Relying on the "Reality" of the Physical, the Practical, the Psychological, and the Philosophical rather Than the Spiritual)

Conditional ethics, values-neutral education, and a host of other confusing and pain-producing notions spring from our efforts to explain and deal with our world without acknowledging inherent good and evil.

While it may not be politically correct to speak about belief in God or in the devil, most people, in some fashion, do believe in both. And the experience of the ages and the logic of our minds tell us that certain core values—honesty, responsibility, fidelity, respect, basic kindness—are essential to the survival of a society and of its institutions, down to and including the family.

> *Years ago, while we were writing our book* Teaching Your Children Values, *we were confronted more than once by media interviews who demanded, "Well, whose values is your book going to advocate?" The implication was that there is some huge pot full of values and each of us selects our own by individual preference. We had*

answers to these questions because we'd done our homework. As we wrote the book, we solicited input from large numbers of parents with diverse backgrounds from all over the world. The bottom line is simple: virtually everyone shares certain basic and universal values and wants those values to be embraced by their children. Based on the feedback we received (the basic question was, "What values do you want most to develop within your children?"), we included twelve values in our book:

1. *Honesty*
2. *Courage*
3. *Peaceability*
4. *Self-reliance*
5. *Self-discipline and Moderation*
6. *Fidelity and Commitment*
7. *Respect*
8. *Loyalty*
9. *Kindness and Friendliness*
10. *Unselfishness and Sensitivity*
11. *Love*
12. *Justice and Mercy*

The essence of this fourth paradigm problem of situational ethics is that while almost everyone pays lip service to these values, we *apply* them selectively and sporadically—and our larger institutions often encourage their compromise. For example:

- Easy credit undermines self-discipline.
- Elaborate welfare systems erode self-reliance.

- Merchandising/advertising downplay self-discipline, moderation, and delayed gratification.

- Complex tax codes encourage dishonesty.

- Macho attitudes and media violence contradict peaceability.

- Media and merchandising-induced trends and peer pressure undermine kids' courage to be themselves and follow their own standards.

- Loyalty to family is replaced by economically mandated loyalty to job.

- Respect and unselfishness are replaced by the exploitation and expediency it takes to get ahead.

- Kindness and friendliness are knocked out of us by suspicion and fear.

- Media amorality and the glamorization of stereotypes of recreational sex discourage fidelity and chastity.

- Self-help and pop psychology emphasize self-fulfillment and strategy at the expense of love and mercy.

Contributing to the expanding idea of situational ethics is the whole self-help and pop-psychology industry, which often seems to suggest that we can each make up our own rules. As the stress and complexity of daily life has increased over the last half century, the two recurring "solutions" thrown at us by quick-fix and rely-on-yourself culture have been *positive mental attitude* and *time management*. "You can do anything," goes the positive attitude thesis. "You deserve more and better than what you have." "Every day in every way you are getting better and better!" "Whether you think you can or think you can't, you're right!" "Whatever the mind of man can conceive and believe, it can achieve." The time-management solution tells us to plan everything, control everything: "Act, don't react." "Never be surprised." "Live by your list."

The notions of self help and time management are comforting—and motivating—but neither is completely true or reliable, and in the long run, they set us up for a fall. The fact is that we *can't* do everything. We're actually pretty limited in what we can do on our own, and, sorry, we just don't get better every day in every way. As much as we might like to control everything, plan everything, and never be surprised, life doesn't work that way. Unpredictability is the only truly predictable thing.

In fact, it is our human inadequacies that can make us humble, faith-filled, and ultimately powerful through a higher power. And the surprises, opportunities, and unplanned, spontaneous "serendipities" are what make life interesting and entertaining. Family life, especially, doesn't work in a predictable, scheduled, or even always positive way. When a child needs help or has a question at an inconvenient moment, we can't "pencil him in" for another day. Families have ups and downs; they test the extremes of our emotions in both directions.

As much as we might like to control everything, plan everything, and never be surprised, life doesn't work that way. Unpredictability is the only truly predictable thing.

This paradigm problem of "self-help" is more than a matter of applying the wrong techniques. It is a problem of false realities. When we make the mistakes of thinking of the spiritual as less real than the physical, of impressions as less reliable than sensory evidence, of guidance and inspiration as something exclusive to monks or gurus, of spirituality as less important than psychology or philosophy, we give up what is most real within us. As Pierre Teilhard de Chardin said, "We are not human beings having a spiritual experience; we are spiritual beings having a human experience."

Trying to explain everything physically and empirically is actually a phenomenon of the last few centuries. Before that, most perspectives and explanations were spiritual. In the renaissance, science and "enlightenment" became a temporal alternative to excessive religious power and unsatisfying, simplistic spiritual explanations. Today, many view the secular, "scientific" explanation as inadequate and shallow and look ever deeper at the spiritual.

A favorite writer and thinker of ours is Francis Collins, one of the world's leading scientists, who headed the Human Genome Project and who is now the Director of the National Institutes of Health (NIH). He puts it this way:

> It became clear to me that science, despite its unquestioned powers in unraveling the mysteries of the natural world, would get me no further in resolving the question of God. If God exists, then He must be outside the natural world, and therefore the tools of science are not the right ones to learn about Him. Instead, as I was beginning to understand from looking into my own heart, the evidence of God's existence would have to come from other directions, and the ultimate decision would be based on faith, not proof.[4]

Very few of us, deep down, want to be a "material girl" or a "material guy." Our desires are spiritual, and our finest hours often come in the enlightenment and courage of faith rather than the limited and fearful insistence on self-reliance.

Ultimately, "self-help," in the psychological or the scientific sense, is an oxymoron. We can work to be our best; we hold within us powers of self-improvement. But to truly lift to another level—to go beyond our very finite and limited abilities, to see realities that are beyond our senses—we need non-self-help. We need help from a higher source, from a spiritual source—from God.

It is less empowering to say, "I can do anything," than to say, "I can do very little by myself, but I have faith in a higher, stronger, better power that can guide and illuminate and help."

Simply acknowledging this, simply releasing the false paradigm of one-dimensional self-help and self-reliance, liberates us and lifts a weight from our heads. It is less empowering to say, "I can do anything," than to say, "I can do very little by myself, but I have faith in a higher, stronger, better power that can guide and illuminate and help."

As mentioned in the last chapter, faithless pop-psychology pushes us toward three nice-sounding but highly problematic pursuits:

1. Control
2. Ownership
3. Independence

Each of these accepted (and almost worshiped) pursuits constitutes part of a serious false paradigm.

1. While we should certainly try to control some things (our temper, our checkbook balance, our various appetites), attempts to control all of our circumstances and all of the people around us result in frustration and in the destruction of relationships and of families. To a person of faith, the goal should be *guidance* rather than control. Indeed, the central tenant of all religions is to put God's will above our own and to acknowledge God's control. Seeking divine will always lead us to prioritize values and family, whereas following our own desires for power and control often leads us away.

2. Ownership may be a good and necessary economic paradigm in free market politics, but it is a disastrous spiritual paradigm in families. Ownership and the desire for *things* turns our hearts away from family. First of all, materialism and the "all I want is the land next to mine" mentality sucks away time and attention from families. Second, parents who live in this

paradigm often begin to think of their children (and their spouse) as their *property*, thus treating family members with less respect and less nurturing.

3. Independence, too, is nice politically but disastrous spiritually. "I'm on my own" and "I can do it alone" can become presumptuous and even atheistic comments. We are, in actual fact, completely interdependent. We need each other. No man is an island. We need our families, and they need us. We need faith and we need God.

DANGEROUS NOTIONS STEMMING FROM CONDITIONAL OR SITUATIONAL ETHICS AND THE OXYMORON OF SELF HELP:

- "Do whatever you want because there is no absolute right or wrong."
- "We need values-neutral education."
- "Poverty causes the destruction of values." (rather than the reverse)
- "I can do anything I want and have anything I want."
- "I am number one."
- "All of my problems are emotional and mental, not spiritual."
- "You need professional expertise to teach kids."
- "Religion is self-serving and self-righteous."
- "We can understand and explain everything."
- "There is no ultimate source of good or of evil. No God, no culprits."

Don't underestimate false paradigms, and don't say, as a friend of ours recently did, "Thoughts and ideas can't hurt me—because they aren't real."

In fact, they are the most real, and the most influential, things in our lives. Replacing false paradigms with true principles is a huge step in revaluing our families—and in upgrading our own inner lives.

In every conceivable manner, the family
is link to our past, bridge to our future.

—ALEX HALEY

PART TWO

TURNING
BACK

*Over the last several decades, for a myriad of
reasons, too many hearts have turned away
from family. The question is simple: What will it
take to turn them back?*

Introduction to Part 2

This book now moves from problems to solutions, from analysis to action. What remains to be discussed are the positive aspects of families in today's society—the *celebration* of how great families can be, the *cure* of making our family cultures stronger than the cultures that surround them, and the *case* for banding together in a movement to restore and support families. Chapter 8 is a reminder of the awesome things we are fighting for—the beauty of a family-centric life. Chapter 9 is a comprehensive set of recommendations to parents on how to "fix" and protect their own individual families. Chapter 10 is a reasoned argument for why larger institutions should do all they can to protect and preserve families—and suggestions for specific things these "culprits" can do in order to stop weakening and start strengthening families. Chapter 11 is an overview of how a coalition and movement for stronger families might come together and might begin to influence and impact the way we view and prioritize families at every level within society.

A Metaphorical Summary of Cause and Culprits

Having used just about every simile and metaphor we could think of to explain the destruction of families by bigger institutions and false paradigms (symptoms, illness and germs, big things swallowing little things, boats and currents), let us use one final comparison: war.

In warfare, a force goes through three steps in the conquering process:

1. *Propaganda* to weaken and soften the resolve of the enemy.
2. *Strategic attack*—going after the enemy one element at a time— undermining its defenses, knocking out its communication, blasting away at its operations and its main cities.
3. *Actual take over* of its government, its functions, its operations.

The war on families, while often unintentional, is being waged in exactly this way. The false paradigms are powerful propaganda, which weakens the commitments and priorities of families. The strategic attacks are the things big institutions actually do to undermine and destroy families—from over-taxing married couples to selling families things they can't afford. And the actual takeover is where larger institutions begin to assume the roles and responsibilities that have always belonged to families—nurturing, making decisions for families, disciplining, teaching false or incomplete values, and generally removing parents and families from the loop.

But we are not powerless in this war. There are ways that we can fight back, both in the micro of our own homes and families and in the macro of forming coalitions to influence large institutions to change their tunes and change their policies and actions and messages with regard to the families of their employees and the families of their customers.

The goal is to turn back; to make reverse course; to re-orient our direction, both personally and as a society, toward the family.

There is no doubt that it is around the family and the home that all the greatest virtues, the most dominating virtues of humans, are created, strengthened, and maintained.

—WINSTON CHURCHILL

CHAPTER EIGHT

THE CELEBRATION

The Best Way to Live Is also the Happiest Way to Live

cel·e·brate *noun* \ˈse-lə-ˌbrāte\

1. to do something special or enjoyable for an important event, occasion, holiday, etc.
2. being glad, acknowledging victory

Enough of castigating our civilization for all of its problems and deficiencies.

Enough of the curses and the crises and the causes.

Time to leap the stream of doubts and woes

And to enter the land of happy homes,

And to celebrate the commitment of family.

HOPEFUL SIGNS

One of our main speaking clients over the past couple of decades has been The Young Presidents' Organization (YPO), a worldwide organization of Presidents and CEOs. To join, you must be forty or younger and head a company with revenues in excess of ten million dollars. By definition, these are young, educated, aggressive, type A personalities who want to be the best at everything they do, including their parenting and their marriages. They are, in a way, the prototype of a new kind of marriage and parenting, and a new kind of family, that combines the best from the past and the best for the future.

They are—as evidenced by how often they bring us in to present to them in their various chapters around the world—very, very interested in developing strong and lasting marriages and families and in raising responsible and highly motivated kids.

Their divorce rate is low, and their kids are, generally speaking, solid, polite, and high achieving. These parents prioritize their families and devote a lot of time and mental effort to their relationships and their parenting. And while we can't take much credit for any of it, most of them are poster families for the mission statement of our writing and speaking company, which is "FORTIFY FAMILIES by celebrating commitment, popularizing parenting, validating values, and bolstering balance."

Curiously, what is happening in the world today is that more highly educated, more economically successful families are prioritizing and committing themselves to marriage and parenting with much more regularity and dedication than lower-income, less-educated parents. Frankly, hands-on parenting and real partnership in marriage is becoming "the thing to do" among young, upwardly mobile couples.

According to Richard Reeves, writing in *The Atlantic*, "A new version (of marriage) is emerging—egalitarian, committed, and focused on children. There was a time when college-educated women were the least likely to be married. Today, they are the most important drivers of the new marriage model. Their marriages offer more satisfaction, last longer, and produce more successful children. Against all predictions, educated Americans are rejuvenating marriage."[1]

Fathers, in this new model of marriage, spend much more time with their children and are much more likely to share household duties with their wives.

Fathers, in this new model of marriage, spend much more time with their children and are much more likely to share household duties with their wives. And the great thing about it, at least from our observation, is that these committed, aspiring families are not doing it out of duty but out of joy—they are working at their relationships because they have concluded that their family is what matters and what will make them happy.

Generally, it is the very demographic we are talking about here—the better-educated, higher-income group—who set patterns and start trends that are then followed by more and more of the population. We can only hope that this will be the case with more lasting and celebrated commitments and more popular and energetic parenting.

Not So Hopeful Signs

Our YPO clients mentioned earlier—genuinely committed to their marriages and their families—are in their 30s and 40s. They are Generation Xers—born between the early 60s and the early 80s—and it seems that the better educated they are, the more effort they are putting into their families.

But, when we find ourselves speaking to and interacting with Generation Y, or "Millennials"—the generation that ranges from late teens to early 30s, born between the early 80s and the year 2000—the story changes. Even among those in graduate school, the idea and even the desire for marriage and children is not nearly as strong.

In the book *Baby Bust*, Wharton Business School professor Stewart Freedman reveals that only 42 percent of the 2012 graduating class plan to have children—compared with 78 percent who answered positively to the same question in the graduating class of 1992. This means that, in only twenty years, the percentage of graduates wanting to have or adopt a child has declined almost by half.[2]

It's not just that well-educated Millennials are planning to have smaller families and fewer children; it's that more than half of them, at least in the Wharton graduating class, plan to have no children at all. The phenomenon of childless by choice is partially driven by the belief that a solid financial base should be in place before children come, and that in today's world, obtaining and keeping that financial base is essentially incompatible with the time required to raise children.

One of the problems is that Millennials are exposed to so much frightening hyperbole about how much it costs to raise a child. You have probably read headlines like this: "Cost of Raising a Child Ticks Up" or "The Half Million Dollar Child" or "Cost of Children Higher than Ever Before."

If you google "cost of raising a child," you will get dozens of articles, most of them aghast at how much money children cost these days and many of them implying that few can afford to raise children at all.

Most estimates range from a quarter of a million dollars per child to half a million, depending on whether college is counted, although *Today's Parent* ran a 2014 article called "Million Dollar Babies." There are two problems with this type of article: (1) they discourage parents, and (2) they are simply not true!

We suppose it would be possible to spend a half million dollars raising a child, but we don't know anyone who has! In fact, we know families who have raised several children for less than that lofty estimate, and some of those children have gone to Harvard!

Even the *Wall Street Journal* got in on the myth, with an article saying it costs $222,360 to raise a child to age seventeen. And this without anything added in for college. Where do they get these numbers? Well, at least the *Wall Street Journal* was good enough to break it down for us. They said, "Child care accounts for 17 percent of the total spending, and education for 16 percent of the total. The cost of housing makes up nearly one-third of the total; this is gauged by the average cost of an additional bedroom." You see what a big myth it is?! A third of the $222,000 is housing, a house you already have and would have with or without the child.[3]

Millennials need to see more of the positive and joyful aspects of family, and less of the scary and expensive ones. They need to see and appreciate more good reasons for having families. They need to see more people celebrating commitment and popularizing parenting.

And what all of the articles forget to tell us is that there are economies of scale. A family with three or four kids certainly spreads the cost and clearly does not spend four times as much as a family with one child.

The other thing these articles leave out is that kids can actually work. They can pay part of their keep. Older kids can pay part of their education costs. They can even pay part of the cost of their clothes and their electronics (and, in fact, they should). Since when did kids become 100 percent consumers and 0 percent producers or earners? Since this age of entitlement, that's when!

It's time for us to quit indulging and entitling our children. It's time to help them become productive, gradually more and more self-sufficient kids who have financial savvy and who know how to earn and budget and save and give. It's time for us to start thinking of our children as part of the solution rather than part of the problem. And it's time to stop

The fact is that a mom and a dad, living together with children, is the most economical as well as the most secure and joyful way to live.

listening to the discouraging myths of how impossibly expensive it is to raise a child.

To come to the same pro-family and pro-marriage conclusion that highly educated Generation X persons have, Millennials need to see more of the positive and joyful aspects of family and less of the scary and expensive ones. They need to see and appreciate more good reasons for having families. They need to see more people celebrating commitment and popularizing parenting.

LIGHTING A CANDLE
FOR WHAT'S RIGHT

Speaking more broadly, the challenge of strengthening families is not so much about what we are against as it is about what we are for. It is fine to be against drugs and violence and youthful sexual experimentation and everything else that undermines families, but we have to be at least as committed and vigorous in what we are for.

It is said, "It is better to light a candle than to curse the darkness."

What the world needs is more examples and more celebration of the secure and happy lifestyle enjoyed by those willing to commit, to sacrifice, and to accept the responsibility of family.

And, despite what some say about a nuclear family being a luxury that only the rich can afford, committed family relationships are available to anyone who really wants them. The fact is that a mom and a dad, living together with children, is the most economical as well as the most secure and joyful way to live.

Turning Back and Turning Forward

We are not advocating a return to the days of *Ozzie and Harriet* or *Leave It to Beaver*. We don't romanticize the 1950s with a father breadwinner and a homemaker mom raising the kids. Why feel nostalgia for the old when there is an emerging new that is better? Good marriages today are well-thought-out partnerships with common goals and shared responsibilities, along with the conscious choice to prioritize kids and to accept the tradeoffs that come with being "tied down."

An alternate title for the second half of this book could be: "Turning back (and forward) to family"—a better kind of family than has ever been possible before.

> *This is the shortest chapter of the book, but it may also be the most personally important. It is also our chance to editorialize a bit—to get up on our soapbox and make a good little campaign speech for the simple JOY of families. We believe that our mission statement of celebrating (and loving) commitment, popularizing (or prioritizing) parenting, validating (and teaching) values, and bolstering (and living by) balance is not only the best lifestyle, it is the happiest lifestyle.*
>
> *Let me, Richard, be a little personal here. I know my own nature, and I freely admit that it tilts toward selfishness, comfort, and personal gratification—even indulgence. Frankly, I hate to think about the type of person I would be without the refinement and sacrifice that marriage and children brought into my life. To have other people who you love more than yourself does wonders for*

your perspective and your priorities, and I have come to believe that marriage partners, in a truly and deeply committed state, are the epitome of synergy.

Synergy is where one plus one equals more than two—where marriage partners work effectively together and complement and play off of each other in ways where the total is greater than the sum of its parts. Two people, well-matched and completely committed, can possess a combination of skills that cannot possibly exist in one person. There is something to the concept of the yin and the yang, the masculine and the feminine, combining to bring about a "oneness whole" that works and that is more efficient and effective than two people going solo could ever be.

Good marriages today are well-thought-out partnerships with common goals and shared responsibilities, along with the conscious choice to prioritize kids.

This new marriage model combines the best of the old, traditional marriage model and adds to it a more realistic and equal partnership. It rises above the debate about equality by stressing the superiority of the oneness and synergy of a true yin/yang partnership. It rises above the debate about independence and dependence by opting instead for interdependence—both partners needing the other—and admitting it.

So when I think of my family, even with all the challenges, it is a thought dominated by the moments of joy, and infused with the secure, relaxing peace of unconditional commitment—an atmosphere in which creativity and resilience can flourish.

The Real Reason

Ask the question: what is the prime reason or purpose or motivation for strengthening families?

Is it to improve our economy?

Is it to reduce our government?

Is it to repair social problems?

These are good reasons and worthy causes, and each is an "effect" clearly traceable to the "cause" of stronger families. But there is an even greater personal reason to commit ourselves to and to work tirelessly for stronger families. And that reason is JOY!

Nothing will influence your long-term happiness more than the strength and unity and love within your immediate and extended family.

In this age when independence and the individual are so valued and fought for and honored, almost to the point of worship, we all need to step back a little and turn our attention and our hearts a little more away from ourselves and a little more toward our families.

Because the selfless, committed, sacrificing happiness of family is vastly greater than the selfish, indulgent "freedom" of independence.

It is fine to protect our own marriages and families out of duty and obligation, but it is so much better to celebrate them as the single grandest source of joy that exists on this earth.

Offense over Defense

The problem is that advocates and proponents of man-woman marriage and natural families have not sounded or acted much like advocates and proponents. Instead, we have been sucked into the defensive posture of being "opponents"—fighting against gay marriage, against abortion, against cohabitation, against having kids out of wedlock, against divorce, against waiting too long to marry or to have children—against, against! We have become so busy with what we are fighting *against* that we start to forget what we are fighting *for.*

We need to celebrate our lifestyles, and just generally remind ourselves and the world around us that we have found the most joyous, most rewarding, most satisfying way to live and to share and to love.

Nothing will influence your long-term happiness more than the strength and unity and love within your immediate and extended family.

The consequences of focusing only on correcting what's wrong rather than celebrating what's right are beginning to manifest themselves. While same-sex couples clamor for the honor and privilege and right of marriage, the rest of us too often take it for granted or don't avail ourselves of it at all. While special interest groups and lobbyists are fighting for business and individual rights, few are advocating or pushing for family rights.

We have forgotten that the best defense is a good offense!

Viewing the individual as the basic unit of society and fighting for individual rights, individual freedoms, and individual options is fine to a degree, but when it is overemphasized, it leads to selfishness and self-centeredness at the expense of the sacrifice, responsibility, and commitment that goes with having a family. Societally, the sand of individual rights is not as good a place to build as the rock of family rights.

Part of Celebrating Is Giving

Those who are blessed enough to have a reasonably functional, reasonably happy family often feel the desire to help others have and feel the same joy. Just as "misery loves company," so does happiness.

We are aware of more and more families who have the goal of "giving back" in a family-centric way. Many of our clients sponsor "Habitat for Humanity" projects where homes are built for families in poverty; many participate in humanitarian expeditions where first-world families go together to third-world locations to build schools or clinics or to help poor families gain access to clean water or achieve smoke-free huts.

We see others joining "big brother" or "big sister" organizations or volunteering to read with underprivileged kids or help them with their homework.

If we really want to celebrate families and contribute directly to the root of the ultimate solution, we may each want to consider helping parents directly to help themselves and their children.

Sometimes the problem with programs that are set up to help kids or rescue adolescents is that the work can become a substitute for family or it is simply a pain reliever or Band-Aid, providing some comfort but ignoring the bigger problem. Working with parents and helping them do a better job with their kids is true preventative medicine that can arrest or correct a problem before it spills out of the home and into society. We think it would be wonderful if a functional family could link up one-on-one with a dysfunctional family—finding ways to mentor and teach them parenting skills and other family-saving, family-preserving skills.

But even beyond extending personal help to other families, the most important thing we can do may be simply to celebrate and talk about our family commitments and the joy they bring us. Young people and others need to see that joy and optimism—to see marriage and parenting as the happiest and most blessed thing they can do. They may have grown up without that example, so it may be up to us as neighbors, volunteers, and mentors, to give it to them.

Rejoice with your family in the beautiful
land of life!

—ALBERT EINSTEIN

CHAPTER NINE

THE CURE

Making Your Own Family Culture

Stronger than All Competing Cultures

---

cure *noun* \ˈkyùr\

1. something that defeats an illness, ends a problem or improves a bad situation

It bespeaks the end of something bad.

And the start of something good.

A cure is most often a personal thing, and in many cases something that we can create for ourselves.

What Families Can Do
to Save Themselves

This chapter is written primarily for parents and grandparents who, recognizing the threats posed to their own families by false paradigms and larger institutions, want to be proactive in creating a personal family culture that withstands and supersedes the peer culture, the media culture, and every other competing culture to which their children are exposed.

The ideas here may also appeal to those who wish someday to become parents.

In either case (current or future parents) it is important to be encouraged rather than discouraged by the suggestions that follow. Trying to implement everything, or feeling guilty if you don't, will lead to discouragement. But picking a few ideas—just the ones you think might work for you right now—will be encouraging, even empowering.

If you are fortunate enough (and rare enough) to come from a highly functional family, many of the suggestions in this chapter may seem natural, even obvious. And for the many who come from dysfunctional or almost non-existent fam-

If we put forth the effort, seek the right help, and persist, we can be the predominant influence in our own families and with our own children.

ilies, these ideas may seem daunting, if not impossible. But look at it this way: if you can just begin—if you can try harder than your parents before you, if you can deliberately turn your back on bad family habits and start developing some better ones—you may change the culture of your family for generations to come.

Any concerned parent, who has become aware of the dangers of larger institutions and false paradigms, has three options:

1. Give up and give in to entities and influences that are so much bigger than we are.

2. Try to organize and fight against the "enemies" (using anything from boycotts to letters to our congressmen).

3. Create a family institution strong enough to resist the dangers posed by the larger institutions and false paradigms.

This chapter focuses on the third option. Not that there is anything wrong with option two—in fact, there are some ideas on organizing in Chapter 11. But most of us, as parents, know that the thing we have the best chance of influencing, in the short term, is our own families. After all, we are with them on a daily basis, and we have the most influence on change when we operate in our own sphere. We also know, deep down, that if we put forth the effort, seek the right help, and persist, we can be the predominant influence in our own families and with our own children, countering, preempting, and superseding the negative influences of peer groups, larger institutions, and false paradigms.

We heard this story from a father:

> *I remember one of my first personal experiences with the alternating helplessness and hopefulness that all parents feel. Our oldest was twelve and completely caught up with her peer group. She seemed to have total interest in her friends and zero interest in her family. I knew at least a couple of her friends were not providing the kind of influence we'd have wished for. Any time she wasn't with her friends she wanted to spend on the computer, in front of the TV, or listening to music all of which were blasting her with the wrong values and attitudes.*
>
> *"Where's my influence," I thought. "How can I have any effect on who she's becoming?"*

*Then at a parent-teacher conference I saw an essay she'd
written. The assignment (and the title) was, "My Hero," and
she had written about me. I realized that the opportunity
for influence and for the relationship I wanted with her were
there—and they would always be there—but I had to make
it happen.*

The bottom line is that we must *turn our hearts* to our children and our
families. We must come to understand that the larger institutions that were
created to serve us are now demanding too much service from us, as well as
too much time and too much allegiance. We must, as parents, make a conscious decision to give those institutions less of our time and to give them
none of our hearts. Our personal tradeoffs must favor the family. As we turn
our hearts, we will also turn our minds, our priorities, and our time.

Seven Focuses for Strengthening the Family

In earlier times, families survived out of necessity. They were the only institution—their members had no other options for seeking identity, security,
and values.

Today, larger institutions present many alternatives, and families survive only by their own *will* and their own *choice*. Strong families are still
attainable, but only by parents who passionately pledge themselves to
doing what it takes to build and bolster, to protect and prioritize their
families—only by parents who consciously set out to make their family
culture stronger than the peer culture, the Internet culture, the media culture, and all other cultures that swirl around their children.

> *Strong families are still
> attainable, but only by
> parents who passionately
> pledge themselves to doing
> what it takes to build
> and bolster, to protect and
> prioritize their families.*

Here are seven direct and effective approaches to strengthening, protecting, and preserving our families. These approaches have always been important, but now, in the face of all that is happening to the family, they are more crucial and more necessary than ever before. They are listed here as seven suggestions to parents and then explored as seven *steps* that every family can take to save and strengthen itself. They are not precise formulas, but they point in directions that may serve as thought prompters for your own ideas on how to strengthen your own unique family.

1. Make a conscious, personal RECOMMITMENT to the priority of marriage and family and to the seven unique family functions listed in Chapter 1 (procreation, role example, nurturing, personal identity, teaching values, providing permanence, and elder care). Truly turn your *heart* (your priority, your focus, and your passion) to your children.

2. Teach and live by CORRECT PRINCIPLES, which oppose, overcome, and supersede false paradigms. Recognize the error and danger in many of society's attitudes and "norms," and see the wisdom in true and enduring principles as you teach them to your children.

3. Reinvent TIME MANAGEMENT and BALANCE with the priority and emphasis on spouse and children. As you plan your day or your week, set aside and reserve time for family. Set relationship goals and help children understand that relationships are ultimately more important than achievements.

4. Teach understanding and SELECTIVE USE of larger institutions. Teach children to recognize the good and the bad in media, government, and business, and to use the one while avoiding the other.

5. Make COMMUNICATION the constant goal. Implement it, improve it, and insist on it—between spouses and between parent and child.

6. Create IDENTITY, SECURITY, and MOTIVATION for children through family narratives and ancestor stories, through family meetings, family traditions, family rules, and a family economy that shares household responsibilities.

7. Use "VALUES THERAPY," where the focus shifts away from what is wrong and toward the rewards and fulfillment of what is right. Focus on one of twelve basic, universal values each month, and build a family culture that is value-centered.

One: Recommitment to Marriage and Family

A good friend of ours, a country doctor who has attended the last hours of many people's lives, remarked that he had never heard anyone on their deathbed say, "Oh, I wish I'd spent more time with the business," or "If only I'd been able to buy one more new car." The regrets people have at the end of life, as well as their most cherished memories, invariably have to do with family.

And actually, the regrets come well before the end of life. So many people in their fifties, sixties, or seventies, even those who have every material thing they ever wanted, find their lives empty and hollow, lonely and meaningless, because they forfeited family somewhere along the way. They miss so desperately the relationships that they gave up, gave up on, or consciously decided not to have sometime back in mid-life.

Those who chose not to have children or to avoid the commitment of marriage find that the older they get, the more they long for the family ties that they never formed.

And the pattern for many who did start families is so frighteningly predictable: In "early life," we fall in love, begin our families, and know the joys and sorrows that come with the risks of committed, caring relationships. But often, in mid-life, we grow impatient, disillusioned, or just tired, and allow some combination of selfishness, foolishness, and fatigue to turn us away from spouse or child. Or, we simply stop putting forth the necessary effort and let family relationships gradually slip and slide away. Then in later life we may realize that what we gave up was everything and what we traded it for is nothing.

Those who chose not to have children or to avoid the commitment of marriage find that the older they get, the more they long for the family ties that they never formed.

It is in mid-life (sometimes very early mid-life—this time of slippage and selfishness) that we need a purposeful and powerful recommitment to relationships. Deep down, we all know that family is the first priority and that a man named David O. McKay was right when he said, "No other success can compensate for failure in the home." Yet the world pulls us in so many other directions. The false paradigms and the self-preserving larger institutions popularize materialism, self-gratification, and the "freedom" of ownership without obligation.

Family-destructive thoughts come so easily: "My wife doesn't look as good as she used to." "My spouse doesn't take care of himself." "I just don't have the energy to keep track of this kid anymore." "My spouse is so much less stimulating than the people I work with at the office." "My life is so dull compared to what I see on the Internet or on TV." "Think of what I could have if I spent a little more of what I earn on myself." "Once kids are this age, there's not much I can do to influence them anyway." "I'm completely tied down by my spouse and kids." "There's got to be something more to life than this." "It's only when I'm drinking that I can really relax." "I'm just tired of trying to do everything for everyone else and nothing for myself." The thoughts gradually develop into negative language and family-destructive actions.

We need an antidote against the slippage. The prescription we need is *re-commitment*. Real commitment—deep and heartfelt—is a systemic solution. It is the scriptural cure of turning our very *hearts*; it is a solution that moves up through the trunk of parents and extends out to affect the branches and leaves of every child. "Parenting methods" or "marriage techniques" may be effective in the short term, but genuine commitment gets us through the hard times, impacts everything we do, and, more importantly, everything we and those around us feel.

> *"Parenting methods" or "marriage techniques" may be effective in the short term, but genuine commitment gets us through the hard times.*

> *As we have watched couples we know become increasingly tired of each other's idiosyncrasies and choose to separate or divorce or live separate lives, we can't help but notice how stark the contrast is with one dear friend who cares for his Alzheimer-afflicted wife every day, even though she doesn't know who he is. The difference is commitment!*

And if you are one who cannot recommit because you never committed to family in the first place, it is never too late. You can literally start a family and make these commitments at any time and at any age.

> *When I was a young father, the church we went to had a program where the lay members would visit the homes of other members once a month to see how they were doing and to leave a spiritual thought. I was assigned to two families; one happened to be very wealthy and attractive—easy to admire. The man, about ten years older than me, had a successful business, a beautiful wife, bright kids, a large mansion, and a red Lamborghini. The second family was quite a contrast—they were poor, lived in a small house,*

and had only one bathroom for seven people. I looked forward to visiting the first house each month—there was so much style and stimulation. The other house was not particularly compelling. Yet, as the months passed, I found my anticipation shifting. I looked forward to going to the little house because the feelings and the atmosphere were so warm. And what had seemed to be busyness and excitement at the big house was revealing itself to be tension, conflict, and dissatisfaction—everyone was running off in their own direction and trying to find something that fulfilled them—outside of the family. We moved away a year or two later, and I lost touch with both families.

Fifteen years later, I was giving a speech at a university, and afterward, a student came up to me and asked if I remembered her. She was one of the children from the small and humble house. As we talked, I got that same comfortable, quietly confident feeling that I used to feel in their home. I asked about the other family with the big house, and she told me that the parents had broken up and a couple of the kids were in rehab programs. Then I asked about her family and particularly about her father: "What did he do that gave you all such confidence?" I also asked, "What were his parenting techniques? I'm a dad now, and I want that same feeling in my home."

"Oh, we're all fine," she said. "Still not too well off, but everyone is making progress, and we love each other more than ever." She seemed a little amused by my second question. "You remember my dad," she said. "He wouldn't know a parenting technique if it came up and bit him."

"That's true," I persisted, "but what did he do?" "I still remember how it felt in your home, and I see it in your eyes now."

She became more reflective, and I saw something else in her eye—a tear. "You know," she said, "I think it was just that we knew he'd never give up on us. We knew we and our mom were his first priority. He would make mistakes, he had a temper, still does, but he was just always there for us, and he'd tell us that."

I think it was my obvious interest in what she was saying that kept her memories coming. *"I remember he would come and sit on my bed and just hold my face in his hands and look right in my eyes and say, 'I am totally committed to you. You are my first priority. I would do anything for you.'"*

She hadn't ever forgotten those words and that commitment, and its powerful and secure effect still seemed to rest with her.

No Parent Ever Fails until They Give Up

The interesting thing about marriage and parenting and family is that *no one ever fails until they give up.* There will be setbacks and problems—sometimes big, long-term problems—but no one fails until they give up! We see examples of that every day. We see parents who hang in there, who keep trying, keep supporting, keep giving their unconditional love, and keep *telling* their child about it—kids who are in trouble, kids who have run away, kids who won't listen, won't talk—*and those kids eventually come around!* Maybe not tomorrow, maybe not next year, maybe not in ten years, and maybe not quite as their parents would wish, but when the parent never quits, reconciliation comes, and love prevails. Of course, there are exceptions, but the same commitment-magic almost always works between marriage partners. Every imaginable problem may exist, but when no one throws in the towel, and when the commitment is still there, *things eventually get better!*

We tend to undervalue and underestimate commitment. We forget about its pervasive power. When real commitment is felt, and expressed, it has a way of shrinking problems, of making them look manageable.

After giving a speech to a group of parents, we were greeting people personally who had lined up to see us, and I couldn't help noticing a woman progressing toward us who was sobbing. By the time she got to the front of the line she was inconsolable, and all I could do was ask what was wrong and how could I help. Through her sobs, she blurted out that she had lost her son, that he had left home shortly after his eighteenth birthday, that she thought he had drugs, that the authorities wouldn't look for him because he was a legal adult, and that she had not heard from him for nearly a year.

Not knowing how to console her, I said, "So have you pretty much given up?"

Suddenly, her whole demeanor changed. She stopped crying. She straightened up. She got a new look of fierce determination on her face and said, "Given up? He is my son! I will never give up on him!"

In an instant, she changed from weak to strong, from desperate to committed. I took her by the shoulders and made her a promise. "You will find him . . . and you will reconcile. It may take another year, or ten years, or it may happen in the next life, but you have not failed, and you have not lost your son, because you have not given up and you have not lost commitment."

We tend to undervalue and underestimate commitment. We forget about its pervasive power. When real commitment is felt, and expressed, it has a way of shrinking problems, of making them look manageable. When commitment is thought of as unalterable, lasting, and unconditional, problems can't stand up to it—they can't match it in its permanence. Whatever the forces are that undermine relationships and break up families, they tend to back off in the presence of deep, complete commitment as though they had a mind of their own and choose to go work on someone else where there is less commitment and where they can do more damage.

When there is commitment, true commitment, it fortifies a marriage and a family in truly remarkable ways. When adversity strikes a family—be it in the form of illness, accident, economic hardship, or anything else—if commitment is strong, the adversity strengthens that family and brings its members closer together.

On the other hand, families without strong commitment are broken by adversity.

Commitment turns our hearts, *locking* them on the relationships that matter. If we want to fix our families, to shore them up against the false paradigms and the larger institutions, to preserve them for our old age, to immunize them against all of their many potential destroyers, we must start with recommitment. Let the recommitment start in our heart, and then we'll be capable of sending it out through our words and our eyes to reassure and bless the lives of those we love most.

The real question, of course, is how we *apply* commitment. After we profess it to those we love most, how do we demonstrate it in everyday life? The answer, and actually the beauty of it, is that different people will apply it in different ways. If your recommitment is *real*, it will manifest itself in ways that are tailored to your own situation and your own family's unique needs. The techniques are not as important as the heart, the methods are not as important as the commitment.

Too many parents approach the process backwards. They try various parenting techniques in the hope that they will increase their feelings and their commitments to their family. But if the heart is not there—not genuinely and truly *turned* to the family in a prioritized, unconditional love—then the methods, no matter how sound, will be hollow and generally ineffective. One way of implementing commitment to children is to think about them long and hard—even analytically. A method many families use for doing this is called a five-facet review.

Early in our marriage and our parenting, we decided that, once a month, we would go on a special dinner "date" to a relatively quiet place. With no interruptions or disturbances, we had only one item on our agenda—our children. We brainstormed together about the five facets of each of our children, one at a time:

- *How is Josh doing* physically?
- *How is he doing* mentally?
- *How is he doing* socially?
- *How is he doing* emotionally?
- *How is he doing* spiritually?

We talked about potential problems, as well as about opportunities or attributes. We took notes. When we recognized a challenge or a need (or an opportunity), we decided together how to deal with it and who would handle it. At the end of this process each month, we had a clearer picture of each child, a more specific commitment to him or her, and a more sharply focused love for him or her.

It is frequently true that more involvement brings more commitment, and these regular, monthly, five-facet reviews intensified both our mental involvement and our emotional commitment to our children and to each other.

Two: Substitute Correct Principles for False Paradigms

Today's families face a challenge that no other era of parents and spouses has had to deal with: *how to undo or supersede the damage and danger of widespread and pervasive false paradigms.* Families in an earlier age did not have to face a world where a minority masqueraded so successfully as a majority, where materialism and instant gratification were the accepted norms, and where conditional morality and selfish expediency had pretty much overthrown the ideas of absolutes and of spiritual sources of good and evil.

False paradigms have a way of getting in our heads and of staying there until we replace them with something better. As parents, it's hard to overcome the "bacteria" that comes at us from larger institutions if our immune systems are weakened by false paradigms. And children, who are literally surrounded and bombarded by the false world-views, are not going to recognize them, let alone reject them, unless we help them recognize the negative influences and give them real replacements.

But we can't replace false paradigms in kids' heads before we have corrected them in our own.

The most straightforward way to overcome and slip out of the clutches and influence of false paradigms is to openly *assert* your belief in their exact opposites. Do whatever you have to do—make a chart of correct principles, of things as they really are, of

Find your own way to pledge your allegiance to some simple, clear, positive principles that will cut through the smokescreen of the prevailing false paradigms.

what you believe, and hang it on your wall or put it in a family mission statement or make a screen saver out of it for your personal computer. Find your own way to pledge your allegiance to some simple, clear, positive principles that will cut through the smokescreen of the prevailing false paradigms.

There are *four* basic, true principles that can be taught within a family which are the exact antithesis (and the antidote) of the four false paradigms we listed earlier. These principles can set up a foundation on which a strong family can be maintained and strong individual lives can be lived. They will "ring true" to you as you read them because, deep within ourselves, we are all recognizers of truth.

Principle 1: Despite appearances, the majority is always on the side of what is right, and what is light.

(This is the antidote to the false paradigm of popular media posing amorality as the prevailing condition.)

Whether you count angels as part of your majority in your interpretation of this principle, or whether it's just a question of the undeniable might that goes with right, it's a truth that you can rely on and that you can teach to your children. Here are the two things kids need to know in order to accept and live by this principle:

First, the facts run contrary to what is seen and heard in so many movies, TV shows, Internet games, and rock songs:

- Premarital sex is *not* the norm, and there *are* consequences. Slightly more than half of high school students are virgins. And half of kids who have had sex say they wish they hadn't.[1]

- The F-word is *not* the most commonly used word in the English language.

- Everyone worth knowing does *not* drive a trendy new car, wear only name brands, and live in luxury.

- Divorce is *not* something that happens smoothly and easily and without long-term consequences.

- People throughout the world, old and young, *do* continue to value commitments and relationships and character.

Second, most of what we see on the large and small screen and hear in popular music is created by a small cultural elite. Most people in this group are neither as family-oriented nor as religiously inclined as the average person. It is they, not we, who are the minority. But their visibility and influence, magnified a million times by media, makes them appear to be a majority.

Kids who understand these two simple facts will have an immunity of sorts to the compelling "be part of it" influence of media. They will be able to stand aside a bit and see error as error, figure consequences for actions, and take some comfort in the fact that what they believe is more common than it sometimes seems.

Principle 2: What matters is what's inside, what you've worked for and waited for, and what you give.

(This is the antidote to the false paradigm of materialism.)

The world whispers to us (sometimes shouts) that what matters is:

- Outside appearances
- Instant gratification
- How much we can get

Yet almost all of us know that these are not only delusions, they are directly opposite-of-truth lies. What really matters is:

- Who and what we are inside
- Good things worked for (and often waited for), especially relationships
- How much we can give

In surveys, substantial majorities say that family is more important than possessions, and character is more important than appearance. Yet, in so many ways, we believe in one creed and live by another. When the current goes one direction, it takes strong swimming to move in the other. There is real determination and effort required to get to and stay in a place that society seems to be moving away from.

Sometimes the key is as simple as reminding ourselves of who we are and what we believe. As we remind ourselves, we must teach our children. "What matters?" is a topic and a discussion that can't come up too often. Talk about what matters at the dinner table, during a car ride, or in a family meeting.

The biggest manifestation of materialism in kids, and the greatest single challenge of parents today, is the widespread and contagious attitude of entitlement. When children fall into this trap, they begin to feel that they deserve everything. They want whatever their friends have, whatever they see advertised, and whatever they want, they want it right now, without having to work for it or wait for it. It is an attitude that sucks away initiative, motivation, and gratitude and that diminishes their chance for success in virtually every aspect of their lives.

> *"What matters?" is a topic and a discussion that can't come up too often. Talk about what matters at the dinner table, during a car ride, or in a family meeting.*

The antidote to the false paradigm of entitlement and the prerequisite of responsibility is "earned ownership," and the full formula for creating an ownership and responsibility paradigm in your kids' minds is outlined in detail in our last book, *The Entitlement Trap*. See an overview in the "Parenting Resources and Previous Books" summary at the end of this book, and the "family economy" section later in this chapter.

Principle 3: Joy comes from commitment, sacrifice, and delayed gratification.

(This is the antidote to the false paradigm of recreational sex, hedonism, and instant gratification.)

Like any true principle, this one is truly learned and truly taught only by living it. But along with the living should come the straight-forward *telling*. We need to tell our children boldly and clearly that the hedonistic approach of seeking happiness through pleasure and self-gratification is a crock.

> *I was on a several-hour drive one summer with my son from our house to a vacation destination. In his early adolescence, he seemed so vulnerable and easily influenced by everything around him. He wanted to wear the right brands, to have the things that "everyone else" had, to try out and feel everything, right or wrong, that his friends were telling him about. And he wanted to have and be and*

try all of it now. I wanted to use the drive time to talk him out of some of this and convince him of the value of commitment, sacrifice, and delayed gratification, but I knew a lecture on my theories wouldn't cut it.

The only other passenger in the car with us was our chocolate Labrador dog, and we were talking about her. My son loved the dog and was interested in animals and biology in general. It was a safe subject. Somehow, we got from what we were talking about to what I wanted to talk about. Instinct and appetites, we decided, were what made animals accomplish their purposes and find their happiness. Following those instincts, urges, and appetites allowed them to stay alive, reproduce, and keep the biological ecosystem balanced and functional. What made humans different from animals was that we get our happiness and maximize our potential not by following but by controlling our appetites. Animals' appetites control them. Humans must control their appetites.

Then we talked about various appetites—for food, for sex, for possessions, for recognition. I was amazed at how clearly my thirteen-year-old could see how each of those appetites, if allowed to control us, could hurt us and cause unhappiness to ourselves and others. But I was even more impressed that he could see how controlling them could make us better and happier.

So much of our world feeds us (and our children) the disastrous hedonistic attitudes of pleasure-seeking and instant gratification—an animalistic philosophy. We also get bombarded with the notion that "freedom" and "commitment" are opposites, that loyalties to family relationships "tie us down" and limit us in all sorts of ways. By our example and our words, we must help our children see that these messages are simply big lies. We must try both to teach and to exemplify their opposites—to help them

Commitment and discipline expand rather than limit our freedom.

understand that commitment and discipline expand rather than limit our freedom, and that it is indulgence in things like drugs or recreational sex that lead to the bonds and traps of addictions and emotional pain.

In our presentations to parents, we often ask, by a show of hands, how many have had in-depth talks with their kids about violence in media and in computer games. Most hands go up. Then we ask how many have had serious discussions with their children about drugs and alcohol and other addictions. Again, most hands go up. Then we ask the obvious next question: "How many of you have had 'the big talk' about sex?" Fewer hands go up, and there are a lot of shifty-eyed glances between couples and a lot more people looking down at the floor than up at us.

Then we ask them which of the three (violence, drugs, or sex) poses the biggest threat to their kids. When children see violence, drugs/alcohol, or sex in media or entertainment or games, which are they the most likely to emulate or experiment with? Most parents realize that it is early, experimental, recreational sex that poses the greatest threat and the most likely scenario for problems and emotional and physical damage at earlier and earlier ages.

Then we ask one more very telling question: "When do you think you should have the sex talk (and its follow ups)?"

Many parents give the very wrong answer: "When they start asking about it." If parents wait that long, of course, it is probably too late. It will mean that kids get their first information from their peers, the media, and the Internet.

After hearing that so many parents were not proactively speaking to their children, we became so concerned that we wrote a book called How to Talk to Your Child About Sex. *Rather than a lot of advice, it is mostly a dialogue: you say this, your child will say this, then you say this, and your child will say either this or this, in which case you say this or this. The ideal age for the big talk, though certain related things should be talked about sooner, is eight years old. But there are ways to adapt the talk for older kids. Find the dialogue at www.valuesparenting.com.*

Principle 4: Absolute right and absolute help both exist, and both can be found.

(This is the antidote to the false paradigm of conditional ethics.)

The majority of people throughout the world, and more than 90 percent of Americans, believe in God. And among those who do not, many nonetheless believe in families and in consistent principles of morality and of right versus wrong.

While the specifics of belief vary widely, most accept many of the same connected convictions about the nature of deity and about the eternal nature of their own soul or spirit. Although there are many different faiths, when it comes to the basics, various world religions could almost be interpreted by an outside analyst as a game of how many different ways the same things could be said. Certain beliefs of "believers" are virtually universal:

- God exists/lives.
- God is our Father/Creator.
- God is good—the ultimate good.
- God gives truth about how we should live (in scripture and through inspiration).
- God respects our agency (allows us to choose).
- God hears and answers prayers and gives guidance.
- God can forgive, and we can improve.
- We (humans) have within us a spirit or soul that continues after death.

It is important to see and understand the *ramifications* of belief in God and in a life hereafter—to see what it should mean in terms of our general view of life and our rejection of paradigms and attitudes that are inconsistent with spiritual beliefs.

God is the *source* of good, so His principles *define* what is right. (If there were no God, it could be argued that any set of principles would be as good as any other.)

Therefore, *absolutes* exist. God's word or way, and what leads to it, is absolutely good, and what leads away from it is absolutely bad.

A belief in God and in absolutes can simplify life in a positive way, giving us a framework of what is right and wrong, good and bad, relieving us of the oppressive obligation to make every one of those judgments for ourselves.

Beliefs and absolutes are the keys to knowing who we are and to understanding life's purpose. If God is father, we are children. If God is the owner and giver, then we are the receivers and stewards. If God loves us then there is positive purpose in being born into and living through mortality, and there is ongoing life and additional opportunity beyond death. How we live and what we learn here will affect who and what we are there.

This eternal perspective makes life more beautiful as well as more meaningful. Our faith allows us to perceive ourselves as:

- Sons and daughters, metaphorically, if not literally, of God.
- Individuals who came from God through birth (birth which was "a sleeping and a forgetting . . . from God who is our Home"—*William Wordsworth*[2]).
- Recipients of the gift of this mortality. We are physical bodies on a physical earth who have been sent to the perfect school/ laboratory with every option and possibility.
- Choosers of good or evil; we are self-determining.
- Beings capable of love, which precipitates happiness.

- People able to make commitments and create families, wherein lies life's deepest joy.
- Subject to God's commandments (the most important of which involve the taking and the starting of life), which are best viewed as "loving counsel from a wise Father."
- Capable of returning to God, to continue living and progressing in an afterlife.

With these beliefs, shared by a majority but too seldom talked about, what do we do? The best thing to do is to *remind* ourselves and our children of what we believe, of the reality and consistency of what is right and what is wrong, of the need we all have for help from a higher source, and of the happiness that runs so parallel with goodness. We need to remind our children and ourselves often enough and strongly enough that we supersede and outweigh the opposite (counterfeit) messages of the world.

Perhaps, to believers, the best reminder of all is prayer. Most people pray, but too often only sporadically or in times of particular need. As Alfred, Lord Tennyson, said, "More things are wrought by prayer than this world dreams of." Remember that family prayer or prayer with children at bedtime or before a meal, in addition to whatever spiritual help it may bring, is a powerful statement to your child that you believe, that there are absolutes, and that we don't have to depend entirely on ourselves.

THREE: REINVENT TIME-MANAGEMENT AND BALANCE WITH FAMILY AND RELATIONSHIP EMPHASIS

It's ironic that as our cultures have pushed goal- and priority-setting and time management almost to the level of an art form, few of us have figured out how to make it produce any more time for what should be our highest priority—our families. We come up with lots of excuses like "quality time" or making ourselves "available" through texts or social media or smart phones. But real quality time happens when there is an adequate, unrushed *quantity* of time. Our kids don't just need to know how to reach us when there is an emergency; they need to reach us and have us focus on them when there is no necessity other than the need for time together.

The problem with most goal-setting and time-management efforts is that they focus on *achievements* at the expense of relationships, on *work* goals more than on *family* goals, and often on *things* more than on *people*. As one overworked young father said:

> *I was feeling absolutely swamped with responsibilities and time-con-suming projects at work, getting home after the kids were in bed and leaving the next morning before they were awake. I felt espe-cially guilty about not spending more time with my five-year-old son, who seemed to really need a dad. Whenever he wanted some-thing, I'd be gone or about to leave. I blocked off a lunch hour in my old day-timer and wrote "Lunch with Josh." But that morning, something came up.*
>
> *I thought, in those days, that time management was the answer to just about everything, so I simply thumbed ahead a few days in my day timer until I saw a free evening the next Thursday, and I blocked it off for Josh. Almost immediately, I felt a little less guilty. I was scheduling my son, so I really wasn't neglecting him! But when Thursday came, there was a minor crisis at the office, and I had to stay late. No problem; I just penciled Josh in again—for a week from Tuesday. When Tuesday came, I left work a few minutes early and showed up at the house right on schedule (my schedule). Josh was sitting there watching a cartoon when I burst in. "Come on, son, let's go do something fun together!" He looked up at me (probably trying to remember who I was) and said, "Not now, Dad. I'm too busy watching this."*

What a mistake we make when we think we can program our kids or have them want to be with us when it's convenient for us, or schedule them in like a business meeting. Kids need us when they need us, and quality time comes not when we dictate but when circumstances allow a teaching moment—when we're spontaneous enough to answer a question or play a game or tuck a child into bed, even when it's *not* convenient or written down in our calendar. This serendipity of being open and available to children is a hallmark of good parents, and it clearly *demonstrates* to kids that they are the first priority. Open yourself up to these unexpected, unplanned opportunities.

This is not to say we can't schedule some family time. Indeed, doing so may be the most important solution of all. Consult with your kids, take their schedule and interests into account. And when you schedule family time, try to make it your highest priority. With scheduled family time, it is important that the kids participate in the planning so they can anticipate and look forward to it, and start enjoying it even before it happens.

One option is to schedule for family time to coincide with meal time. It used to be that families ate dinner together most nights, and the dinner hour and the dinner table became the time and the place where issues were discussed and feelings were shared. The busyness and conflicting schedules of today make that ideal virtually impossible for most families. But, at a minimum, families with children living at home should set aside one or two regular, set times each week when they will be together. For many families, Sunday lunch or dinner is the best time for a family meeting setting. The next week's needs and schedule can be reviewed, parents can ask about anything from grades to friends, and kids can ask about anything from rules to finances. Family mission statements

> *What a mistake we make when we think we can program our kids or have them want to be with us when it's convenient for us, or schedule them in like a business meeting.*

(see pages 214–216) can be developed. Family meal time is an opportunity to share feelings and to feel the teamwork and identity of family.

> *Whenever we are in Latin America, we find ourselves admiring the family togetherness traditions of most cultures there. Even many of the busy executives in the organizations we present our seminars to seem to find a couple of hours of serious family time almost every day. In one large seminar, we asked how many had dinner or lunch together with their families most every day. Ninety percent of the hands went up. In the United States or Europe or in most of developed Asia, the percentage would have been tiny.*
>
> *The reason we said dinner or lunch is that some of these Latin executives are still able go home in the middle part of the day, often for three or four hours, to have a late lunch with kids just home from school and often to stay for a little siesta before returning to the office for an evening of extended work.*

If Latin American families can get together every day, the rest of us ought to be able to manage one family meeting each week. In addition to the weekly family meeting, every family, wherever they are, ought to try to set aside one weekday evening as a family night where they do something fun together. It could be on the same day or as an extension of the weekly family meeting—something as simple as a seeing a movie or eating pizza or ice cream together. It may not be possible to do this *every* week (or to hold the family meeting every Sunday), but if times are set aside and if only real emergencies or things beyond our control cancel them, they will begin to have a bonding, unifying effect on our families. If a parent is out of town, we have the benefit of Skype or Facetime to join a family meeting. Whether a family consists of two people or ten, blocking out certain times of the week for just each other can make a huge difference.

> *We had been holding Sunday family meetings for years—as consistently as our schedules would allow. But we still didn't feel like*

everyone was having their say or that all were equally involved. Then we heard an idea from another family and began trying it in ours: Once a month, before our Sunday lunch together, we began holding what we called a "family feelings session." Each family member had a chance to take a few moments and talk about his or her feelings—about other members of the family, about school or work, or about themselves. Each could say whatever he or she wanted—their worries, their joys—with everyone else listening and paying attention. The only instruction we gave was that they should center on feelings and use the words "I feel" as often as possible.

The first few times were a little slow—one child was too anxious to express himself, another didn't want to say a word. But we persevered. Linda and I talked about our feelings (especially for the children) and then encouraged them to do so. It became the absolute highlight of our month. There, in the quiet of our living room, with phones and gadgets turned off, we take time to tell each other how we feel. The love level and the trust level have expanded dramatically. We know each other better, appreciate each other more, and love each other more completely than we otherwise would.

Determine the times of the week that are most possible and most predictable for you. Make this a priority, and make these dates in the calendar happen. Real quality time will come gradually, and according to your willingness to set aside time and to be flexible and spontaneous at other times when relationship opportunities come up.

We sometimes get some pushback from parents when we suggest a regular, weekly family meeting. Many say that their demanding schedules, and those of their kids, make this impractical. But they begin to come around when we ask them how many have a weekly staff meeting at the office to prioritize and schedule for the week ahead. Suddenly, it dawns on them that a weekly meeting might

*be a good idea for families as well. It could be a time to re-evaluate
what is going well and not so well within the home and establish
workable family systems. We try to persuade parents that family
meetings are a way to give kids a feeling of equity in the family, particularly when kids can conduct and organize the meetings.*

As kids get older, use the weekly meeting to teach them to set "relationship goals" by writing a brief paragraph describing the relationship they want to have with a sibling or a parent three years from now. As their departure from your home to college or work approaches, teach them that in addition to the deliberate accomplishment of education and career, they should consciously and consistently pursue the goal of finding a marriage partner and being ready to form a committed relationship and to accept the responsibility and the joy of children.

Four: Teach Kids the Selective Use of Larger Institutions

It may sound like a stretched or overdramatized analogy, but we need to think of (and teach our kids to perceive of) big institutions as similar to *fire*. Fire can warm, support, and sustain us, or it can consume and destroy us. Media and merchandising, business and banks, Internet and information can serve us or consume us. It's a lesson our parents and grandparents didn't need to teach us. But times have changed, and it's a lesson we *do* need to teach our children and grandchildren.

We need to remind them that the family is at the heart and essence of all. We can draw on the outer sectors for support, but we should never give up our identity to them, never let them replace or supplant family loyalty, never let them take advantage of or swallow up the family.

Children are capable, once they are seven or eight, of understanding this perspective. They can be taught to identify the larger institutions and begin

The goal is to help our kids become good critics who can see through advertising and promotion, who recognize instant gratification for what it is, who connect action to consequences whether others do or not.

to understand what each one does to help us and what each one does to hurt us. A parent can create a large version of the bull's-eye diagram and help a child fill in the big institutions that fit within each sector, as well as list the good and bad effects that each can have on the family. Such a chart can serve as a "framework of warning" on what to avoid (from "too easy" credit to too expensive tastes, from media amorality to Internet pornography, from all-consuming employment to all-consuming recreation). If your children are older, share with them the information on pages 94–134, and help them to understand the ten different types of large institutions that they should use *selectively* (accepting the good, rejecting the bad).

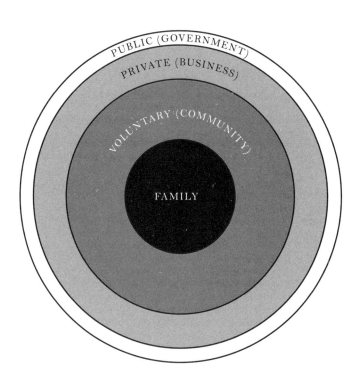

Essentially, the goal is to help our kids become *good critics* who can see through advertising and promotion, who recognize instant gratification for what it is, who connect action to consequences whether others do or not, and most of all, who perceive the dangers stemming from the instinct for expansion (and the greed) of larger institutions. Our own experience convinces us that kids can, gradually, over time, become good critics who see things as they really are.

> *We'd been trying for months to help our kids see the world in the framework of the bull's-eye diagram and to be self-motivated critics of the materialism and amorality that lurks everywhere today. We had little indications that we were getting somewhere when a child, while watching a manipulative commercial on TV would say, "Yeah, sure," or would ask his or her friends if they knew the actual total cost of a car when you bought it on credit. But we really felt we were making progress when we were driving our seventh-grade daughter home from a parent-teacher conference and she suddenly said, "You know, I've just got to go in and talk to my math teacher and tell him why I didn't think that test was fair. After all, he works for us!" We asked her what she meant, and she really told us. "Well, we pay him, don't we? I mean, it's our taxes—he works for us. We own the schools. They don't own us. It's like you've been telling me— schools and stores and companies and stuff, even movies and music and the Internet, they shouldn't be telling us what to do. We should be telling them what to do!"*
>
> *We had to have a little discussion about the right and wrong ways to "tell them what to do," but we were delighted with her growing ability to think things through for herself and her capacity to be a critic rather than a pawn-like acceptor of everything.*

The bottom line (and one that kids can *understand* and feel *empowered* by) is this: Live by your own values. Sift and screen the things media and schools and advertisements throw at you. Learn to recognize when a big institution's self-interests don't match up with your values, your beliefs, and your sense of what's best for you and for your family.

Five: Insist on Communication

Everything depends on communication. It is what solves problems; it is what draws people together; it is how love grows; it is what builds trust and security and identity.

So many marriages and so many parent-child relationships "suffer in silence." Feelings go unexpressed. Resentments or misunderstandings grow because they are unresolved. Pride makes people walk away rather than come together or compromise or apologize. Kids rebel and leave home or "go silent" because they're convinced that parents don't (and can't) understand. When parents try to show interest or ask questions, it comes across as an interrogation. Couples find themselves doing more judging and demanding than real sharing and supporting and communicating.

Even within our families, where the deepest intimacy should exist, we resort to small talk on safe subjects and avoid the real issues, the real needs, the real worries. And bad communication is exacerbated in today's high-tech world where more and more kids find communication through gadgets and devices easier and less threatening than direct voice communication with people. They learn more from movies, reality shows, the Internet, and social media than from their parents because they spend more time in front of a screen and see many more words on their devices than they hear from their parents' mouths.

The simple fact is that parents give up too easily on communication. We expect too little from it. When it gets hard, we back off and move on to something easier and more pleasant. When a kid or a spouse says, "I can't talk to you," we either get mad ("I can't talk to you either.") or sad ("I guess that's just the way it is.") rather than getting *determined* and saying, at least to ourselves, "We've got to find a way!"

One problem, of course, is that real communication takes *time*. In this busy world of over-commitment and trying to do everything—and usually all at once—it is the time for important relationships that is so often lost. We trade relationships for achievements. We trade communication for busyness. We trade time spent talking for time spent running around and trying to keep up with all those we view as competitors. These are always *bad* tradeoffs, but we get in the habit of making them.

Bad communication is exacerbated in today's high-tech world where more and more kids find communication through gadgets and devices easier and less threatening than direct voice communication with people.

The old stalwarts and symbols of communication—family dinners, long walks, bedtime stories, Sunday drives—just don't happen much anymore and are replaced in families by the Internet and social media and sports and technology and gadgets and more tutors and teams and music lessons than our parents ever could have imagined.

Unfortunately, it's not just the places and traditions of communication that are disappearing; it's the desire and the effort to make communication and connection that has gone away as well.

How do we *restore* the desire, the effort, and the traditions of communication? We start with the realization that everything that matters most—our happiness, our values, and our families—depends on communication. Then, once we put communication in the status of highest priority, we *devote* ourselves to it. We put nothing ahead of it, we insist on it, we demand it of ourselves and ask and work and plead for it from those we love.

Studies show over and over again the main reason for the disconnect between parent and child is the lack of communication. Suniya Luther, a psychology professor at Columbia University's Teachers College who has done extensive research on the psychological issues of middle school–aged children of both low-income and affluent families, discovered that most psychological problems begin with a lack of or negative communication between parent and child. For both rich and poor teenagers, certain family characteristics predicted children's maladjustment, including low levels of maternal attachment, high levels of parental criticism, and minimal after-school adult supervision. Among affluent children, Luther found, the main cause of distress was "excessive achievement pressures and isolation from parents . . . both physical and emotional."[3]

Communication Traditions in the Family

Have some regular, repetitive things that you do "in family" that stimulate communication. Develop your own plan that fits your unique family. Here are some examples of strategies that have worked in other families:

- **Bedtime "happys or sads."** As you tuck a child in bed ask, "What was your 'happy' today? Your 'sad'?" Over the course of many evenings, you'll learn a lot about your child's friends, social situations, school, fears, and more. With older kids, ask them about their day's "highs" and "lows" as they are eating dinner. You might also ask them what they learned that day or who they helped. Our questions often influence the directions of our kids' thoughts more than our demands or our advice.

- **Active listening.** Listen actively by paraphrasing back to your child each thing he or she says to you. This shows interest and non-judgment. Instead of interrogating or directing or drawing conclusions, simply rephrase whatever your child says. "So you felt bad when Lisa sat with someone else at lunch." When you listen without directing, kids will jump from subject to subject—often from effect to cause—and will tell you things you'd never think to ask! Practice the same technique with your spouse.

- **Goals and "consulting."** Even fairly small children can set goals for the week. On Sunday, ask a child to set three goals for the week ahead: one for school (a high test score, or a paper turned in); one for personal development (sports, music, hobbies, and so on); and one for family (cleaning room, fixing something, and the like). Set the example by setting your own weekly goal for each of the same three categories (substituting work for school). Then explain your goals to each other. It will lead to a lot of communication about a lot of subjects, and it will feel (to you and to your child) more like a

Have some regular, repetitive things that you do "in family" that stimulate communication. Develop your own plan that fits your unique family.

consultant helping clients with *their* goals and less like a pushy *manager* trying to get kids to follow *your* goals and agenda.

- **Family dinners.** While the old family dinner concept may have pretty well lost out to fast food and over-committed schedules, eating together two or three times a week is still realistic. Use the time to talk about school and events and whatever comes up. Ask each other questions about feelings, dreams, priorities, and concerns.

- **Car time.** All that time we spend driving kids to school, to lessons, and more (time we usually resent) can be "captive" communication time. Keep the radio off and ask "interest questions" ("I'm interested in that new math teacher. How is she?") rather than "interrogation questions" ("How's your grade in math?"). Try to drive car pools when you can—they are an amazing time to learn what is going on because kids seem to forget you are there and talk about all kinds of things that you might otherwise never hear.

- **"Dates."** Married couples who still have a weekly or biweekly date on a set night tend to keep a courtship mentality that prompts better communication and a more lasting romance. A variation on the theme works for kids. Set up a "daddy date" or "mommy date" where the child decides what to do and where to go.

- **"1 to 10."** When kids have a hard time talking about their feelings or if you're getting just "yes" or "no" or "fine" answers to your questions, try the "ranking" technique. Say, "I'm going to mention five separate things to you, and you rank how worried you are about them from 1 to 10." "Ranking" works on everything, from how they did at school that day to how important they perceive various things to be. Once they've ranked something, it gets easier to talk about it and ask further "active listening" questions to better understand where they are coming from.

As a young father, I had an experience that combined the "goal-setting" and "active listening" methods of communication. I read about "active listening" or "Rogerian technique" (named after the famous therapist, Karl Rogers) and will never forget the first time I consciously tried it. Eight-year-old Saydi, rather caught up with her friends and not always easy to talk to, had written for her weekly school goal: "Get a new friend." The normal parental response would have been either a challenge, "Why, don't you have enough friends?" or a lecture, "You know, to have friends you have to be a friend," but I was trying the Rogerian technique so I simply said, "I see, you want to find a new friend this week at school . . ."

"Yes," said Saydi, "because my best friend, Katie, was so rude to me."

Again I avoided the typical parental response, "What did she do?" or "Do I need to call her mom?" I just said, "Oh, I see. The reason your goal is to make a new friend is that Katie hasn't been so nice to you."

Magically, Saydi continued on, telling me everything, really communicating. "Yes. See, she was the chooser in soccer, and she didn't even pick me for her team."

I just kept paraphrasing back what she said, and ten minutes later, I knew more about her third-grade life and about her feelings than I could have learned through hours of interrogation-type questioning.

Breaking Patterns of Non-Communication

When you're not talking and when the trust level and communication level has drastically declined with a child, some more drastic "jump start" techniques are in order.

- **A long trip.** Take a child one-on-one on a long trip (preferably a long car trip). It could be a business trip (it may be expensive and inconvenient, but it can pay huge dividends at the end of the day) or a long weekend trip, or a hike or campout, or anything else you can conjure up. Simply being alone together with a child while traveling allows communication to develop. Don't push too hard; don't interrogate. Use the techniques of "active listening," "ranking," and "interest questions" just mentioned. Be willing to talk about things you're not particularly interested in. Let the connection and conversation develop. Express your joy in being together. Express your confidence and love, and tell the child he or she is your priority and you are committed to him or her unconditionally. Be satisfied with small progress. Don't expect one trip to solve everything.

- **Use their apps and their social media.** Some kids communicate better electronically than with their voices. Text them, Instagram them, Tweet to them, use whatever latest form of social media they are using. And let your electronic communication open up opportunities for verbal communication. (By the way, you need to control your child's technology use directly and unapologetically. If they have a cell phone, have them turn it in before they go to bed. Keep computers in the common areas of your home, not in bedrooms. Know every password and program they have, and tell them that you do have the right to look at everything they look at, and use filters and programs that allow you to do exactly that. Be firm that there are no secrets in your family and that "privacy" does not apply to kids with their parents.)

- **Surrogates.** Sometimes kids will talk better and say more to anyone else but you. If there's an uncle or aunt or anyone you trust who can spend some time one-on-one with a non-communicative child and get him talking, it can furnish you with needed information and can open up future possibilities for your own communication.

- **Persist!** Whichever of these ideas (or others) you try, *tell* your child that communication with him or her means everything to you and that you'll work on it forever. Keep trying, look for opportunities, and make time together. Do whatever it takes to open up the channels.

I've had to call on each of these ideas to salvage communication with my own kids. How well I remember my emails with Josh, my long drives with Noah, phone calls with Saydi. Texts back and forth with Charity. Goal discussions with Talmadge. Different approaches work at different times with different kids. Something will work sometime with every child. Never quit. Make it happen!

Six: Create Identity, Security, and Motivation for Children

All institutions, large or small, require five characteristics to survive and to thrive (and to give their members the identity, security, and motivation to hold them).

1. *Purpose* (a clear reason for existing—a goal, a mission)

2. *Rules/Boundaries/Order* (laws and patterns of behavior that protect other members and preserve the whole)

3. *An Economy* (a way of dividing work and having all members contribute to the bottom line)

4. *Traditions* (which provide enjoyment as well as identity, unity, and permanence)

5. *A history or narrative* (to be proud of and to identify with)

All organizations that last, from a fraternity to a country, have these five things, including the large institutions that are both the culprits and the benefactors identified in this book. Parents must be sure that their own family has all five, too, so they can be as permanent and as strong as the big institutions which they must simultaneously use and fight.

Together, these five characteristics (purpose, rules, economy, traditions, and history) create an "infrastructure" that makes a family work efficiently and that provides individual family members with the support and help (identity, security, and motivation) that they need to be happy, successful people. Like the infrastructure of a city (roads, bridges, water systems, and so on), a family infrastructure takes *time* and *effort* to build, but once it is in place, it saves time and makes everything more efficient.

A Family Mission Statement or Statement of Purpose

Every business seems to have an attractively worded statement of vision and purpose and goals on a plaque, or posted on the wall in a place of pride in the office. Employees are proud of their mission and hopefully do their part to bring it to pass.

Many years ago we met a man who carried two mission statements in the two inside breast pockets of his suit jacket. In the right pocket was his corporate mission statement—he was president and CEO of a highly profitable mid-size company. In the left ("over my heart," he said) was his family mission statement. He told us that he and his wife had taken their three teen and elementary-age children to a resort hotel for a long weekend, rented a conference room there (I was thinking it would have worked just as well on a camping trip) and held several two-hour sessions (interspersed by swimming and activities) where they hammered out a family mission statement. He said they'd started just talking about their family, their love for each other, their desire to stay together and support each other, and how they could use what they had to help others. The dad read them some corporate mission statements and asked if they thought one was needed in their family. At a second session, he and his wife had each written down what was

> *Together, these five characteristics (purpose, rules, economy, traditions, and history) create an "infrastructure" that makes a family work efficiently.*

most important to them and, interestingly, a list of their favorite words, and they encouraged their kids to do the same. At a third session, they spent some time working on simple, personal mission statements reflecting their individual hopes and dreams. At a final session, they pulled everything together and created a family mission statement that incorporated and condensed all of their ideas into a short, clear statement of the purpose and meaning of their family. They had a big, framed copy at their home, and each carried a laminated personal copy.

We were so impressed with the idea that we tried it ourselves. Here is a sampling of what we came up with:

Fifteen-year-old Noah's personal mission statement:

To be looked upon by others and by God with a smile always. To be filled with a joy which others can feel. To find this joy through service. To watch, to absorb, to learn, to find, to discover. To always look forward to the next day.

Following is a portion of our collectively written family mission statement:

Create together an identity-building, support-giving family institution which fosters and facilitates a maximum of broadening and contributing by its members, each of which become strong, independent individuals, committed spouses, and parents; first receiving and then giving the gifts of joy, responsibility, and sensitivity, and approaching the world with attitudes of serendipity, stewardship, and synergy. Help each other to grow up and spin off into independent orbits, still feeling the gravity and light of parents, with whom there is a consulting relationship in which advice is freely asked for, freely given, and used or unused without offense to parent or pressure to child.

Because it was so long, we decided we also needed a "family mantra" distilled from the mission statement that was short enough for everyone to remember. In its gold-leafed version, it now hangs on our family room wall: "Broaden and Contribute." Kids know that the goal is to go out and get the best education and experience possible, to expand and broaden and have a wide perspective and awareness, but then to give back, to find causes, and to contribute to individuals and to society.

A Family Legal System (Rules or Laws)

With hindsight, our first effort to set up family laws was rather comical. As young parents with three young children, we tried to create a list of family rules by nomination (I think, back then, we still thought a family was a democracy!). The kids chimed in with everything from "Don't hit anyone" to "Never plug in plugs—you could get shocked." We dutifully listed every one on a big chart and we soon had thirty-seven "family laws." No one really remembered them or paid much attention to them, and one day, our seven-year-old complained, "Mom, even in the Bible there's only ten rules!"

Over the years, we figured out that we needed a small number of very simple rules, each with a clear consequence for being broken but with a provision for repentance by which they could avoid the consequence or penalty. It finally came down to five key words:

PEACE: (Or you sit on the "repenting bench" with the other "fighter" until you can say what *you* did wrong and give the other kid a hug and ask for forgiveness.)

RESPECT: (Or we'll "start over" until you get it right—give a respectful answer, etc.)

ORDER: (Get your room straight or there will be times when you can't go anywhere until you clean it up.)

ASKING: (We want to always know where you are, so if you forget to ask, the next time you want to go somewhere, the answer will be no. The same penalty applies to curfew.)

OBEDIENCE: (You can ask why, and I'll try to tell you, and possibly even reconsider, but kids must obey their parents. Someday you'll be the parent.)

Looking back now, over twenty or thirty years of trying to establish and live these five family laws, we find that some of our most cherished memories are wrapped up in them (from heated curfew discussions to pitching in to help a child get his room cleaned up so he could go out without breaking a law).

Some of the most interesting memories center around the law of PEACE and the "repenting bench." Somehow, we ended up with incredibly strong-willed children, and "sibling rivalries" is a pretty mild term for describing the competing, arguing, and outright fighting that cropped up so predictably. We came to the "repenting bench" idea because there was no way that we, as parents, could resolve everything. Trying to figure out who was right and who was wrong, being the judge and jury, and trying to decide whom to punish and how was exhausting. And we wanted (needed) the kids to learn how to resolve things for themselves.

Our "repenting bench" is a short, uncomfortable pew that we got out of an old church. The rule is simple: any two family members who are fighting (arguing, yelling, disagreeing, and so on) have to sit together on that bench until each can tell what he or she did wrong (not what the other person did) and can, with a hug, say to the other, "I'm sorry. Will you forgive me?" We stressed that both partners are always partly to blame. Oh, the "repenting" we've seen—from kids who had to sit there for half an hour trying to figure out what they did to kids who repent on their way to the bench so they won't have to sit there at all. The hugs and the "sorrys," even if the child's main motivation is to escape the bench, have blunted bad feelings a thousand times and contributed to our children's love for each other and to their capacity to work out their own conflicts.

Incidentally, when we downsized a few years ago and weren't going to take much of our furniture with us, there was a little competition developing among our grown children for who would get the grand piano, who would get the couch, and so on. In an effort to avoid having to make these decisions, we decided to have a furniture auction. We hired a real auctioneer, complete with microphone and top hat and gavel, and gave each child $40,000 in play money. Two kids who couldn't be there were bidding by phone.

We were amazed how much interest there was when the repenting bench came up for auction. Bidding pushed higher and higher, and it ended up going for $18,000, the biggest bid for anything other than the grand piano. The winning bidder was one of our most feisty kids, and when we asked him why he had spent nearly half of his bidding money for it, he replied, "Hey, I spent half of my life on that thing!"

Family laws need regular discussion and recommitment. Setting them up in the first place needs to be a highly communicative process, and the laws you come up with will fit the unique needs of your family. Kids need to understand that the purposes of laws are safety and happiness and that they show an increase, not a decrease, of trust and of love.

Laws and rules, lovingly set, explained, and implemented, provide children with *security* and with a clear manifestation of a parent's love and concern. Compare them to traffic laws, to civic laws, to school rules. *Tell* them that laws show our love and concern for each other and show our desire to have a good, orderly family that cares for each other and gets us ready for life on our own.

> *Laws and rules, lovingly set, explained, and implemented, provide children with security and with a clear manifestation of a parent's love and concern.*

A Family Economy

Just as they are made more secure by rules and limits, kids are made more confident and competent by responsibility. A strong family institution needs a way to divide and share the work of the household and a way of letting kids earn a small "share" in the family's income. Here is one way to do so in a young family. (Each family should adopt a particular system that works for them. This approach works best for kids between seven and twelve. If you start it during those early years, it can continue to function into the teen years.)

Caution: Don't try to set this up overnight. It will take a lot of discussion and some trial and error. Remember that infrastructures take time to build, but then they facilitate the operation of the institution.

1. Create a big chart of all the household work that needs to be done in your home. List *everything*, from doing the breakfast dishes to sweeping the patio. Explain that those who do a share of the work should get a share of the money that comes into a family. While everyone should take care of their own room without pay, there are plenty of "common areas" in the house and yard that need to be taken care of, as well as daily tasks that need doing.

2. Tell the kids that this approach will allow them to *earn* more money than they could get as an allowance and that with their earnings they can buy their own clothes. Kids aged seven to eleven are *flattered* by responsibility. (Note that this system doesn't require any additional money. Parents are simply taking the funds they spend on children's clothes and channeling that money *through* the kids who "earn it" and make their own purchase decisions while learning economic and motivational lessons through the whole process.)

3. Explain that there are four things each person can get "credit" for each day: (1) getting up and being ready for school on time; (2) cleaning or straightening one "zone" or area of the house or yard (not their own room); (3) finishing homework (and music practice, if applicable) for the night; and (4) being ready and in bed by bedtime. Each day, they can fill in a "slip" (on their *own* initiative and hopefully without a lot of reminding from you) with a "1," "2," "3," or "4," depending on how many of the four they did. The parent must "initial" the completed slip to make it official.

4. The slips go in a box or "family bank," and Saturday becomes "pay day," where a child receives an amount proportionate to the total of her slips. She can take her payment in cash or leave it in the family bank. She is given a check book (an old or extra book of your checks) with which she can deposit money to the family bank (with a deposit slip) or draw it out (with a check). When she goes shopping with you, she brings her checkbook and check register and writes a check out to you so you, in turn, can pay for what she buys. She keeps track of her balance in her check register. Whether she will ever use a checkbook in real life, using one with the family bank is great training for keeping track of her balance and thinking about what to put in

and take out of the bank.

5. This "family economy" can be enhanced in a number of ways. A child can have an interest-paying savings account, as well as a checking account in the family bank. Parents may want to pay a high interest rate on the condition that the savings be used only for college. When a child turns sixteen, real checking and savings accounts can be opened for him at a local bank or a discount brokerage, and all the money in his family bank account is transferred in. Children might also be encouraged to donate a certain percentage of what they earn to church or charity. Details about alternative ways to set up a family economy can be found by going to www.powerofmoms.com and searching for "money system."

This type of "family economy" has been a huge blessing in our family. Kids have learned principles that will serve them well for the rest of their lives.

*. . . About **self-reliance**. (I recall nine-year-old Jonah calculating how much he'd have by age sixteen at the 10 percent per quarter interest we paid on his "education only" family bank savings account. I also recall the look of pride on his face as he wrote out a real check for his full freshman year tuition.)*

*. . . About the **dangers of instant gratification**. (Eight-year-old Saydi spending $120 of "her own" money on a pair of designer jeans and wanting to "turn them back in" or sell them to someone the next day because she realized she had no money left in her checking account to go to a movie with her friends.)*

*. . . About **depreciation** (Josh wanting to "sell-me-down" rather than hand-me-down the outgrown clothes he'd bought to his little brother who wanted "a good deal.")*

*. . . About **restraint** (Ten-year-old Talmadge saying he'd decided*

to ask himself three questions before he bought anything: "Do I
want it?" "Do I need it?" "Can I afford it?")

   *. . . About **saving** (Twelve-year-old Shawni observing that "If I*
put some in savings right when I get it, it's like I never had it, so I
don't miss it.")

Good as the "money lessons" are, it's the life lessons that really count . . .
lessons about responsibility, about self-reliance, and about doing your share.

Family Traditions

Everyone, particularly every child, needs an identity larger than himself—
something he belongs to, feels part of, and gains security and protection
from. It is kids who do not get this identity from families who are drawn
to the rituals, "colors," and traditions of gangs or other substitutes for families.

Strong traditions exist in every lasting institution. Nowhere is this more true
than in the family. Traditions are the glue
that holds families together. Kids love and
cling to family traditions because they are
predictable and stable in an unpredictable
world.

Almost all families have traditions that
often center on holidays or other special
occasions. But parents who come to real-

Everyone, particularly
every child, needs an
identity larger than
himself—something he
belongs to, feels part
of, and gains security
and protection from.

ize the importance of traditions and their ability to teach values to improve
communication, to give security to kids, and to hold families together can
refine and redefine their family traditions and give them true and lasting
bonding power.

Start by assessing and analyzing your family traditions. What do you do
on each holiday? How do you celebrate family birthdays? Are there some
things you do on each special day each year? Are there some monthly

traditions, such as going over the calendar and the family's schedule for the month ahead? Do you have some weekly traditions, such as a special Sunday dinner? Make a list of your yearly, monthly, and weekly traditions.

Then, as a family, ask yourself three questions: How much joy, how much fun comes from each tradition? What values are taught by each? Are there some gaps—some months without a holiday or birthday tradition? With these questions in mind, *revise* and redesign your family traditions. Formalize them by writing them down on a chart, calendar, or in a special book.

Here's a sample of what happened to us as we went through this reassessing process.

1. We *revised* some traditions (i.e., our Thanksgiving tradition had essentially been to eat way too much and watch football all day on TV). We decided to shift the emphasis to *thanks* by making a collective list (on a long roll of cash register tape) of all the little things we are thankful for. Each year, we try to "break the record" of the previous year for the number of things listed.

2. We decided we needed at least one major family tradition each month—to look forward to and anticipate. Most of these centered on a birthday or holiday, but we had no set event to celebrate in May or September so we started a "Welcome Spring Day" (a hike) and a "Welcome Fall Day" (a picnic).

3. We listed all the traditions, by month, in a big, leather-bound book. A little description of each tradition appears on the left, and a child's illustration of that activity appears on the right.

4. We worked some of our ancestors (the kids' great grandparents) into our traditions because we wanted our children to have that extra layer of identity of knowing where (and who) they came from. We wrote some simple bedtime stories based on real experiences of these ancestors (especially experiences

that illustrated honesty, courage, or other values), and we now have a little "ancestor birthday party" for them which includes "their story."

Family Genealogy and Family Narrative

Columnist and family advocate Bruce Feiler wrote a column in the *New York Times* in 2013 called "Stories That Bind Us." He had become interested in what held some families together while others were falling apart.

After several years of gathering information, along with other researchers, a surprising theme emerged: The single most important thing you can do for your family may be the simplest of all: develop a strong family narrative.

Researchers developed a "Do You Know?" questionnaire with twenty questions that they asked children, which included: "Do you know where your grandparents grew up?" "Do you know where your mom and dad went to high school?" "Do you know where your parents met?" "Do you know an illness or something really terrible that happened in your family?" "Do you know the story of your birth?"

After researchers studied four dozen families, Feiler records that they discovered that "the more children knew about their family's history, the stronger their sense of control over their lives, the higher their self-esteem, and the more successfully they believed their families functioned. . . . The 'Do You Know?' scale turned out to be the best single predictor of children's emotional health and happiness."[4] Interestingly, one of the best indicators of resilience in children was that those who knew stories about ancestors who had overcome hard times in their lives were better able to bounce back and overcome disappointment in their own lives.

Words like "history" and "genealogy" don't strike some of us as particularly exciting. Yet looking back into our ancestor identity is perhaps the most powerful and effective approach of all for building strong and confident *identity* within our children.

Anyone with a sense of where she came from (and *who* she came from) has a kind of security and a kind of motivation that can't exist otherwise. Children are quick to grasp and understand that they *descended* from their parents, their grandparents, and their great-grandparents, and that they *inherited* a big part of their physical, mental, and emotional selves from these ancestors. By teaching our children a little genetics and a little genealogy, we can help them understand who they are and why they have certain gifts, characteristics, interests, and abilities. A child who grows up feeling connections, ties, security, and identity from and within a family will feel no need to seek these same things from a gang or an Internet chat room or someone portrayed on TV who doesn't share your family values.

The more children knew about their family's history, the stronger their sense of control over their lives, the higher their self-esteem, and the more successfully they believed their families functioned.

It's truly beautiful to see a child or adolescent who is proud of his nose or her hair color or his stature because it's a lot like a grandparent's. Or who feels she can do well in math because her great-grandfather was good with numbers. Or who makes a decision to be honest because of a story he has heard about an ancestor who made a difficult honest choice.

Kids easily make a connection to the notion that "blood is thicker than water" and that who they are comes from their family. The trick for parents is to make genealogy and family history interesting so that kids gravitate to it joyfully and naturally.

Family Tree and Ancestor Stories

One of the best things we ever did in our family was to make up a big "family tree" with pictures of our children's parents (2), grandparents (4), great-grandparents (8), and great-great-grandparents (16). We actually painted a big, old oak tree on a 3 x 4-foot framed canvas. The tree has nine branches, each with a picture of one the children. Branches go out from each of these nine, suggesting the children they will someday have. Our own two pictures (mom and dad) are on the trunk. Four roots go down from the trunk, each with a photo of a grandparent, each of these splits into two so there is a total of eight smaller roots, each with a picture of a great-grandparent. In our case, we were lucky enough to find photos of the next generation back—sixteen great-great-grandparents, which are glued onto the next and lowest set of sixteen sub-roots.

This painted tree, with its quaint, old-fashioned pictures, is remarkably reassuring to our children. They look at it more than you would imagine. I'll never forget our seven-year-old one day, idly tracing a path with his finger from his limb down through the trunk and into the roots. "I'm one-fourth like you," he said, pointing at one of his grandpas. "And I'm one-eighth like you," as his finger went down to one of his great-grandmothers.

It was the popularity of the ancestor tree that led us to take the next step—writing our personal family Ancestor Stories Book. It consists of a big, bound book of blank pages on which we've written some simple bedtime stories based on actual experiences of people on the ancestor tree. There is "The Honesty of Grandpa Dean" (a story of how he hit a parked car one night on the way home from a date. The dent was small, and no one saw, so he drove on home. But he thought about it, went back, found the owner, and offered to pay). Or there is the story of "Great-Grandma Margret's Trip to America" (how she emigrated from Sweden on a rat-infested sailing ship).

As our children were growing up, these "ancestor stories" became their favorites. Each connected in some way to a value—courage, responsibility, respect, sensitivity. They were always told the stories with the ancestor tree in clear view. ("I'm one-eighth that person . . . . I must have some courage in me, too.")

You don't need a complete gallery of four generations to do this in your family, nor do you need photos. Creating a tree with grandparents will do. And the stories can simply be retellings of any experience you've heard and can be about any incident that shows some positive things about an ancestor.

Create your own variations of "ancestor identity." We know one family that makes video tapes of living grandparents telling about their childhoods. Another takes short vacations to the places where their ancestors came from. Still another celebrates birthdays of dead ancestors, complete with a birthday cake and candles, remembering and passing on all they know about them. The main thing is to create positive connections and to help your children feel a security and a *heritage* that they are proud of, that they are motivated by, and that they can identify with.

If you'd like some help in tracing your family tree back a few generations, assistance is readily available through various genealogy or family history associations. A quick way to get started is to go to www.familysearch.org on the Internet. With a minimum of name and birth or death date and location information, you can quickly access what data is available on each root of your family tree. Often, there are pictures and stories that other, unknown relatives may have sent to the site that will give you additional insight about your ancestors.

Simple Genetics Lesson

Something that may help your children feel more connected and more appreciative of their extended family is a short discussion of basic genetics. Explain that when a baby is born, he or she has certain genes from each parent (and in turn from the parent's parent). These genes determine everything from height to eye color. Go as far as your child's interest on this.

Use the genetic discussion to lead into a broader discussion: "If you can get eye color from an ancestor, do you think you could get courage, or musical ability, or a quick temper? What do you think you got from each of your grandparents?"

If you wish, carry the idea (and the discussion) one step further and into a more spiritual realm, pose the question: "If we can inherit all kinds of things from our parents and grandparents, is it possible we could also inherit something from our Heavenly Father, from God?"

Explain that all people have something called a *conscience*, which is something in their *spirit* that helps them know when something is right and when something wrong. People who follow these feelings are happier. They have the courage not to do something they sense is wrong, no matter how much pressure there is, and they dare to do what they feel is right, even when it goes against the crowd.

SEVEN: USE "VALUES THERAPY" TO BUILD A SELF-IMAGE FOR LIFE

The trouble with so much of what we call "parenting" is that we operate defensively rather than offensively or proactively. The "experts" seem to say, "If you have this problem . . . try this solution," or "If Johnny does this, you try that." The old adage of the best defense being a good offense isn't applied very much. Most parents don't have a plan!

The best offense in today's world is a plan for teaching our children values, which will protect them, maximize their chances to be happy, and help them avoid some of the problems that require a more defensive stance.

If you ask a business manager or owner what his or her goals and plans are, he or she will hand you vision statements, sales targets, pro forma financials, an *offense*. But ask a parent about his or her family goals and plans, and the answer is likely to be much more general, "To *raise* my kids," "To keep them out of trouble," "To have a happy family." How impressed would you be if the business person answered the question so generally? "To have a nice company." "To avoid going bankrupt."

Today, more than ever, parents need clear and specific goals and plans for their families. We need an *offense* good enough that we're not forced to constantly react and to always rely on our defense. The best offense in today's world is a plan for teaching our children *values*, which will *protect* them, maximize their chances to be happy, and help them avoid some of the problems that require a more defensive stance.

> *As mentioned previously, we surveyed and questioned parents and came up with a list of twelve values, one for each month of the year, that were so universal that virtually every parent everywhere would desire them for their child and that, together, would create the kind of character in a child that would maximize his or her chance for a happy and productive life. Here is the same values list cited earlier, but with brief value-descriptions:*

1. *HONESTY: Truthfulness with other individuals, with institutions, with society, with self. The inner strength and confidence that is bred by exacting truthfulness, trustworthiness, and integrity.*

2. *COURAGE: Daring to attempt difficult things that are good. Strength not to follow the crowd, to say no and mean it, and to influence others by it. Being true to convictions and following good impulses, even when they are unpopular or inconvenient. Boldness to be outgoing and friendly.*

3. *PEACEABILITY: Calmness. Peacefulness. Serenity. The tendency to try to accommodate rather than argue. The understanding that differences are seldom resolved through conflict and that meanness in others is an indication of their problem or insecurity and, thus, of their need for your understanding. The ability to*

understand how others feel rather than simply reacting to them. Control of temper.

4. *SELF-RELIANCE AND POTENTIAL: Individuality. Awareness and development of gifts and uniqueness. Taking responsibility for own actions. Overcoming the tendency to blame others for difficulties. Commitment to personal excellence.*

5. *SELF-DISCIPLINE AND MODERATION: Physical, mental, and financial self-discipline. Moderation in speaking, in eating, in exercising. The controlling and bridling of one's own appetites. Understanding the limits of body and mind. Avoiding the dangers of extreme, unbalanced viewpoints. The ability to balance self-discipline with spontaneity.*

6. *FIDELITY AND CHASTITY: The value and security of fidelity within marriage and of restraint and limits before marriage. The commitments that go with marriage and that should go with sex. A grasp of the long-range (and widespread) consequences that can result from casual, recreational sex and from infidelity.*

7. *LOYALTY AND DEPENDABILITY: Loyalty to family, to employers, to country, church, schools, and other organizations and institutions to which commitments are made. Support, service, contribution. Reliability and consistency in doing what you say you will do.*

8. *RESPECT: Respect for life, for property, for parents, for elders, for nature, and for the beliefs and rights of others. Courtesy, politeness, and manners. Self-respect and the avoidance of self-criticism.*

9. *LOVE: Individual and personal caring that goes both beneath and beyond loyalty and respect. Love for friends, neighbors, even adversaries. And a prioritized, lifelong commitment of love for family.*

10. *UNSELFISHNESS AND SENSITIVITY: Becoming more extra-centered and less self-centered. Learning to feel with and for others. Empathy, tolerance, brotherhood. Sensitivity to needs in people and situations.*

11. *KINDNESS AND FRIENDLINESS: Awareness that being kind and considerate is more admirable than being tough or strong. The tendency to understand rather than confront. Gentleness, particularly toward those who are younger or weaker. The ability to make and keep friends. Helpfulness. Cheerfulness.*

12. *JUSTICE AND MERCY: Obedience to law. Fairness in work and play. An understanding of natural consequences and the law of the harvest. A grasp of mercy and forgiveness, and an understanding of the futility (and bitter poison) of carrying a grudge.*

There are many simple and effective methods, techniques, stories, games, and other ideas to teach each of these values to kids, but the most important and overriding method is simply to *focus* and *concentrate* on one single value each month. Make it the "value of the month" in your family, and look for opportunities (in everything from the media you watch to the everyday situations you find yourself in) to talk about it and to point it out to your child. Assign one value to each month, and when the year ends, start over (your eight-year-old is now nine and will learn each value on a new level). Here is our family's list:

January: HONESTY

February: COURAGE

March: PEACEABILITY

April: SELF-RELIANCE AND POTENTIAL

May: SELF-DISCIPLINE AND MODERATION

June: FIDELITY AND CHASTITY

July: LOYALTY AND DEPENDABILITY

August: RESPECT

September: LOVE

October: UNSELFISHNESS AND SENSITIVITY

November: KINDNESS AND FRIENDLINESS

December: JUSTICE AND MERCY

Resources for Monthly Values

A special program of twelve monthly audio sets is now available. (See www. ValuesParenting.com or www.PowerofMoms.com.) Each set (one for each value) contains a parents' segment with methods, stories, games, and other ideas to teach that value to different aged children and a child's segment (called Alexander's Amazing Adventures) where kids learn the value through an imaginative and musical adventure story. See the afterword of this book for more information.

Properly approached, this "values offense" does not create a burden of "one more thing to worry about." Quite the contrary, it simplifies things for you when you want to be the source of teaching your child values. It gives parents one clear subject to concentrate on for the month rather than worrying about everything at once. This approach is not a panacea nor is it something that has to be worked on every day. The beauty of having a "value of the month" is that when you've got a minute, when you find yourself with a child in the car or in the kitchen you bring up the value and work on it *with* your kids. You can mention your own need for it, quest for it, problems with it, and so on. Daily life and media will present plenty of chances to discuss the value. The effect becomes cumulative. The way your family thinks about and puts these values into action gets a little better each month, a little better each year, building a base of shared and understood values that become a lifetime defense against the false paradigms and larger institutions that threaten to swallow up our children and our families.

Making Decisions in Advance

Our family has a method for bringing all twelve of the values together and seeking their practical application in our children's lives. We call it "making decisions in advance," and it works like this:

1. During the first two or three years of elementary school (ages five to seven), we try to talk a lot with a child about *decisions*. We discuss how fun they can be and how important they are. We also use the word *consequences* a lot and help the child see how consequences are tied to decisions. We try to let the child make as many decisions as possible for himself—anything from which shirt to wear to which kind of juice to have for breakfast.

2. When the child is ten or eleven, at the back of his journal or diary (something every child should have), we have him write the headline, "Decisions I Have Already Made." Then we talk about two kinds of big decisions: the ones you can't make until you know all of your options and are older (college, marriage, profession, and so on) and the ones that are actually best made *in advance* (whether to do drugs, whether to cheat on tests, whether to smoke, whether to graduate from college, etc.).

3. Even when the child understands the idea, we ask him to *wait* and not to write down any "decisions in advance" just yet. We encourage him to think about it for a week or two. Then, at another "meeting," when we're not rushed and really have some

time, we ask the child if he's got any decisions in advance that he wants to write in the special place at the back of his journal. We explain that when he writes it, he should sign his signature by it and date it so it's like a contract or promise to himself.

4. When he comes up with a decision in advance say, "Wait. Before you write it and sign it, let us tell you a story about what might happen to you in a few years." Then we try to create the most difficult possible scenario for the decision he's proposed. Essentially, this is a role-playing or case-study exercise. For example, if he's said his decision in advance is never to do drugs, we'll have him imagine he's at a party when he's sixteen and a group of his friends want him to try a pill. "Come on— we've all taken one—they make you feel great." The girl he's with takes one—everyone's looking at him—what does he do? What does he say? If he feels sure he could handle the situation we say, "Great—now I think you're ready to list it and sign it."

As we've done this exercise over the years with our children, almost every value has come into play. It is a way for them to commit themselves to the practical and future application of each value. It works well with ten- to fourteen-year-olds, but you will know the best time for your own kids, according to their maturity. The list can be added to over the years as they encounter other conclusions and commitments. It's not a panacea or a guarantee, but it increases a child's chances of making good choices for years to come.

The ancient Greeks had a word for the cultivation of character, values, and virtue in a child. The word was *"paideia."* We call this "values therapy" because we have observed what a healing, security-giving, therapeutic effect it has on children. Kids who understand basic values well enough to incorporate them mentally into their concept of who they are develop strong, healthy self-images and self-esteem.

Whatever we call it, it is something that can be done, and doing it can make all the difference for your child.

AFTER YOU DO ALL YOU CAN DO

The seven approaches are the best ideas we know for an individual family to counter, within itself, the family-destructive influences of the broader society and larger institutions. Parents who make serious attempts at each of these seven principle focuses will protect and preserve their own families.

If these are the best ideas for *individual* families, what are the best ideas for *collective* families? Can parents band together in some effective way and persuade larger institutions to do more to help families and less to hurt them?

Maybe so. In the final two chapters, we will try to make the case for serious revaluing of families by all sectors of our society and some possibilities for your involvement on a broader scale—in a parent's "movement" that might be hard for larger institutions to ignore. The first step is to make the *case* for greater help for families from the bigger parts of society.

The most important work you will ever do will be within the walls of your own home.

—HAROLD B. LEE

CHAPTER TEN

THE CASE

For Greater Family Focus within the Public, Private, and Non-Profit Sectors

---

case *noun* \ˈkās\

  1. the evidence supporting a conclusion or judgment—or a convincing argument for a policy, action or direction

When we want to change something and recruit others to help in that change, we must make our case, and make it convincingly!

FAMILIES TO INSTITUTIONS:
"SAVE YOURSELF BY SAVING US"

We admit to having something of a one-track mind when it comes to seeing stronger families as the solution to practically everything. One friend frequently reminds us that we are like the guy with a hammer in his hand—to whom everything looks like a nail.

We admit to being family focused! But we can't deny that our whole life experience leads us to the conclusion that societies can't operate very long or very well without functional families. In our travels we are occasionally exposed to a company or a country that understands this connection and genuinely focuses on it. We have observed corporations who have decided to do whatever is in their power to keep marriages together and find ways to help employees and sometimes customers to be the best parents they can be. They offer generous maternity leave, part-time and flex-time and job-sharing options for new moms who want to continue to work. They take into account family needs as they formulate office hours and corporate culture policies. They genuinely understand that company loyalty should take a back seat to family loyalty.

We also occasionally find ourselves in countries or provinces whose governments have decided that preserving families is the key to preserving themselves. Malaysia has a Ministry of Women, Family, and Community Development; India and Bangladesh both have a Ministry of Health and Family Welfare; British Columbia has a Ministry of Children and Family Development; Singapore has a Ministry of Social and Family Development; Hungary has a Ministry of Social and Family Affairs; countries like Australia and states like Virginia are attempting family-impact statements on legislation and legal actions. And so it goes in many parts of the world as larger institutions wake up to the fact that they can't thrive or even survive without healthy families.

Building stronger individual families is the cure, and that has to happen one at a time in individual homes. But fixing our own families doesn't mean we can't also cry out to larger institutions and ask them in every forcible way we can think of to stop any practice or policy that threatens families and to encourage them to start giving us more values-based help in raising the children that are their future as well as ours.

As we've discussed, the natural instinct of larger institutions, as they pursue their own preservation and expansion, is to unconsciously undermine, supersede, and substitute for families in a hundred ways. However, none of them can exist without the foundation of stable households, which provide the human resources and become the end consumers of every good or service that the larger institutions produce and provide. The survival of all the large institutions we have created depends entirely on the survival of solid, individual households and families.

Some still argue otherwise: "Who needs families?" they say. Individuals are consumers, individuals are employees, and individuals can make up the larger institutions. Who cares if they are married or if they live together as families? Some even suggests that when marriages fail or families are broken or divided, it doubles the number of "consuming units" and expands the market.

Statistics and common sense say otherwise. Married individuals earn more, produce more, and consume more than single individuals—30 percent more.[1] Try to imagine any business or government surviving a thirty percent decline in sales, in production, or in tax base. Try to imagine a society reproducing and successfully raising its work force and its consumer base without functional, nurturing families.

Parents provide a huge service to society by raising its next generation, its next work force, its next tax payers, its next universe of consumers. Yet society (or our larger institutions) does little to repay families. In fact, there are

Parents provide a huge service to society by raising its next generation, its next work force, its next tax payers, its next universe of consumers. Yet society (or our larger institutions) does little to repay families.

punishments, ranging from higher taxes to job and career disadvantages, for establishing a family.

The bottom line is that we all depend on families. And as surely as we depend on them individually, we depend on them institutionally.

When larger institutions have policies or practices that weaken or harm families, it is almost always a classic example of trading long-term viability for short-term gains. It is a macro example of choosing instant gratification over permanent stability. For their sakes, and for ours, our larger institutions need to become more family friendly, and the first stop is for them to recognize anything and everything they are doing that hurts families—and to stop it.

Stop It

We once attended a church where the lay bishop was, by profession, a plumber. Despite his lack of training, he did his best to counsel and advise his parishioners. In the same congregation, there happened to be a high-priced, highly educated therapist/psychiatrist who had many congregation members as his paying clients. On several occasions, people dropped him as their doctor and therapist, explaining that the plumber/bishop was helping them more. Finally, in frustration, he went to the bishop and asked him his secret. "How do you, without any training, help people more than I do? What do you tell them to do?"

The bishop gave a typically blunt and simple answer: "It's what I tell them not to do," he said. "I just ask them questions until I figure out which of God's commandments they are breaking. Then I tell them to stop it."

Similarly simple, the first message we need to get to larger institutions is "stop it." Stop undermining and sabotaging the family! Put an end to any policies or practices that weaken or threaten families in any way.

Keep in mind that none of these institutions intend to damage or weaken families—at least, not directly. But the goal of their own preservation and expansion occupies them and is not consciously or conceptually tied to the necessity of the strong family base. *Consciousness* of mutual dependency is what we need more of in our larger institutions. If it were possible to wave a magic wand and change one thing, the most productive wave would be to cause the policy makers of every institution to be conscious and responsible of the impact that their actions and policies have on families. This one focus, this one awareness ("How does what we are doing impact families?") could literally change the world and protect and preserve our larger institutions by saving our foundation of real homes and stable households.

> *This one focus, this one awareness ("How does what we are doing impact families?") could literally change the world.*

A Wish List for a Family-Friendly World

It is interesting (and almost inspirational) to imagine each of the other sectors operating with the conscious goal of supporting, strengthening, and bolstering the family. Some of this vision is already happening, but picture a world where the outer rings literally transform and revitalize themselves by returning to their original purpose of serving their constituency of the bull's-eye of families. It may sound a bit unrealistic, but just image a world where the outer rings support and magnify the bull's-eye:

Community and Voluntary Ring: Neighborhood organizations and churches teach parenting skills and orient part of every aspect, from worship services to Little League, toward family participation and involvement. Ministers take strong stands for marriage partners staying together and for restraint and responsible sexual behavior among youth. Civic clubs focus on helping and supplementing families, and service organizations encourage parents and children to volunteer together to help other families. Extended families and genealogical societies work to give children a sense of their roots and heritage.

Private Sector (Business) Ring: Employers adopt family-friendly policies for maternity and paternity leave, for transfer practices, for flex time and job sharing, and even for education and elderly care assistance. They find that these policies are more profitable over the long run. Marketers and advertisers replace the tone of self-fulfillment and instant gratification with a slant toward the warmth and joy of family and commitment and find that this approach sells better, anyway. Media and website creators, producers, and participants opt away from obsessions with greed, sleaze, and dysfunction and toward themes of commitment and loyalty and the striving for family solidarity and find that this ultimately draws more viewers and sells more tickets, anyway.

Public Sector (Government) Ring: Every policy, law, judgment, and priority is weighted by the question, "Is the family served?" Public codes, from tax law to welfare policy, are rewritten and interpreted with the promotion of stable families as the goal. Education policy is shaped to give families choice and input and control and to actually teach ethics, values, marriage, and parenting skills in support of what kids learn at home. Marriage and adoption laws are rewritten to prioritize staying together and growing together and to take the unnecessary delays out of the adoption process. Politicians campaign on family issues and propose family-strengthening ideas at the heart of their campaigns.

We see glimpses of changes in these directions in all three sectors, yet their full fruition still looks like some sort of unobtainable utopia. It can come about only through a consistent, wide *overlay* of family consciousness, a clear awareness of family consequences by larger institutions. This will not come about easily. We've been moving away from it for decades. And no specific list of recommendations would cover the full breadth of the problem. Nevertheless, the suggestions in the next section, even if partially adopted and implemented, could make a difference to families and make it easier for us all to *turn our hearts.*

> *Large private, public, and nonprofit institutions make countless thousands of decisions, policies, and choices of direction and orientation every day that affect families.*

Large private, public, and nonprofit institutions make countless thousands of decisions, policies, and choices of direction and orientation every day that affect families. If every manager, every policy maker, every decision-making officer of every large corporation could be implanted with a tiny microchip that did nothing but maintain awareness of family importance and consistently pose the question, "How will this impact families?"—that would, in fact, *turn the hearts* of policy makers in the direction of family needs. The world we live in would rapidly begin to become a different and better place.

Because this isn't possible, we'll try the "thorn" approach. Each "directional recommendation" that follows is intended to be an attention-getting thorn in the side of decision makers in a larger institution to prod them to consider their products, their pitches, their procedures, their priorities, and their patterns in light of the net effect they are having on families. What follows is a set of things most parents wish larger institutions would do to help (or to stop hurting) families. Most of them aren't likely to happen anytime soon. But while we're fixing our own families, we can wish, we can wait, and in some cases, we can demand.

FAMILY-SUPPORTIVE SUGGESTIONS FOR WORK AND PROFESSIONAL INSTITUTIONS

Families are being squeezed harder than ever before by corporations and business interests. The corporate preoccupation with profit and stock price is causing short-term policy that will hurt everyone in the long run.

What should corporations do for families? In essence, they should wake up to the fact that taking advantage of their employees is a very bad long-term policy for everyone, including stockholders and top managers. The companies that emerge on top in the new millennium will be those that can attract and hold a loyal work force. As the number of available workers declines, companies with reputations for greedy top management, low worker wages, long hours, and poor family benefits and flex options will be the big losers. Those who are getting away with it now will not get away with it for long.

At the very least, any mid-sized to large corporation should seek to offer its employees:

- A fair wage and other compensation commensurate with the company's overall profitability (a truly enlightened company will enact a tighter limit on the ratio between the compensation of its CEO and its lowest paid worker).
- *Real*, well-publicized, and accessible job flexibility options that can accommodate the needs of parents and kids. These policies can include the whole gamut from flex time to job-sharing, from telecommuting to child and elder care, and from maternity and early childcare leave to shorter work weeks. All should

be considered, fine-tuned, and incorporated. Companies need to turn these empty promises into accessible realities.

- Location and transfer policies that do not uproot families against their will.

- Job security that can be interrupted or threatened only by extreme incompetency on the part of the employee or extreme profitability stress on the employer.

FAMILY-SUPPORTIVE RECOMMENDATIONS FOR FINANCIAL INSTITUTIONS

Nothing destroys families like debt. By making high interest credit card debt so easily available to everyone, and particularly to young parents and college-age kids, banks and other financial institutions are putting huge stresses and strains on families even as they increase the default rates that result in higher costs and interest rates for everyone.

Instead of offering "pre-approved" credit cards to us all and competing with each other to see who can create the most debt and charge the highest interest rates, financial institutions should take more responsibility for assisting families in learning and practicing sound fiscal policies and savings habits.

All any bank officer needs to do to be more family supportive is to treat and advise all customers like he would his own children.

All any bank officer needs to do to be more family supportive is to treat and advise all customers like he would his own children. If his married daughter and son-in-law asked about credit cards, he would say, "Use a debit card for now and avoid any debt except for education or to buy a house." If his college freshman son received unsolicited, pre-approved credit cards in the mail at his dorm, the father would say, "Cut them up and throw them away!" or "If you want to use one to establish credit, get one with a low limit, not more than $1,000, use it for only one purchase a month, and pay the bill each month before there is any interest."

If that same banker and his counterparts everywhere would give the same advice to everyone, countless families would be saved and spared the devastation of heavy consumer debt. The same kind of thinking should prevail on other credit. We have all felt the collective pain of what happens to an economy when unqualified borrowers are allowed mortgage loans for homes bigger than what they can afford.

The best goal banks and other financial institutions could adopt that would benefit both themselves and their customers over the long run would be like a coin with two sides:

- Avoid any policy or practice that endangers or hurts families, and
- Actively develop and implement programs to assist and help families.

In their best light, financial institutions and their services are enormously important and helpful to families. They allow the purchase of homes; they facilitate savings; they give security and provide for retirement. Yet by making credit and debt too easy, they destroy so many of the very families they could have helped. Banks ought to take a longer and closer look at the market segment that uses credit unwisely and offer everything from simple educational tools to highly-promoted debit cards as an alternative to credit cards. Financial institutions ought to begin to judge themselves not by how high their average interest rate is but by how many stable family economies they can assist, knowing that those families will become lifetime customers with resource levels that produce bank revenue through long-term growth and investing rather than through gouging short-term consumer interest.

FAMILY-SUPPORTIVE SUGGESTIONS FOR ADVERTISING/MERCHANDISING INSTITUTIONS

Advertising/merchandising institutions hurt families in two broad and basic ways:

- Through marketing strategies that induce greed, encourage instant gratification, and cause the kind of over-extension that endangers families economically and turns parents' attention and priorities outward rather than inward.
- By creating ads, marketing messages, and other images that glorify casual sex, violence, and materialism—the very things that damage and divide families most.

Trying to imagine our advertising/merchandising institutions reversing these two things is so difficult that the two following suggestions or calls will be instantly labeled impossible if not laughable. Still, we feel compelled to make them—first, because that is what this book is about, and second, because this group of institutions and any company within it would actually gain substantial long-term benefits by following them.

1. Advertisers/merchandisers should honor moderation and actually advocate and teach delayed gratification. They should push the benefits and well-being of saving and waiting rather than the quick thrill of credit buying. They need to list the full, honest price and promote the savings of paying cash rather than hyping the half-truths and false promises of monthly payments. Over time, short-term losses would be overcome by the long-term benefits from loyal consumers who appreciate the honesty and the motives.

2. Advertisers/merchandisers should create messages and images that center on the themes of values and positive emotions like

love, loyalty, and personal integrity. These ads and messages probably cost more and require brighter creative input, but over time, they will help implant the same respect, loyalty, and love *from* the consumers that they portray to them.

These two dramatic shifts, impossible as they sound, could benefit most marketing institutions over the long haul, *and they would help save the family.*

FAMILY-SUPPORTIVE SUGGESTIONS FOR ENTERTAINMENT AND MEDIA INSTITUTIONS

It is obvious that media has *enormous* influence over how we perceive ourselves and our world—and over how we live within that world. Those who say otherwise are trying to defend the indefensible.

Perhaps the two most self-serving, delusional public lies of the last half century have been (1) the tobacco industry saying smoking is not addictive, and (2) the movie, music, and television industries saying they don't *influence* public or individual morality and behavior, they only reflect it and report on it.

We have a basic question (with a surprising answer) that leads to some challenging recommendations:

- *The Question*: Why is so much of our programming, our movies, TV, music, and other media so full of violence and sex? And why is really good portrayal of values, families, and positive role models so hard to find?

- *The Answer*: It's not as simple as "sex sells" or "people are drawn to violence" or "producers give people what they want." The fact is that really good movies, about positive and powerful things *do* sell. As do uplifting Internet apps and video games, as does truly great music and value-oriented, even spiritually-related television. Even upbeat, positive-slanted news is well received if it is well reported and well produced. Yet there are nowhere near enough of these. Why? Simply because the baser the emotion, the easier and cheaper it is to portray. You don't need a great script or great actors to depict sex and violence. It takes much more subtlety and much more artistic talent to get audiences or listeners to feel faith or fidelity than to feel titillation or terror. Violent, sexual video games are easy to produce compared to more subtle approaches that actually teach values. Media institutions, in it for the profit and for their own preservation, churn out the easy formula. They deliver the stuff they can produce for cheap and that they know can't miss.

- Our appeal to writers/producers/directors: Have the courage to attempt the portrayal of the more positive (and more difficult) emotions and characteristics. Take the risk of making something about honor or truth or courage rather than the "safe bet" of more sex and violence. Show the real and honest consequences of things. Actually think about the effect and influence on the consumer. Meet the challenge that is inherent in all creation: think more about the ultimate *quality*, *effect*, and *legacy* of what you make and less about the short-term profit.

- Our appeal to actors, artists, celebrities, "role models," and their agents and publicists: Show the significant rather than the seamy. There are so many celebrities with strong families and strong views about priorities. We don't often see this side of them, partly because of privacy and partly because it doesn't seem sensational enough to sell. In fact, there is a hunger for human-interest stories that we can connect to and identify with. If people knew as much about the "good" as about the "bad," we might all be amazed (and reassured) that there is more of the former than the latter.

- Our appeal to news producers and directors: If every news director or Internet producer had a child he really loved, say a ten-year-old, and if he knew that child would see and hear everything he created, we would probably reach far higher standards in what comes at us as news and information. Show the good and the hopeful as well as the bad and the hopeless. Don't sugarcoat anything, but don't drape it in black either.

- Our appeal to funders and benefactors, and to resources that are not "players" now but could be: Most of what ends up on the big or small screen, or in apps or games, starts off as *writing*. And writers write what they think will *sell*. Often, the only buyers are those who subscribe to the theory that sex and violence are the only big sellers on the public market. Grants and prizes, both of recognition and of remuneration, can stimulate a lot of better writing. Foundations, corporations, endowed universities, or churches—any entities with resources and with a desire to impact entertainment positively—could (and should) set up some form of writing prize for scripts or books or lyrics or games or reality shows that portray positive, family, and character-strengthening emotions and storylines. Any philanthropic or alternative-minded organization looking to maximize its reach and impact would have a hard time finding a more powerful way to allocate its resources.

Err to the Light

We were featured guest speakers at an Aspen, Colorado, retreat with top Disney corporate officers and division heads. We wrote a brief "parents' plea" for the occasion, attempting to articulate the appeal we felt all parents would want to extend to the Disney organization

in light of some of their recent moves away from the family enter-
tainment that made them famous. We called it "Err to the Light":

> *We appeal to you now, today, as parents, as "everyparent," from a*
> *part of the heart that only parents know. We have been with you*
> *in these convention sessions, looked around, and tried to calcu-*
> *late the influence in this room. You reach every American family*
> *and every American child and beyond, to the whole world, not*
> *periodically, but daily.*
>
> *Because of your size and who you are, because of media's*
> *stretch and subtle stimulus, you may have more influence than*
> *any other company, even more, perhaps, than any other single*
> *institution of any kind, perhaps more than the Presidency, more*
> *than the Congress. Actually, "influence" is too small a word. You*
> *have stewardship. You reach our children every day. They may*
> *listen to you longer and with more concentration than to us.*
>
> *What we say to you now is born not of statistical analysis or*
> *profit-margin expertise (although we promise you that "goodness*
> *sells"). It comes from a simple clarity bestowed only on parents.*
> *Because, you see, while our own personal commitments and val-*
> *ues, our desires and dreams, may quiver with ambiguity, they*
> *take on a firm, sharp focus in what we want for our children.*
>
> *As mere people, we are confused by complexity when we look*
> *at our world. But as parents, we are touched by simple, pure*
> *wisdom when we look at our child. In that wisdom, we see the*
> *joy of right decisions, the wonder and trust of selfless love, and*
> *the nobility of simple courage. We see the good and love in the*
> *world reflected in our children's eyes. We feel the deep desire to*
> *pour all that is good into their lives. And we feel the need for help*
> *because we also see the damning dangers of the dark dimming of*
> *sensitivity, the callous desensitizing and loss of wonder that not*
> *only robs them of their childhood but steals their awe and hope.*

So, first, we thank you for the times you have portrayed the light better and stronger than others portray the dark (and when you portray the dark, for showing it accurately, for making it lose); for the times when you have reached the deeper realism of right that is truly stronger than might. Thank you for escapes into fantasy that are not to places outside ourselves, but to the deepest and truest parts of our own hearts. Thank you for the times you've shown the courage to speak of and to the spirit and softly and carefully of a higher, better being to go with a higher, better way. Thank you for the times you have avoided the mindless amorality, which is, in its public face, more widely destructive than immorality.

Media, goes the old poppycock, doesn't influence a society's values, it only reflects them. Is that why prime time ads cost a million a minute—to reflect? Media influences us and our children so profoundly it cannot be measured. "With influence comes responsibility" goes the old cliche. A stewardship? A burden to bear? But isn't it more an opportunity, an opportunity to lift, to love, to help us all live in a higher realm?

As parents, our plea to you is so basic: Help us. Help us remind ourselves and our children of who we really are and who we really can be. Help us to see the light within ourselves. Help us to be better parents by being our ally, by giving our children heroes and role models, by creating good that is both beautiful and believable.

If you err, err toward the light. Be willing to earn 15 percent instead of 20 percent by avoiding the dark. Light brings strength, and a sure-footed, clear-headed creativity and confidence that makes up (financially and otherwise) much more than the missing 5 percent. Err to the light, not only in turning down a bribe or a sweatshop or a tax dodge. . . . Err to the light in turning down

*an amoral script, or a superfluous excess of foul language or vio-
lence, or a tarnishing comedy that makes fun of what is right. Err
to the light in telling stories about the noble human spirit rather
than the pseudo-sophisticated "realism" of the underside. Err to
the light by believing and portraying that human beings are still
good at their core.*

*From parents to Disney: err on the side of right; err on the
side of light.*

FAMILY-SUPPORTIVE RECOMMENDATIONS FOR INTERNET, INFORMATION, AND COMMUNICATION INSTITUTIONS

The much-heralded information age in which we live gives us access to virtually everything. Unfortunately, there seems to be *more* access to the sensational than to the deeper values and virtues of life. There seems to be no end to the filth, violence, and anti-value attitudes that flow through our smart phones and onto our monitors or into our eyes and ears from the Internet or through our 4G connections.

Here is a classic situation where government is needed to step in and protect people from other people. The Internet should be regulated and restricted at least to the same degree that network television is.

With these online institutions, it's hard even to know where to direct our parents' appeal. There is no CEO of the Internet. Unlike media, merchandising, or financial institutions, there is no centralized, small number of people who make the decisions about the messages that will be sent out. Everyone can put something on the Internet, and it seems like everyone does! We can throw out a general appeal about how vulnerable our children are and how dangerous these messages can be, but not many of those whose preoccupation is violence and raw, random sex are going to listen.

Here is a classic situation where government is needed to step in and protect people from other people. The Internet should be regulated and restricted at least to the same degree that network television is.

The three standard arguments against such regulation are:

- Regulation represses freedom of expression.

- People choose to pay for and receive the Internet, so they should be able to get what they want.

- You can't regulate something that has so *many* diverse suppliers.

The arguments are all weak. Freedom of expression should always be stopped or regulated when it endangers others. We don't have the freedom to yell "Fire!" in a crowded theater. Lots of things we pay for, from magazines to movies to the mail, are regulated if children could have easy access to them. And despite how many providers or suppliers there are of various types of filth, the beauty of the information age is that we know exactly where to find them. If fines and criminal penalties were stiff enough, most of the worst material could be eliminated over a fairly short time frame.

FAMILY-SUPPORTIVE SUGGESTIONS FOR POLITICAL/GOVERNMENTAL INSTITUTIONS

Government on all levels needs to reprioritize and reorient itself to the service, protection, maintenance, and motivation of society's basic building block: the family. As always, there are two sides to this coin.

First, we need to review and eliminate policies that harm, undermine, or weaken parents and families. Second, we need to create policies, incentives, and options that protect, encourage, and strengthen families.

We suggest reversing family-unfriendly policies by:

1. Eliminating any form of "marriage tax" so two married people

never pay more tax than those same two people would as single individuals.

2. Getting rid of no-fault divorce and other divorce laws that favor the convenience of the spouse rather than the welfare of the child.

3. Rolling back any law that limits parental input and responsibility regarding educational choices for their children.

In their place, family-friendly policies can be created that would:

1. Raise child deductions on income tax to their 1950s levels in today's dollars.

2. Create and improve school/college IRAs and other deductions that allow families to pay for college with pre-tax dollars.

3. Regulate the Internet.

In the long term, public policy could and should go even further. There are two things government could do that would have enormous positive impact on families. They seem almost laughingly naive and totally politically unrealistic, but even thinking and talking about them may bring about the kind of public thinking that prioritizes families and recognizes strong families as the goal of the public sector.

1. Give each parent of one or more under-eighteen children one additional vote (in local and national elections). This kind of parental power at the ballot box would cause politicians to work for families like never before and would no doubt unleash a stunning list of creative, family-friendly ideas and proposals.

2. Eliminate all federal and state income taxes, substituting value-added sales taxes on everything but food. This would reward saving and work, strengthening society and rewarding families

for the very prudence and industry that could strengthen the overall economy. It would also eliminate the enormous IRS and state income tax bureaucracies and refocus a huge section of the legal and accounting establishments.

FAMILY-SUPPORTIVE SUGGESTIONS FOR EDUCATIONAL INSTITUTIONS

We live in a society that requires licensing or training or registration for almost every conceivable activity. We even need a license to fish. Yet anyone, with no license, no training, and all too often no sense of responsibility, can assume the most critical and important role that exists in society: parenthood. Our schools are probably the only institution close enough and influential enough to collectively wake kids up to the responsibility and importance of parenting. Yet our schools have done very little to help young people appreciate and be prepared for the role of parents, and they do much that is negative and counterproductive concerning sexual responsibility and commitment.

When schools and teachers think of their role and their job as one of helping parents raise responsible and educated children, schools become better, parents become better, and most importantly, children become both better and happier.

The most sweeping and positive thing all public and private elementary and secondary teachers could do is to *see* themselves as the closest, most accessible, and most important backups, safety nets, and teammates to parents (not as *substitutes* or *surrogates*, but as *supplements* and *supports*). When schools and teachers think of their role and their job as one of *helping* parents raise responsible and educated children, schools become better, parents become better, and most importantly, *children* become both better and happier.

Here's what schools should strive even harder to do for parents and for kids:

For Parents:

1. Offer evening or weekend classes on parenting and specifically on how to help a child succeed academically.

2. Put on even more family functions where kids come to school with parents. This could be anything from the traditional sports, plays, and social events to creative academic and community events and from read-a-thons and back-to-school nights to service projects. Offer special family prices to every school function which has an admittance charge.

3. Improve parent-teacher conferences and schedule options where parents can come in with their child to work out a team-work approach to learning.

For Children:

1. Have a mandatory course on ethics and values in the seventh grade. Plenty of good curriculums and programs exist. *Rotate* the teaching (a math teacher teaches it one semester, a history teaching the next) thus "outreaching" and "transplanting" values into the texture and content of other classes.

2. Have a required class on parenting and family responsibility for all high school juniors. Teach communication and parenting skills, budgeting, and personal economics, but also teach family and relationship priorities.

3. Incorporate personal and family responsibility into all sex education classes. Reorient the curriculums to include the importance of commitment and responsibility. Within this framework, sex education, human intimacy, and reproductive

facts take on a whole new and more positive slant. *Involve* the parents who are willing to get involved, and at least *inform* the rest.

The most far-reaching and predictable way to get parents more involved in the education of their children is through a voucher system of educational and school choice. When we turn parents into consumers by giving them an educational voucher that they can "spend" at any accredited school that they choose, it forces even the most uninterested and disinclined parents to think at least a little bit about what they want from their child's education. This changed mentality and accountability inevitably makes schools more accountable and more creative in trying to meet parents' expectations and creates the closest thing we will ever get to a market-driven education system.

> *The most far-reaching and predictable way to get parents more involved in the education of their children is through a voucher system of educational and school choice.*

FAMILY SUPPORTIVE SUGGESTIONS FOR COURTS AND LEGAL INSTITUTIONS

We're dealing with two related but separate institutions here: first, the court system of America and its judicial process, which has increasingly and progressively interpreted laws with overemphasis on individual autonomy at the expense of what is best for families and parents; and second, the institution of private law firms and attorneys, which has made divorce, separation, and litigation too prominent on the family landscape.

Judges and their courts need to:

1. Re-enshrine the family and reflect (in their opinions) interpretations of laws that respect the responsibility and stewardship of parents.

2. Favor the welfare and well-being of children rather than the convenience of parents in divorce or other domestic disputes.

3. Strive for better balance between protecting the rights of individuals and children and preserving the unity, autonomy, and priority of families.

With regard to private legal practice, we need to:

1. Close down a few US law schools—America needs to quit producing so many litigators. Or, as an alternate to fewer law schools, discontinue some of the divorce law and litigation courses and substitute more instruction on arbitration mediation and alternative conflict resolution. The United States should operate more like Canada in this regard.

2. Do all we can to persuade the family law legal establishment that their job is to save families, not pull them apart. Focus more on win-win arbitration and less on win-lose (or lose-lose) litigation, and always view divorce as a last resort.

FAMILY-SUPPORTIVE SUGGESTIONS FOR RECREATION AND SOCIAL/CULTURAL INSTITUTIONS

Play, diversion, and social and cultural activities—the very things that should bring families together and add richness and diversity to family life—have begun to do the opposite.

Recreation and social life used to not only revolve around the family, it used to occur primarily within the immediate and extended family. Today, enormous recreational and social/cultural complexes consume what used to be family time and fracture the family because of different interests and options that take family members in different directions.

A new *mindset* by those who manage and run the institutionalized recreation and cultural establishments could make a positive and powerful difference to families. Directions that ought to receive consideration:

1. Stop scheduling everything on Sunday. Sundays are still the best chance for most families to be at home (or at church) together. With everything from soccer games to kids' birthday parties and recitals spilling into Sunday, private family time is often the thing that is eliminated.

   We lived in England for four years in the late '70s and early '80s. In that era, everything was closed on Sundays. No stores were open—except the occasional emergency pharmacy—and no sporting or musical events occurred. Even the British Open golf tournament and Wimbledon had their finals on Saturday and had no play on Sunday. This had a remarkable effect on our family. Our only option was to do family activities together. We went on long walks, played family games, and went to church together. Sundays became a true and refreshing change of pace—something we have never been able to duplicate here at home in the United States.

2. Give "real deals" to families who attend events together. If more spectator events—from high school sports to movies—offered family passes or major discounts for family groups, it would increase ticket sales at the same time as it brought more families together.

3. Encourage volunteering—especially volunteering as a family. There is nothing quite like volunteering as a family. Working together for a good cause, whether it's serving food at a homeless shelter or cleaning up a park or roadway, truly brings parents and children together. Voluntary agencies and

community service organizations should aim more of their outreach and recruiting at families and create projects where parents and children can volunteer together.

> *One of our daughters worked for Family Matters, the family volunteering arm of the Points of Light Foundation in Washington, DC. Their effort was to reach out and encourage families to sign up for volunteer projects together so they could combine family time and parent-child communication opportunities with the community service they render.*
>
> *Parents who became involved indicated that, in addition to the satisfaction of service and the quality family time, they have had amazing opportunities to teach values like empathy, love, and self-reliance to their children.*

4. Create recreational options that revolve around family and the parent-child relationship. To balance the camps, sports leagues, church outings, and music retreats that take kids away from parents, organizers should try to come up with occasional alternatives that let parent and child attend and participate together.

FAMILY-SUPPORTIVE RECOMMENDATIONS FOR NON-PROFIT AND RELIGIOUS INSTITUTIONS (AND PSYCHOLOGICAL, SELF-HELP, AND COUNSELING SECTORS)

For all the good they do, NGOs and charitable and humanitarian groups often find that their efforts in education, health care, nutrition, clean water, and microlending are not sustainable because they focus on individuals more than on families. Every NGO project or initiative should include some kind of family impact statement.

Historically, it is religion that people have looked to for help with their families, as well as their spiritual well-being and their outlooks and philosophies of life. During the last several decades, self-help, psychiatry, and other secular counseling have become important factors as well.

The question is, are any doing their jobs? Are they working? Are religious and counseling institutions playing as strong and prominent a role as they should in saving, safeguarding, and stabilizing families? Or are some aspects of these institutions working against families by stressing and glamorizing individual freedom and autonomy at the expense of family connections, responsibilities, interdependencies, and commitments?

We hear far too little of churches speaking out strongly against anti-family messages, models, and media. We see divorce becoming easier and more acceptable in faith communities. We see all sorts of affairs, amorality, and alternative lifestyles being tolerated, if not sanctioned, by some religions. It seems that many of our religious institutions have become so anxious to attract and recruit people and so over-committed to *tolerance* that they no longer try very hard to make it clear what is right and what is wrong—both in the eyes of God and in terms of what is good and bad for the family.

Counseling and self-help entities, on the other hand, are more and more involved and prominent in "fixing what ails us." Yet, so often, what they offer is a "quick fix" that essentially sets us up for a fall.

Essentially, our churches, synagogues, mosques, and other religious institutions have to *step up* and be stronger and bolder in their advocacy of the family and in training, assisting, and helping parents. At the very least, churches should:

1. Formally and emphatically make recommitments to the sanctity and pivotal importance of the family, reminding all that family priority and mutual fidelity lie at the heart of God's teaching.

2. Establish more extensive programs for parenting education, for teaching family communication, and for providing spiritually-based marriage and family counseling.

3. Speak out more strongly and vigorously against early, casual, recreational sex (scripturally "fornication") and marital infidelity (scripturally "adultery"). Talk more openly about the devastation sexual irresponsibility brings to families.

By the same token, secular counselors, authors, and analysts need to understand that individual "solutions" without some connection or acknowledgment of family are doomed to failure over the long term.

Too much is being written (and spoken) about avoiding co-dependency, developing self-confidence, and building wealth, and too little is being written and said about building positive family interdependency, developing empathy and faith, and building strong families. Writers, therapists, and "gurus" of all kinds should:

1. Ponder the long-term and the ultimate importance of family relationships to be sure their recommended "quick fixes" don't work at odds with what really matters.

2. Examine their own motives to be certain what they are preaching and recommending stems from their genuine belief in what is best for people over their whole lives and not from their own desire for short-term profit and popularity.

The suggestions and directions of this chapter just scratch the surface, and their intent is to prompt more and better "family thinking" by the larger institutions of society and to give some simple examples of the directions that kind of thinking could go. To motivate this type of direction on a significant level, it will take a movement—a true turning of hearts. A few thoughts about how that movement might come about is the topic of the concluding chapter.

The family is the first essential cell of
human society.

—POPE JOHN XXIII

Society is not a mere aggregation of
individuals, but the outcome of relationships between people—husband and
wife, parents and children, siblings—the
foundation of which is to be found in
family life and the bonds of affection
deriving therefrom.

—POPE BENEDICT

CHAPTER ELEVEN

THE COALITION

Building a Movement

from the Inside Out

---

co·a·li·tion *noun* \ ˌkō-ə-ˈli-shən\

1. a group of people, organizations, or countries who have joined together for a common purpose

There is no shortage of people who care about families, but there is a severe shortage of people organizing anything to do something about it. We need a movement, and movements can start with coalitions.

WHERE WILL THE HEART TURN?

Whether or not the forgoing family-supportive suggestions are ever implemented (or even taken seriously) by policy makers of larger institutions really depends on where the *hearts* of these individuals are. So we conclude this book back where we started—back with the admonition from the last page of the Old Testament. When our hearts are turned to family, we feel warm longings and tender feelings that come from the best part of us. When we experience these feelings of unconditional love and undying commitment to our children and our spouses, we begin to make a difference in our own homes and in our broader roles in the larger society.

This book won't convince a film producer to make a more moral, more uplifting movie, but his love for his own child might. A printed suggestion won't persuade the CEO of a bank to cut back on easy credit, but her love for her own family might.

And so it goes. Everything starts with the heart. As parents' hearts turn to children, and as children's hearts turn to parents, families change; and as families change, the world changes, the curse lifts, and life has meaning.

Sometimes, with the right combination of motivation and publicity, something called a "movement" can start and can become persuasive enough to begin to change the hearts that can change the minds at the larger institutions that compose a culture's engines of change.

And sometimes, with the right combination of motivation and publicity, something called a "movement" can start and can become persuasive enough to begin to change the hearts that can change the minds at the larger institutions that compose a culture's engines of change. In this final chapter, we will overview one course that such a movement could take.

Coalition Building

The most direct way to start a movement is to create a coalition. Creating co-alitions strong enough to actually create a societal shift toward greater family priority will require a carefully orchestrated two-phase effort.

Phase I involves the external effort to build a coalition and a grassroots movement (let's call it CSF or "Coalition for Strong Families") which links major existing pro-family organizations with religious, academic, phil-anthropic, voluntary, and civic groups to share information, ideas, and outreach. Then they can reach out to individual people and families through the churches, neighborhoods, clubs, and schools—uniting them, both in small community groups and online, bonded by a love and priority in family that supersedes cultural, political, economic, and religious differences.

Success will require good public relations, publicity, and branding/imag-ing which establishes CSF (or whatever it gets named) as a known entity with a clear and compelling message that appeals to the additional thousands of established pro-family organizations, progressive academic societies, com-munity and school organizations, and others who, once they know of the movement, will want to join it; and which develops pro bono music, movies, video, and social media that celebrates and emotionalizes the joys of mar-riage, parenting, and family relationships.

Phase II involves institutional intervention by influencers where opin-ion leaders and power brokers from all "engines of change" within society are recruited, tapped for support and fundraising, and committed to reach into their sphere of influence to build awareness of the viability of micro, grassroots, family solutions to global economic problems. At this stage, CSF expands into CBU (let's call it the "Coalition for the Basic Unit") as rep-resentatives from each of societies power matrixes are recruited into the movement. Task forces can then be made up of members from both the "grassroots" and "influencer" elements of the organization and which draw from the movement and from the intervention, and develop and locate the programs, materials, methodologies, and ideas which the larger institutions of all and varied kinds can use to lift, teach, motivate, and inspire parents and families.

Much of the coalition building, particularly in Phase II, revolves around effectively reminding larger institutions of how much they, and the broader society, ultimately depend on the basic unit of the family. Examples of the kind of fact-dissemination and reasoning to be used with various sectors include:

- (Companies and Corporations) Married adults earn more, save more, spend more, and have a much higher net worth than their single counterparts.

- (Economy and Society) Virtually every measure of economy-disrupting dysfunction, from school drop-outs to drug abuse, is markedly higher in broken families.

- (Economy and Government) Once problems spill out of the family and into the welfare and justice systems, they become impossibly expensive and expensively impossible to solve.

- (Civil society) Children from single-parent homes have substantially higher rates of crime, mental illness, and suicide.

- (Civil society) The United States has the highest incarceration ratio of any country, with a highly disproportionate number of inmates coming from broken homes.

- (Economy and Civil society) Unmarried couples are less likely than their married counterparts to be college graduates, to vote or engage politically, to go to church, and to earn a living wage.

- (Education) Kids from married homes complete two more years of education, on average.

- (Government) Welfare costs soar for persons from broken homes.

- (Poverty) Poverty rates track in parallel with fractured families.

- (Personal) Poll data shows married parents to be the highest demographic for "happiness," "personal growth," and "life-satisfaction," and the lowest for "depression" and "frustration."

Coalitions and Movements

In Phase I, the Coalition for Strong Families (CSF) is a coming-together and mutual sharing of religions, institutes, think tanks, foundations, agencies, and every other entity that focuses on the needs and well-being of families.

In Phase II, the Coalition for the Basic Unit (CBU) both influences and infiltrates corporations, schools, media, blogs, charities, firms, communities, clubs, publications, governments, and every other institution made up of and directly or indirectly dependent on the basic institution of families.

The coalition-building approach hearkens back to days when neighborhoods gathered in the village church or the town hall or the school auditorium

The coalition-building approach hearkens back to days when neighborhoods gathered in the village church or the town hall or the school auditorium to tackle problems, to teach sound principles, and to assist families in need.

to tackle problems, to teach sound principles, and to assist families in need. Today's gathering places may often be online or in cyberspace, but the solidarity and urgency and unity of purpose should be no less.

There is no reason that a micro, grassroots, bubble-up model should be thought of as obsolete or old-fashioned. Our neighborhood churches and civic clubs and schools still exist and can still deliver the kind of help and support to families that they once did. In addition, and in some ways even more efficient, online solutions, information exchange, best practices, and electronically-connected task forces can be set up that seek real, grass-roots solutions and make them available—through churches and clubs, through companies and schools—to families.

And these coalitions, like the silent plurality that they truly are, can develop task forces and corporate support and fundraising and even a public relations and image-building publicity arm that lets parents everywhere know that they are important and that their hope to raise responsible kids and to escape the misdirection, violence, amorality and entitlement of the broader society is not the exception, but the norm, and that help is on the way!

Phase I: CSF

There are countless organizations and groups trying to assist children and parents and families, ranging from Boys and Girls Clubs and scouting programs to research institutions and think tanks and from community service organizations to church auxiliaries. They do good work, but they often lack resources and frequently are not communicating, sharing, synergizing with, or learning from each other.

In many cases, their long-term effectiveness and sustainability suffers from the fact that they often substitute for and supersede parents rather than supporting them. If all of these elements could be loosely linked, brought together under the banner of a Coalition for Strong Families (CSF), and made more aware of each other's efforts and ideas, all could benefit. Many of them might be motivated to clarify and refine their goals around the ultimate objective of strengthening households as they adopt the umbrella vision statement of FORTIFYING FAMILIES *by celebrating commitment, popularizing parenting, bolstering balance, and validating values.*

A maturing CSF, through its publicity, image, and public relations arm, could raise awareness and favorability of many of these existing grassroots entities, and could complement and recognize them via a sort of "good housekeeping seal of approval." (ie., "a CSF approved and affiliated organization.")

Ideally, over time, CSF will also become a funding source, a publicist, an idea sharer, a cheerleader, and a recognizer of any and all groups that work for the betterment of families and households.

The first step, and the one that will facilitate and make possible all successive steps, is to gather the top twenty to thirty existing pro-family or dedicated family-strengthening organizations and demonstrate and prove to them that there are significant advantages in working together and pooling resources and constituencies.

Adopt the umbrella vision statement of FORTIFYING FAMILIES by celebrating commitment, popularizing parenting, bolstering balance, and validating values.

The most important and demonstrable advantage lies in using not only each other's data, but each other's bandwidth and outreach. Each of the organizations about to be listed has significant "material," ranging from research and papers to short- and long-form movies and well-crafted electronic and social media messages. Getting this material to an exponentially larger audience holds deep and immediate appeal.

The coalition might begin with US organizations, with the view of expanding internationally as the initial American movement catches on and gains traction. As the initial coalition is formed and each organization brings to the table its outreach, from email lists to subscribers and from social media followers and "friends" to media station audiences, each member entity becomes instantly capable of reaching out to a collective audience or a public that has combined and increased geometrically.

Beyond that, each entity learns from the others, and the quality of the message and of the media increases. Subtle competition begins as each member hones and develops its messages and its targeting. Over time, the broader reach attracts commercial interests, from writers to artists to ad agencies, who compete on an even higher creative level to develop messages that more powerfully and more emotionally convey the love and the importance of family.

The first meeting should be thought of as a "steering committee" out of which will grow a larger potential member list, and a second, strategic planning and organizing session can be held with an expanded group perhaps six months later.

A sampling of the organizations that should be considered to be included in the "pilot" coalition or steering committee includes:

- AARP—Family Arm
- A Better World Foundation
- The Ad Council
- Adventist Community Services
- AfterSchool Alliance
- The Alliance for Children and Families
- The American Society of Genealogists
- The Annie E. Casey Foundation, Kids Count, and the Family
- Association of Jewish Family and Children's Agencies
- Association of Junior Leagues International, Inc.
- Boys and Girls Clubs of America
- Brookings Institution—Ron Haskins
- Catholic Charities
- Citizens for Family
- Christian Coalition of America
- Family Research Council
- Family Watch International
- Fatherhood Coalition
- Focus on the Family

- Generations United
- Harvard University—Kathryn Edin
- International Conference on Strengthening Families Strategy
- Johns Hopkins University—Andrew Cherlin
- Kids Included Together (KIT)
- Learning for Life
- Mentor International
- National 4-H Council
- National Genealogical Society
- National Human Services Assembly
- National Marriage Project—University of Virginia—Brad Wilcox
- Nonprofit Leadership Alliance
- One Million Moms and the American Family Association
- Pro-Family Alliance
- Strengthening Center
- Urban Institute—Robert Lerman
- The World Congress of Families
- YMCA and YWCA

The initial steering committee meeting, composed of representatives from most of these organizations and others like them, should be held in a central and "neutral" US location, perhaps Chicago or St. Louis, over a Friday-Saturday, two-day format.

An honorary advisory committee could be considered, made up of "names" from entertainment, sports, balanced politics, and other visibility-lending sectors. It is surprising how much some celebrities will do when asked to speak up for families.

Each steering committee member entity should bring to this initial meeting the "outreach statistics" for his or her organization and show a representative sample of the kind of research and policy work they do, as well as a sample of any family strengthening media they produce and would like wider distribution for.

Someone, of course, or some group, has to assume the role of founding catalyst, with the underlying attitude of "Someone had to get the ball rolling," even if they want to eventually be viewed as simply one of the organizing members, "exactly equal to the rest of you."

Phase II: Link and Expand CSF into the Larger, Power-Based CBU

It is one thing to form a coalition of organizations and voices already committed to the improvement and well-being of children, parents, and family, but it is another thing altogether to convince society's largest and most powerful institutions that they are ultimately reliant on the basic unit of family and that they should do all they can to support and strengthen those basic units.

In Chapter 6, we called the larger institutions that sabotage and supplant the family "the culprits." Here, we want to recruit those very institutions to the cause of strengthening families, convincing them that their own long-term survival depends on doing exactly that, converting them from "culprits" to "champions."

From business to media to education, these larger institutions will now be referred to as "The Nine Engines of Change" because of their potential to save families.

The aim of Phase II is to tap into the uniting, universal support for family that can be found across all of society. Parents, at all levels, because of their common hopes and fears for their children, are potentially more united than they are divided by economics, politics, or religion. Finding such persons in the leadership of the major players within the Nine Engines of Change is the key to kicking off Phase II. This is not just a search through the traditional and conservative types often thought to be the strongest supporters of family. Several studies suggest that "progressive liberals," who are highly educated but generally are not religiously affiliated, are a group as large and as pro-marriage and pro-family as the "faithfuls" who attend church or synagogue or mosque each week.

The idea is to try to set up this influence-centered coalition and its task forces in a way that focuses on motivating and facilitating more involvement by each of these "engines" in better serving the families of those who are their constituencies or their employees (creating ideas and offering resources and catalyzing efforts to do less that harms families and more that helps them.)

The problem has long been that although families are the foundational institution, and although parents are the largest special interest group, they are not organized in any comprehensive way that allows them to

Although families are the foundational institution, and although parents are the largest special interest group, they are not organized in any comprehensive way that allows them to have lobbyists, collective advocates, or image and branding consultants.

have lobbyists, collective advocates, or image and branding consultants. In short, families are too often the unfortunate victims of societal change, not the initiator or originator of it.

It is organizations with products, with money, with reach and influence, with large membership, and with growth agendas that have the weight to dictate cultural change. And it is these engines of change that we must engage to bring about the positive transformations that are needed for families and households.

1. Business and Industry Engine

2. Philanthropy and Non-Profit Engine

3. Government and Politics Engine

4. Media, Sports, and Entertainment Engine

5. Education Engine

6. Professional and Self-Improvement Engine

7. Intellectual Properties, Writing, Journalism, Advertising, and Public Relations Engine

8. Internet and Grassroots Engine

9. Church and Religion Engine

Once a steering committee is set up involving at least three prominent members from each of the Nine Engines, they can be charged with doing some very simple and straightforward things:

1. Meet or talk with as many of their peers as possible to introduce and explain an overview of CBU and review the connections between strong families and a strong economy and society.

2. Find five other "influencers" of equal status within their engine, possessing a diversity of backgrounds and personal beliefs, and invite them to the next CBU meeting to be held six months after the initial meeting.

3. Be part of a FAB Talks initiative where they are given opportunities to speak in a TED Talks–like setting on "Family, Awareness, and Balance," on their own personal family life, and on their efforts to blend their professional and family lives. These lectures would be recorded for broadcast and Internet release with the goal of going viral.

"INFLUENCERS" AND ENGINES OF CHANGE

CBU will be most effective and most efficient when it moves beyond its umbrella and coordination function and begins to work as a catalyst with the goal of giving encouragement and ideas to large institutions about how they can be effective in strengthening the smallest, most basic institution on which they all rely. Each of the Nine Engines of Change has the resources and reach and influence to change the norms and priorities of its elements and members and to orient them all more toward the mission of *FORTIFYING FAMILIES by celebrating commitment, popularizing parenting, validating values and bolstering balance.*

At the first steering committee meeting of CBU, after its mission and vision is well aired, the progress of Phase I and the CSF coalition can be reported, and plans for going forward can be brainstormed and developed.

Representative opinion leaders from each "engine" should begin by discussing what could be done within that engine or sphere of influence to protect, popularize, and strengthen family life.

Attendees can be commissioned to locate and recruit five additional influencers representing diversity within their "engine" and to invite them to the next gathering six months later. In both meetings, CBU should be positioned as an entity growing out of a profound and unmet need, a coalition to do what legislation and policy and judicial action has not been able to do, and to create a movement from the grassroots, micro level that can accomplish things we have failed to do from a government, macro level, and that has the potential to save both our economy and our freedom and our way of life one family at a time.

THE POTENTIAL IMPACT AND DIRECTIONS OF EACH ENGINE WITHIN THE CBU PHASE II APPROACH

Representative opinion leaders from each "engine" should begin by discussing what could be done within that engine or sphere of influence to protect, popularize, and strengthen family life.

Conceptually, the idea is to assemble a group of highly influential and well-placed individuals from each of the nine engines who essentially be-come the "champions" of efforts and creative, family-friendly policy that safe-guard their own institutions by protecting and strengthening the house-holds and family units that constitute their sector.

In order to reach out effectively, steering committee members will need a concise letter or document that overviews the mission of CBU within their own sector. What follows are sample early drafts of that kind of summa-ry statement or brief overview of the approaches that could be considered within each engine. They include much from the ideas already discussed, but in letter or email format. These templates can be fleshed out, expanded, and finalized during both the "first wave" and "second wave," organizing and steering committee formation gatherings of Phase II and the CBU.

CBU

Coalition for the Basic Unit

Private Sector Champions for the Natural Family

PARADIGM: The family is the basic unit of our economy, and only families can provide the stability that enables businesses to flourish.

We all owe a great deal of the quality of our lives to the innovation and efficiency of the corporate world, and the quality of life that families enjoy is largely attributable to entrepreneurs and enterprise. Conversely, it is stable families that provide private business with its employee and customer base.

Despite this symbiotic relationship, many business institutions—particularly large ones, motivated by self-preservation, profit, and growth—have unwittingly begun to undermine the very family institutions they were created to supply, support, and supplement. They have also, to a degree, taken over some of the functions that should only belong to families and have fostered the impression that families are losing relevance. They have stolen away the time and loyalty of parents. They have promoted an anti-family materialism and debt with hedonistic advertising and have enabled and encouraged it further with liberal lending policies.

Businesses must come to better understand that it is in their best interest—financially and principally—to do all within their power to preserve and promote strong and stable families, wherein the values of self-sufficiency and responsibility are exemplified and taught. In doing more of this, businesses can spawn and develop and stabilize not only their present and future customers, but also their present and future workforce (employees and managers). Like the cells of a body, the health and viability of families determines the vibrancy and vitality, as well as the longevity, of the larger business and economic organism. Corporations that ignore the plight and the needs of families do so at the peril of their own survival . . . and are slowly but surely dismembering themselves.

By creating a company culture that demands all of an employee's loyalty and absorbs all of his or her energy, businesses orphan families into millstone appendages. Instead, companies can win loyalty by being less demanding and allowing employees to have the flexibility to spend more time with their families. As President Obama said in June 2014, "Some businesses are realizing that family-friendly policies are a good business practice, because they help build loyalty and inspire workers to go the extra mile."[1]

With marketing that poses wants as needs and creates demand out of envy, marketers and merchandisers manipulate families to mortgage their time and traditions for status. Instead, businesses need to protect their own consumer base and employee pool by encouraging, both internally (among their employees), and externally (among their customers), the classic values of delayed gratification, respect, responsibility, self-reliance, honesty, and family priority that make a market economy thrive.

Businesses of all sizes need to recognize that a high percentage of consumer money is spent on family-related goods and services, and customers (as well as workers) are drawn toward and develop loyalty to companies with family-oriented images and with a precedent of serving and supporting family values.

A clear way to see both the damage corporations can do to families and the good they could be doing more of is to think in the model of a simple grid about what companies should stop doing and what they should start doing—internally for their workers, and externally for their customers:

STOP DOING: INTERNALLY

- Requiring long, exploitive work hours
- Assigning evening and weekend work
- Enacting "mommy track" penalties
- Fostering a work-over-family culture, mentality
- Uprooting families with transfers, job shifts
- Paying CEOs 500 times the average worker's salary

START DOING: INTERNALLY

- Creating family-friendly employment policies (parental leave, job sharing, flex time, etc.)
- Holding courses on parenting, marriage, life balance
- Providing parenting helps (communication ideas)
- Assuring more job and location stability
- Giving educational assistance, savings matching, etc.

STOP DOING: EXTERNALLY

- Making credit too easy and too available
- Using "covet-based" advertising and promotion
- Using manipulative, materialistic marketing

- Excessively emphasizing Sunday shopping

START DOING: EXTERNALLY

- Participating in joint efforts with schools, communities
- Offering parents family/child teaching materials
- Sponsoring a "family value of the month"
- Holding debt avoidance training and policies

Certain types of corporations bear a particularly large part of the burden for damaging and endangering families:

Marketing, Merchandising, and Advertising Corporations have created a collective mentality of excess and materialism that, in the words of the head of a large ad agency, "makes people think they need what they really only want." This mentality leads parents to make the wrong choices in the constant "things and recognition versus time and relationships" tradeoffs and dilemmas of everyday life. It is these same merchandising businesses that have the opportunity to help families by basing their promotions on values, positive and altruistic emotions, and images of commitment within families.

Banking and Financial Corporations offer easy and excessive credit via charge cards and home mortgage loans which lets families consume at levels that necessitate both parents working, often at multiple jobs, plunges them toward bankruptcy when any one of the jobs is lost, and makes it impossible to give up any of the jobs voluntarily in favor of child-rearing priorities. It is these same financial institutions that have the opportunity to encourage saving and to motivate and reward the prudent and provident financial practices of families.

Retail Businesses constantly promote impulse-purchase items that families don't need and offer extended hours that crowd into times that should be family time. Staying open all day and all night, on weekends, and particularly on Sundays, pulls families away from time together and time in church. It is these same stores and shops that are perfectly positioned to offer, at promotional prices or as premiums, the kind of child- and family-oriented products that could help parents and kids.

Companies who think about and factor in the long-term good of the families of customers, clients, and audiences will preserve and retain those consumers to buy another day.

The bottom line really is the bottom line. Corporations which become more sensitive and concerned with the welfare and stability of the families of both their workforce and their consumers will reap a stronger long-term bottom line even as they fulfill their responsibility to the most basic institution of the broader society.

CBU-BUSINESS, ORGANIZING COMMITTEE

CBU

COALITION FOR THE BASIC UNIT

Non-Profit Sector Champions for the Natural Family

PARADIGM: The family is the basic beneficiary of and target at which aid, assistance, and philanthropy must be aimed if it is to be sustainable and to bring about lasting improvement in people's lives.

Most people generally think of non-profits, NGOs, humanitarian organizations, philanthropies, social entrepreneurs, and volunteerism as a chief advocate and supporter of children, but they are often not as sensitive as they should be to the effects they are having on families, and they sometimes unwittingly do things with good intent that are disruptive to families or that unintentionally substitute for families or make families redundant by replacing some of their functions. Charitable organizations often need to be reminded that their efforts to help people will be sustainable and beneficial in the long run only if they encourage and empower parents and families to take care of themselves and to gradually become more self-sufficient and less dependent.

The desire and duty so many people feel to "give something back" and to support charitable causes needs to be tapped and redirected toward global efforts to strengthen and empower families. It is unfortunate that over 90 percent of private philanthropic giving in most developed nations stays "in country" rather than going to assist the extreme poverty that affects nearly a fifth of the families in our world; and on the public side, it is most unfortunate that less than 1 percent of most national budgets goes to third-world humanitarian aid.

Among non-profits and humanitarian groups that do focus on third-world and developing countries, there is a continual debate on the question of what kind of aid is most effective and most sustainable. The question is, in situations of extreme poverty, where virtually every need exists, where does one start, and what kind of assistance will trigger and motivate additional aspects of development and lead toward ultimate self-sufficiency? Some say it must start with clean water, others say basic food and nutrition must come first, others advocate education as the first step, and still others say basic health care must be provided first. Some push micro lending and the development of small enterprises, especially among women, as the key to independence and self-sufficiency, while others insist that the elimination of racial and gender bias, which is the cause of so much violence, has to be tackled first. Some say we first just need to rescue orphans and feed starving children. Still others argue that political crisis intervention and the establishment of democratic rule opens the door for all the rest.

Certainly all of these are worthy efforts; all are integral elements of a stable and developing society and essentials of basic quality of life. But none are sustainable or capable of gaining a "life of their own" without stable families. Families create the economic incentive, the civil responsibility, and the educational, health, and physiological motivations that bring about the thirst for and the maintenance of each of the other kinds of initiatives.

Sometimes, when a particular "improvement" is pushed too hard without regard for its effect on families, it can backfire. For example, micro lending groups that insist on giving their loans only to women (with good reason) may inadvertently disrupt families and totally undermine the usefulness and image of fathers.

All humanitarian groups working in the villages of the third world should do at least an informal "family impact analysis" to see how their efforts are affecting families, and they should have the constant, underlying goal of unifying and strengthening families and the parent-child relationship. Often, with just a little thought and focus on this priority, ideas relating to health, education, nutrition, and every other approach can be adjusted so that they bring families together rather than pulling them apart or making them less necessary.

Among non-profits and charitable organizations that focus their efforts more locally and more domestically, the same kind of thinking should apply. For example, "big brother, big sister" and other mentoring programs admirably try to do things for kids that their families are not doing, but may, unwittingly, make parents feel unneeded and superfluous. Instead, there should be more "parent-to-parent" and "family-to-family" efforts where the goal is to teach parents to be more nurturing and to accept more responsibility.

Pairing up a reasonably functional family with a less functional or "in trouble" family is a win-win situation because the helping family works to improve its own example and has the joy of service even as the receiving family learns from the association and begins to improve its own performance.

Of course, there will always be kids with serious needs that their own families (if they have a family) are not meeting, and where rescue- and intervention-type programs are necessary. But in addition to that "medicine," we should be trying to go back a step and work harder on prevention. We should have more efforts aimed at helping families become functional enough to deal with more of their own needs rather than just waiting to pick up the kids who fall out of the nest.

There are an increasing number of non-profits that help families very directly by focusing on drug- and alcohol-abuse prevention, and on helping kids avoid violence, pornography, and early, recreational sex. These organizations should be applauded and supported, but they also should be encouraged to make homes and families their first line of defense and to instruct and support and assist parents in teaching (and exemplifying) these lessons themselves.

Bottom line: We need to factor in the family impact of every kind of aid or charity we are giving, making the effort and giving the thought necessary to tailor each intervention to be family friendly and supportive. And we need more private non-profit entities whose central mission is the strengthening of families—NGOs who are developing new ideas and concepts aimed directly at motivating parents and discovering and solving kids' problems within families before they spill out into society.

CBU-NON-PROFIT, ORGANIZING COMMITTEE

CBU

COALITION FOR THE BASIC UNIT

Public Sector Champions for the Natural Family

PARADIGM: The family is the basic unit of government and the grassroots element that makes up communities, cities, counties, states, and nations.

Government and the "public servants" who maintain it would be well served (and would serve us well) if they would adopt a family prioritizing perspective in which the prime objective of all public institutions is to strengthen, support, and stabilize the private institution of households. The well-being and welfare of families should be the guiding principle of all public policy at all governmental levels, and should be factored into all executive, legislative, and judicial decisions and guidelines.

We must remind our public servants that they are the servants of families, and that if the basic and foundational unit of family continues to break down, it will cause the larger units of the public sector to weaken and crumble also. We must understand that family rights are as important as individual rights, and that it is households, not individuals, that give us stability.

Politics and the public sector is, by definition, a "macro institution," established to deal with and support the population at large and to set policy that benefits everyone. Therefore, we should think in terms of curtailing and preventing any governmental practice or public policy that adversely affects families; and we should think in terms of conceiving, developing, and implementing governmental practices and public policies that benefit and strengthen families (and of incentivizing and rewarding such practices when they occur in the private sector).

Government has the role of protecting and advancing individuals, but must also recognize that individuals who are not franchised and integrated into a functional family are at greater risk to become economic drains and judicial risks within the broader society, and much less likely to make substantial contributions.

Think of it this way: All of society's social problems stem from breakdowns in families. If all families functioned perfectly, if all mothers and fathers were committed to their children and fully accepted their parental responsibilities, then all children would be taught proper values, all elderly people would be cared for, there would be no abandoned or abused children, and families would group together to provide services and do things as a neighborhood that they couldn't do on their own. There would be little need for social services or juvenile justice or welfare or any of the impossibly expensive "solutions" that we must resort to when problems spill out of and over the basic unit of family. Therefore, the best thing government can do to promote its own solvency and survival and to advance economic and societal well-being is to protect and strengthen traditional, functional, lasting families.

Some national governments are beginning to recognize this. Australia has adopted a policy of attaching a "family impact statement" to all proposed and pending legislation, forcing lawmakers to consider how various policies will affect families and households. Other nations are beginning to recognize and acknowledge the enormous economic contribution of a family in raising a child as a productive and law-abiding member of society, and as a result, are increasing the tax deduction and exemption for each child in a household and abolishing any form of "marriage tax," which causes married couples to have higher tax rates than two adults living singly. And governments all over the world are trying—although not making as much progress as we would like—to find appropriate ways to protect children and families from everything from pornography and violence to health risks and excessive taxes.

But with all the well-intentioned "defensive" efforts aimed at protecting families in various ways, local, state, and federal governments and public agencies are not doing much creative or proactive thinking about ways to promote families and support parents in the increasingly difficult job of raising children.

The most important proactive steps that government can take are things that empower families and that symbolize the perspective of parents having the ultimate responsibility and decision-making authority for their own children, with the public sector as the supporting and enabling entity. A good example of this is educational vouchers, which would allow parents to decide where their children go to school and give families the economic clout to reward good schools and penalize (and even close) schools that are not making the grade.

Perhaps the most dramatic way to get all of us (particularly elected office holders) to think more creatively about how to help and support parents and families would be the radical step of giving parents of one or more underaged children an extra vote at the ballot box. That would give such political clout to parents that politicians would scramble to come up with pro-family legislation and policy ideas of all types and unleash a torrent of creative, pro-active ideas for strengthening and supporting families. This is unlikely to happen any time soon, but the point is that a pretty good case can actually be made for the notion that parents, since they support and pay for their children, ought to have an extra vote to cast for them, too.

Sometimes the best way to impact and change the public sector is to make demands and look for answers at the political/election level. Political parties would do well to frame their issue positions in family terms and to develop proposals that support parents. If political candidates feel that there are votes to be gained by addressing the family issues that parents care most about, they will begin to look harder for answers and become more sympathetic and empathetic to the challenges normal, everyday families face. It could be well argued that the biggest special interest group of all is parents, and any candidate that positions him or herself (hopefully with real intent) as a champion for families and for the concerns of parents might actually win enough support to be able to divorce himself from the demands and excesses of the more common self-interest groups.

CBU-GOVERNMENT, ORGANIZING COMMITTEE

CBU

COALITION FOR THE BASIC UNIT

Media and Entertainment Champions for the Natural Family

PARADIGM: The family is the basic consuming unit of all forms of media and the basic user and potential beneficiary (or victim) of all existing and emerging technology.

The mainstream consciousness, the collective of our individual paradigms and perceptions, is enormously influenced by our all-pervasive media industry, in which amoral minorities masquerade as majorities and suck away traditional values and family priorities and balance, creating a moral vacuum where faith, commitments, and a clear-headed sense of what is important are hard to cling to. The face of the media/technology juggernaut is a shiny but distorted mirror that changes the shape of how we see ourselves and causes us to worship false gods and graven images.

Media spokespersons have often said things like, "We don't influence people's values; we only reflect them." But anyone who is observant, and particularly anyone with children, knows that the values (or lack thereof) portrayed across our small and large screens have an enormous impact on viewers, especially on children. Those who run the media and entertainment world generally are not typical, mainstream Americans, and they do not have typical, mainstream values. Yet the reach and influence of their media allows them to pose what they produce as "the norm" and cause members of the real and silent majority (those who don't jump into bed on the first date and don't treat violence with indifference) to wonder if they are out of step and old fashioned.

A way must be found to bring about fundamental change within the six electronic mass media juggernauts: (1) drama/comedy movies and TV series, (2) commentary and news, (3) reality and talk shows, (4) interactive computer and TV games, (5) music and recording, and (6) sports. The ideal, of course, would be to transform their content from being the sucking vacuums that create values voids to being blowers that bolster and beef up the beliefs and balance of strong traditional families, thus popularizing parenting and creating a new mainstream consciousness where it is cool to be committed and popular to be family-prioritized. In the meantime, what can realistically be done to minimize the damage they are doing to society? A brief look at each of the six:

Drama and Comedy (movies and TV series): We need some kind of recognition or awards for scripts and programs and movies that portray universal values and show them as mainstream. We also need a new rating system for movies that takes into account the motive and message of the movie rather than basing itself only on some formula of what is shown and said. (For example, a lot of PG-13 movies portray a light, comedic form of amorality that is far more damaging to kids than dark and identifiable immorality.) Some enlightened producers and directors are starting to recognize how huge the market is for movies and shows that uplift and inspire, or that least deal with moral or even spiritual subjects.

Commentary and News: We need more balance, and specifically more a moderate middle ground in our news coverage and commentary. So many programs, stations, and channels become too linked to either the extreme conservative right or the far liberal left, and thus, both news and views go out that seem to suggest that there is no middle ground. And we need more optimistic, "glass-half-full" news . . . though not necessarily sugar-coated, and not at the expense of the reality of pessimistic or worrisome news; and more outlets and editors who believe they have the responsibility to cover the positive as well as the negative. There are so many good things going on in the private and public sector that never get mentioned—lots of pro-family initiatives that need but never get either coverage or editorial support.

Reality and Talk Shows: It is essential to look for celebrities and other potential opinion leaders who exemplify and speak well for the joy and excitement as well as the satisfaction and peace of families, balance, and values . . . and get them on shows where they can express their views and set their example. It is amazing how many people who are famous for one narrow skill or notoriety are also great and committed parents. Yet no one has ever asked them about their kids or their home or their priorities in life, and they would like to be asked. And when it comes to reality shows, some enlightened producers are just starting to realize that real reality is about families and hopes for a better life, so we are starting to get shows which at least begin to look at "good that could happen" rather than "bad that has happened."

Interactive Computer and TV Games: It is important to think of computer and video games as part of the entertainment engine because so many of them are linked to other media forms and to the creators and producers of electronic media. These also need a better rating system, more government regulation, and most of all, more good writers and producers turning out games that teach values rather than violate them.

Music and Recording: Perhaps of all the anti-family and anti-values messages out there, the most blatant and egregious are in the lyrics of rap and other modern genres of music. We need to object as loudly and powerfully as possible to music or any other type of media that offends the basic, universal values that 99.9 percent of us hold. It has been said that the proper response to outrageous behavior is outrage. We also have to support the production of well-done music that inspires and promotes introspection, improvement, and good decisions.

Sports: It is hard to overestimate how important and influential sports are on our society, particularly sports that are carried and glorified by the media. Much work needs to be done to encourage and help sports figures to accept and responsibly fulfill their place as role models. The very young sports hero icons need mentoring on how to handle their celebrity status. And more teams and other sports organizations need to be prompted and motivated to seek ways to ensure that the personal influence of their athletes on the broader society is helpful and unifying rather than disruptive and dividing.

Most parents think of media as an adversary rather than an asset with regard to their families and their parenting. And it will not change overnight. But as the basic consumer of media, families have more power than they know, and they simply need to find more effective and viable ways to use it. And media decision makers need to be helped to understand that appealing to values that families already have is better (and ultimately more profitable) than trying to alter or mold people's values to match their own.

CBU-ENTERTAINMENT, ORGANIZING COMMITTEE

CBU

COALITION FOR THE BASIC UNIT

Education Sector Champions for the Natural Family

PARADIGM: The family is the basic supplying and receiving unit of all practical and formal education, and parents, not governmental agencies or schools, are responsible for their children's education.

School systems and educational institutions play a powerful role in the lives of most families, and they have become an engine of enormous and often controversial reach and strength. But while the internal and external debates rage about what and how schools should teach, what is often left out of the equation and the formula of what education should be are the most important factors of all: (1) how to get parents more involved, and (2) how to incorporate the basic principles, values, and skills that will help kids to one day have successful families of their own.

It has long been recognized that our educational establishments, in addition to teaching academic skills and imparting intellectual information, have a responsibility to teach social principles and impart practical life skills. The most important elements in this second category can be reduced to (a) personal values and character, (b) parenting and family prioritization, and (c) work/life balance. Of the three, only the first is receiving significant attention (as many districts mandate some form of character education).

While few would disagree with the importance of the other two (family/parenting and personal life balance), a popular mainstream consensus that these can and should be taught in schools has yet to be created. It is fine to argue that family and parenting skills should be learned in families and from parents, but the problem is that bad family situations and poor or nonexistent domestic skills become a continuing cycle in many families. We know that most neglectful parents were neglected as kids. We know that harsh, ineffective, harmful parenting flows from one generation to another just as predictably as genetics. And we know that the crime, poverty, substance abuse, and nonproductive, noncontributing traditions that stem so predictably from inadequate families are incredibly costly to society. This is why society and its educational establishment is justified in and should be willing to institute required courses on family skills and on work/family balance in high school and on values and ethics in middle school or junior high. This kind of subject matter doesn't need to involve complex psychology or behavioral science, just basic information on how children grow, what they need, ways to teach responsibility and discipline, common mistakes parents make, the dangers of temper, how to get help, and so on. And there is already a broad choice of available ethics and values curriculum.

While they are at it, secondary schools should offer evening classes on the same two subjects for adults. We should use school buildings (and public school teachers) after hours to help parents gain the skills their parents didn't teach them, and to link what the kids are learning about ethics and families with what parents can elect to learn. This could also provide some much-needed extra income for teachers.

And while we are on public school teachers (and the shortage of them), it would be a positive step to develop a provision for alternative certification whereby a person with a field of knowledge and natural teaching ability—particularly retired persons—could be hired to teach within their field of expertise. It is absurd to think that teachers, colleges, and education departments of universities are the only source of good teachers. Small stipends could also be paid to bright students who would apply and compete for "student tutor" positions. Though they would need direction and careful selection, student peers are sometimes more effective in helping fellow students than are much higher-priced special education teachers.

But how do we get parents more involved in their children's education (and strengthen individual families in the process)?

One place to start the search for this answer is simply to acknowledge that private schools achieve more results with less money and get parents far more involved than do public schools. Test scores are higher in private schools, parent satisfaction and participation is more common, and far more "educational efficiency" (or bang for the buck) is achieved. On surveys, parents rate private schools "simpler," "friendlier," "more autonomous," "less constraining," and "clearer in their goals." So how do we get more private schools, make them more affordable, and make public schools more like them?

Perhaps the most involving element of all would be to create public education vouchers (where each parent has a voucher equal to the amount the state spends on each student which can be "spent" at whatever school the parent chooses). Besides generating far greater interest and involvement on the part of parents, a properly conceived voucher plan can provide increases in per pupil expenditures and teacher pay and decreases in class size. Vouchers essentially make students and their parents the "paying customers" who drive the whole system by the power of the free market. A voucher approach funds students, not schools. And it makes schools autonomous, creative, and responsive to real needs and desires. It gives low income families some of the same freedom of choice that has traditionally belonged only to the wealthy. And most importantly, it puts parents in charge, gives them real ownership in their kids' education, and draws them into meaningful choice-making and participation.

Most essential is the conviction that *parents*, and not schools, have the ultimate responsibility and stewardship for their children's education. Thus, along with trying to make schools better, parents need to be committed to providing the educational elements that the schools leave out. Parents need to assess and analyze what their kids are and are not getting from the schools they attend, and then supplement it accordingly. We will set up task forces within this committee to develop home-based programs for teaching values, family skills, and "the other three R's" of **responsibility**, **relationships** (interpersonal communication skills), and **right-brain learning** (creativity and "out of the box" thinking).

CBU-EDUCATION, ORGANIZING COMMITTEE

CBU

COALITION FOR THE BASIC UNIT

Professional Speakers Sector Champions for the Natural Family

PARADIGM: The family is the basic unit of client groups, patients, congregations, and audiences, and is the transmitting and receiving element of all oral tradition and word of mouth.

There is a great deal of speaking and meeting and group discussions going on in the world. People gather in associations, in clubs, in congregations, in book groups, in civic gatherings, in corporate retreats, and in all kinds of other settings and combinations. And teleconferencing and video conferencing just increases the whole phenomenon. The trouble is that the subject matter is too much devoted to individual-focused topics—from self-improvement to investing to time management to personal leadership to dieting to cooking to salesmanship to technology use and application to a hundred other things.

We join groups and associations and clubs of all kinds, but there are too few that are aimed at family and at parenting. It's easy to find instruction on almost anything these days, to study and become "qualified" for anything from flying a plane to trading stocks online. You have to have a license to do most everything, even to go fishing. But no license is required to have a child . . . or to raise one. Family skills, the most important of all, are too seldom talked about, met about, or spoken about.

More ways need to be found to get parents together, to learn and discuss family needs and parenting skills, to hear each other's ideas. Community-based profit and non-profit entities, from hospitals to insurance companies, should sponsor parenting presentations and speeches. Businesses should put on seminars for their employees, and related public agencies should focus more on the "preventive medicine" of family and parent instruction to help cut down the need for intervention. Professional associations should hold more conferences on how their industry can help families more. The bottom line is that family topics need more talk, more speaking, more word-of-mouth.

Professional associations, from doctors and lawyers to trade unions, can become focal points for proactive efforts to support and strengthen families.

CBU-PRESENTERS, ORGANIZING COMMITTEE

CBU

COALITION FOR THE BASIC UNIT

Written Communication Sector Champions for the Natural Family

PARADIGM: The family is the basic emotional unit of most classic fiction, comedy, and drama; the basic measurement or manifest of much self-help and non-fiction writing; and both the basic subject and basic consumer of journalism.

Writing and commentary is a powerful engine for change, not because of the money or resources it can throw at problems, but because of the ideas and concepts and insights it can illuminate, because of the insights it can conceptualize, because of the truth it can reveal and the feelings it can stir.

Writers today should be anything but worried about other media and electronic forms because everything that is developed is just another outlet for writing. The "old outlets" of letters, books, newspapers, and scripts for plays have been joined by the "new outlets" of the Internet, email, texts, e-news, e-publishing, and all kinds of scripts for movies, TV, computer games, and more. And additional outlets for writing are coming along all the time. Most of what we call the information age is writing. Written language is becoming more important, not less, and even what we think of as "non-written" usually started with a script or notes or some other written way of capturing ideas or conveying emotion.

Few would question the massive and universal influence of writing. What we should question, however, is the way and the direction in which it is influencing us. So much writing today is aimed at selling. Books are written to titillate and entertain and shock, not to uplift or teach principles. Scripts are written about violence and sex because they are easy to sell (and easy to write). It takes far less skill to write about base emotions, or to act or portray them in movies, or report them in the news, than it does to write about higher, finer emotions like love or loyalty, or about the nuances of difficult choices or moral dilemmas, or to report the good news in the world as well as the bad. To make the engine of writing become more beneficially influential in the lives of families, we must somehow get it to write better things!

What may be needed even more than prescriptive parenting books, though, is writing that creates a more positive and popular image of families and of the parental role and the family-oriented lifestyle. No matter how important people know their families are, if they live in a world where devotion to home and children is not glamorous, or not regarded with respect or admiration, or not "the thing to do" in the popular culture, it is hard to stay motivated and committed. And it is not the writers of parenting books who will popularize parenting; it is the writers and producers of the entertainment media of the mainstream culture. And these are the writers that are writing to sell, using the proven formula of sex, violence, smut, gossip, celebrity idolization, reality shows, hedonism, and amorality in every imaginable form—all of which can be churned out quickly and sold easily.

It's not that the good stuff—the material that is based on the higher, nobler emotions and ideals—won't sell. Indeed, when it is done and done well, it does remarkably well in the marketplace. When a writer or a producer with real talent (and lots of funding) really sets out to do something with deep roots, real values, family-centered emotions, and a right-over-might mentality, it becomes a best-seller or a 200 million dollar movie, a Tony award-winning musical, or a "surprise hit" TV series. (Think of your own favorites in each category.) The problem is that there are not enough of them—not nearly enough.

What it really comes down to is that writers are working for the publishers and producers and marketers rather than the other way around. A "seller" says, "Sex sells" or "Violence sells" or celebrity or reality or materialism or whatever sells, and writers crank out what they are asked to write. How much better would it be if writers captured truth and light, wrote about the highest and best that is in us, and accurately portrayed the things that are good and right as well as the things that are wrong in ways that people could feel? What if publishers and producers and marketers worked for the writers in distributing and promoting the best they could find to the public?

What would it take to make more of this happen? What would encourage and motivate the best writers to write about the best things? We have often wished that some kind of Writers Awards could be established, perhaps by a well-endowed foundation, to give recognition (and substantial cash awards) to writers who produce the best materials (in all sorts of different writing categories from fiction to journalism to dramatic or comedic scripts) depicting different universal values or exploring important moral questions or portraying realistic, family-oriented lifestyles. We believe that if the truly good manuscripts are written, they will get published; if the truly good scripts get written, they will get produced; if the truly good computer games are conceived, they will get manufactured; and if the truly good news stories, columns, and editorials are written well, they will get as much ink as gossip columns and stories about crime and natural disasters.

Advertising and public relations and the art of "branding" also needs to be turned loose in all its subtlety and emotion on the task of celebrating commitment and popularizing parenting. Family- and relationship-charged vignettes and short viral videos, well-written and beautifully produced, can tug at heartstrings and motivate individuals to prioritize their family relationships higher and to afford them more time and more mental energy.

CBU-WRITERS, ORGANIZING COMMITTEE

CBU

COALITION FOR THE BASIC UNIT

Cyber Sector Champions for the Natural Family

PARADIGM: The family is the basic unit of cyberspace and of all grassroots organizations. The Internet and social media that we often think of as a parent's enemy can instead be the inclusive web that connects families to each other, shares ideas, and allows parents to encourage and motivate each other.

Unfortunately, unless it is controlled and channeled, the Internet is today's single biggest worry of parents, the most ominous threat to family values, and the scariest mental and emotional danger to kids. In our justified scramble for filters and blocks and other ways to protect our children (and ourselves) from the direct access of pornography, predators, and perversion of all kinds, we must not lose sight of the enormous possibilities for positive influence, for constructive self-improvement, and for proactive good that are presented by the Internet.

Unique among the main engines of change in society, the Internet not only influences, impacts, and affects families—it can involve families in that influencing, allowing parents to give as well as receive strength, ideas, and encouragement to and from other parents.

For this to happen effectively and efficiently (as well as

consistently), there needs to be a focal point and a central "magnet" that draws parents and families toward a cyber center where they can meet and motivate each other even as they communicate and commiserate and find common ground. In this kind of linked family of families, this siblinghood of households, CBU and its members must create an extraordinary website which not only gives security and a larger identity for parents, but instructs them, gives them tools and proven parenting programs, and encourages them to share with and help each other.

This website will get better in the same way that it gets bigger—by the involvement and contribution of more parents and the linkage to other valuable online family resources. The equivalent of a seal of approval can be developed wherein CBU endorses other good web-based resources for families.

Today, "grassroots" essentially means the Internet, and geography and distance, and even cultural, economic, or religious differences, no longer present boundaries or divisions. Among parents around the world, differences are overwhelmed by the similarities and common ground they have as parents. Essentially, we all want the same things for our children, and we all have the same worries, the same hopes, the same dreams. And being connected online helps us to accept, understand, deal with, and sometimes solve our parental worries, even as it reinforces, emboldens, and gives us practical tools in pursuit of our family hopes and dreams.

All this certainly does not lessen the huge need to protect our kids from the Internet, and CBU will be active in demanding more regulation and governing law in cyberspace.

We will appeal in every way we can discover to Internet content creators and providers, and we will attempt to make it clear that wholesome content is, in the long term, more profitable than its amoral alternative.

CBU-INTERNET, ORGANIZING COMMITTEE

CBU

COALITION FOR THE BASIC UNIT

Religious Sector Champions for the Natural Family

PARADIGM: The family is the basic unit of eternity as well as the basic unit of churches, synagogues, temples, and mosques throughout the world; but more importantly, for all who believe in a benevolent God, the family is the basic unit of happiness, the fundamental element of God's family, and indeed, the very structure of the government of God's kingdom.

One useful model for looking at the world is a bull's-eye style target made up of concentric rings. At the center, in the bull's-eye itself, is the family—the fundamental and basic unit of everything. Then the rings go out from there, each one representing an element or level of society that supports the family and assists parents in the raising of children: the community, the private sector, the public sector, and so on. In this model, the ring immediately next to the bull's-eye, the one that is second only to the family itself, should be the church or place of worship.

As churches take a leading and catalytic role in pulling together representatives from the other major engines of change in society, it may be helpful to visualize religious entities as the bull's-eye of CBU.

Some examples of family-related initiatives already being discussed in many churches:

1. More family-focused social media, public service spots, and viral videos for the media.

2. "Family lectures" that can be taped and distributed, held in some iconic place for each particular religion, where well-known members (from athletes to actors to authors and etc.) talk about their families and the successes and failures they have had (or are having) as parents. (FAB Talks—"Family, Awareness, and Balance")

3. "Family implementation" paragraphs added in sermons and other spoken or written messages.

4. Values lessons for families that are parent-friendly and non-denominational. And encouragement of families to hold a once-weekly Family Home Evening. A possible prototype exists at www.familynightlessons.com.

5. Churches, synagogues, temples, and mosques used as neighborhood family resource centers. Too many religious buildings sit empty and dark six days a week. By staffing them with church volunteers and organizing their existing libraries and media equipment, these well-placed, neighborhood buildings could be turned into family resource centers during the week where parents could come for ideas and information and stay-at-home moms could organize playgroups and mothers' groups.

By taking steps like this, churches and other religious institutions can focus their attention, and the initiative and creativity of grassroots members, on finding more and better ways to magnify our roles as parents and partners. We can get away from the neglect of marriages and families that sometimes occurs with those who have demanding and time-consuming church responsibilities. And we can reclaim the family-focused image and reputation in the world that churches may have lost a little of in recent years.

Additionally, by doing all in their power to prioritize the role of spouse and parent above all other roles, religious institutions can put themselves in a position where they can call for more attention and priority to be given to families by other influential institutions in society.

For starters, churches can move strongly to promote ten ways in which we all depend on families (Macro to Micro):

1. (Economy) Married adults earn more, save more, spend more, and have a much higher net worth than their single counterparts

2. (Economy and Society) Virtually every measure of economy-disrupting dysfunction, from school dropouts to drug abuse, is markedly higher in broken families.

3. (Economy and Government) Once problems spill out of the family and into the welfare and justice systems, they become impossibly expensive and expensively impossible to solve.

4. (Civil society) Children from single-parent homes have substantially higher rates of crime, mental illness, and suicide.

5. (Civil society) The United States has the highest incarceration ratio of any country, with a highly disproportionate number of inmates coming from broken homes.

6. (Economy and Civil society) Unmarried couples are less likely than their married counterparts to be college graduates, to
vote or engage politically, to go to church, and to earn a living
wage.

7. (Education) Kids from married homes complete two more
years of education, on average.

8. (Government) Welfare costs soar for persons from broken
homes.

9. (Poverty) Poverty rates track in parallel with fractured
families.

10. (Personal) Poll data shows married parents to be the highest demographic for "happiness," "personal growth," and
"life-satisfaction" and the lowest for "depression" and
"frustration."

By promoting these ten societal problems and areas for change,
churches can help rebuild the basic unit of happiness—the family.

[signature]

CBU-RELIGION, ORGANIZING COMMITTEE

TIME TO TURN

In an ideal scenario, CSF and CBU would form on all levels. There would be national coalitions, state coalitions, community coalitions, and even groups representing individual churches or civic clubs. While this may seem far-fetched and unrealistic, the beauty of the approach is that anyone or any group on any level can begin the process. A single individual in a single neighborhood can meet with other like-minded parents and begin to reach out to local institutions with ideas, suggestions, and appeals for more family-friendly policies. Existing family-supportive organizations of any size can be in touch with other parallel organizations in an effort to be more symbiotic and helpful to each other in meeting family needs. Public officials or business executives on any level can form small coalitions with others within their own "engine" and explore or share ideas on family strengthening ideas affecting their employees or their customers.

Over time, we hope www.The-Turning.com will become an ongoing resource for large and small CSF and CBU coalitions where ideas can be exchanged.

The important thing for now, (and for you as you finish this book) is to do *something*, to change something, to add something, to improve something! Start with the "inner" of your own family by creating a family culture that is stronger and more lasting than the other cultures that surround your children. Then look for "outer" opportunities to meet with others who also feel the importance of strong families—with an eye toward the possibility of creating some kind of coalition.

Consider finding or forming a personal support group for the "inner" as described in the Afterword; and begin thinking about the "outer" by meeting with a current or newly created book club that reads this book together and goes through the outline and questions in the reader's guide that follows in Appendix I.

Our most basic instinct is not for survival but for family. Most of us would give
our own life for the survival of a family
member, yet we lead our daily life too often as if we take our family for granted.

—PAUL PEARSALL

AFTERWORD

FIND A SUPPORT GROUP

Parents who finish this book with a genuine desire to protect and improve their families—parents whose hearts turn—are going to need one thing more than their own rededication. They are going to need some kind of support group to encourage and sustain and bolster their rekindled parenting and family efforts.

The adage, "It takes a village to raise a child," while used too often and too politically, nonetheless is absolutely true in the sense that parents need other adults—individually and in groups, as allies and as support mechanisms—in their effort to raise happy and responsible children. For one thing, we all need moral and emotional support and encouragement (and commiseration). Parenting can be a lonely process, and we are prone to think that nobody has problems or challenges like ours. Sometimes just knowing other parents who *do* struggle gives us the courage to keep trying. And secondly, we just frankly need help in the form of other caring adults who will genuinely try to help teach our kids the same things we are teaching them. As parents, we know that our children will often accept something from another adult more quickly and more easily than they will accept it from us. It's the concept of "other mentors" and "other examples" that give weight and credibility to what we try to teach.

Frankly, the best parental support groups are usually neighborhood churches, synagogues, or mosques. Through Sunday schools, youth activities, and various other forms of guidance and mentoring, children receive solid secondary support. And parents get instruction, insight, and encouragement, along with the ability and opportunity to share ideas and concerns with other parents. This certainly is not the only reason for finding a place of worship in which you can be comfortable and active, but it is one very good reason.

An additional form of support and motivation can come from joining some kind of parenting co-op or organization. Some exist in communities, some on the Internet. We have our own, called Values Parenting (http://www. valuesparenting.com), which we organized more than twenty years ago, and which now has a membership of over 200 thousand parents. At Values Parenting, you can find all kinds of parenting and family helps, including:

- A monthly family and parenting newsletter
- Materials for neighborhood "Joy Schools" where parents alternate as the volunteer preschool teacher of a curriculum of twelve social and emotional "joys" (e.g., the Joy of Sharing and Service, the Joy of Imagination and Creativity, etc.)
- A set of twelve monthly "values units" involving a child's and parent's audio on each of twelve basic values.
- Ideas for setting up a family economy, family legal system, and productive family traditions and rituals.

The most important benefit of Values Parenting groups is that they bring parents together where they can share ideas and concerns, as well as the responsibility of helping out with each other's children. More and more, Values Parenting will also be involved with attempts to push for implementation of some of this book's "Family-Supportive Suggestions" in larger institutions. Values Parenting will, in this book's terminology, help parents participate in the "cure" and band together to make the "case."

Use the "contact us" button at valuesparenting.com to request further information or a free membership information packet.

APPENDIX I

READER'S GUIDE AND DISCUSSION QUESTIONS

Once you have read the book, you may wish to consider some of its topics and issues with your spouse, family members, friends, or book club. Below are questions, taken in sequence from the book, to help you think about what you have read, talk about the issues, and consider some actions you might like to explore

Seven Functions, Four Elements (pp. 5–9)

- These can become measuring points and "touch stones" in terms of how an individual family is doing and how it can do better. Rank your own family from one to ten in terms of how well you think you're doing in each of the seven purposes and on each of the four elements. Where do you need the most improvement and the most focus? (This book, as you read, will provide help on all eleven.)

- Discuss (or think about) what happens when other, bigger institutions try to assume the seven basic purposes or functions of the family.

Concentric Circles (pp. 9–12)

- Discuss this "world view" and the concentric circles diagram. Adolescent or high school-aged children will have an interest in (and most likely an opinion on) the model.

- Do you feel the three outer circles of society are helping or hurting your family?

Social Problems and the Breakdown of the Family (Chapter 3)

- Think about (and discuss) the connections between "social problems" and family breakdown. Which is the cause and which is effect?

- How do stronger families impact social problems? Where else but in the family can these issues be successfully addressed and solved?

A Nation at Risk (pp. 31–33)

- Discuss the two different uses of the term "nation at risk." Which constitutes the greatest risk—educational deficiencies or "social problems"? How are the two related? Which is the most serious threat to your family?

Startling Statistics (pp. 33–38)

- Discuss these statistics. Which do you find most shocking? How do they affect your family, even if you're not a statistical part of them? Which of the problems do you and your kids confront most directly?

Future Projections (pp. 33–38)

- Discuss where you'll be in 2025. Will your grandchildren be part of these projected statistics? How does your parenting today affect the kind of parents your children will be to your grandkids?

Curse, Crisis, and Cause (pp. 46–53)

- Discuss how the curse of social problems is traceable to the crisis of family breakdown, which in turn is caused by hyper-individuality, materialistic entitlement attitudes, false paradigms, and the take-over of larger institutions. Do you agree with the cause and effect? Is it a worldwide phenomenon? Can it be stopped?

- Discuss why the crisis of family decline and the call for family values needs to come not just from the right, but from across the political and economic and religious spectrum.

Family, Values, and Society (pp. 53–56)

- Discuss the relationships and connections between families and basic values, and between families and values and the larger society. Where is the best starting point? Why? Why does the horizontal arrow go both ways?

Parenting Today (pp. 56–58)

- Discuss why it is harder to be a parent today than ever before. Does it have to be so hard? Can we reprioritize? Do we have the freedom and flexibility to make tradeoffs that put more time and thought into our families?

- What do you think of the "subcontractor" parenting model? Do you find yourself following it—relying on others, from teachers to coaches—to give your children what they need?

Institutions and the Family (pp. 76–78)

- Discuss the theory that big institutions are destroying small ones (family). How are they doing so? List as many big institutions as you can. How many of them existed a generation ago, when you were growing up? How many existed a hundred years ago?

- What would have been your reaction if you were in the audience described above? Do you agree that it's harder to be a parent today than ever before?

Public-, Private-, and Voluntary-Sector Pressures (pp. 79–81)

- Discuss the private, public, and voluntary sectors or "rings" of the diagram. What should they be doing for families? What are they doing instead? Which institutions are becoming substitutes for family? Which institutions undermine families and tear down the values that hold families together?

Faux Families (pp. 82–85)

- Discuss *why* and *how* the care-giving, value-instilling, and teaching roles of parents are being assumed by larger entities in all three "outer ring" sectors. How is this "diminishing of the family role" different than what happens in China? How is it the same?

- What do you think are the results (and the dangers) as parents influence their children less and less and government, business, peer group, and media influence children more and more?

Hits to the Family (pp. 86–118)

- Discuss the "hits" your own family is taking from the outer sectors. What percentage of smart phone games, TV shows, movies, and rap songs help you in your parenting and your effort to teach values?

- What do you think is the net effect of advertising on your children?

- How much does the Internet scare you?

- How hard is it to find time to spend together as a family?

- What do you think of government welfare and tax policies that make people financially better off when they split apart their families?

Paradigms (Chapter 7)

- How would you define a "paradigm?" Discuss the importance of paradigms. How do false paradigms get started? How do people come to accept them?

- What do you think influences our paradigms most (media, advertising, peer groups, what we perceive to be the "norms" around us, etc.)? What should influence them most (our values, our conscience).

- What is the main danger of false paradigms to a family?

Four False Paradigms (pp. 141–160)

- Discuss the "amorality as the norm" coming from media and Internet, the dangerous obsession with materialism and entitlement, the deception of recreational sex and instant gratification, and the confusion of situational ethics. How do these false paradigms deceive us? Do you think they can be replaced with the positive "antidote" principles from pages 189–198?

Celebrating Family (Chapter 8)

- Discuss the long- and short-term pros and cons of having and prioritizing a family. Do you agree that it is both the right way and the happiest way to live?

- What are the hardest things about having a family today? What are the things that make it worth it?

Creating a Family Culture Stronger than All Other Cultures (Chapter 9)

- Discuss the various cultures that our children are a part of. Which of these influence them most? Can families compete against these forces?

- What are the key ingredients in a family culture?

Seven Ways to Save Your Own Family (Chapter 9)

- Briefly discuss the seven "keys" listed on pages 181–182. Which ones do you think are the most important? Which are the hardest? Are these doable, or are we suggesting a formula that requires too much time that parents do not have?

Nine Engines of Change (pp. 275–276)

- Discuss how these nine societal sectors influence us and impact our families. Which of the nine affect your family most? How is it that these nine institutions were called "the culprits" in the first part of the book and "the solutions" in the second half of the book?

What Each Does to Hurt Families and What Each Could Do to Help Families (pp. 275–276)

- Pick three of the nine "engines of change" that you find most interesting. What do you think each of the three do that is harmful to your family? What could each of the three do to help and support your family?

APPENDIX II

PARENTING RESOURCES AND PREVIOUS BOOKS

Readers are invited to visit the following websites:

- www.The-Turning.com
- www.EyresFreeBooks.com, where many of the books listed below are available for free
- www.TheEyres.com, for Richard and Linda's speaking schedule and topics
- www.PowerofMoms.com, the organization co-founded by Saren Eyre Loosli
- www.71toes.com, the "mommy blog" of Shawni Eyre Pothier
- www.ValuesParenting.com, the official website of the Eyres' parenting programs
- www.Familius.com, for articles and books dedicated to making families happy
- www.DeseretNews.com/author/22926/Linda--Richard-Eyre. html, for the Eyres' weekly column
- www.byuradio.org/search?q=eyre, for the Eyres' weekly radio show

Previous Eyre books* related or supplemental to *The Turning* are below:

- *Teaching Your Children Values*
- *The Entitlement Trap*
- *Three Steps to a Strong Family*
- *Teaching Children Responsibility*
- *How to Talk to Your Child about Sex*
- *The Happy Family*
- *Teaching Children Joy*
- *A Joyful Mother of Children*
- *Teaching Children Sensitivity*
- *LifeBalance*
- *Spiritual Serendipity*
- *Stewardship of the Heart*
- *I Didn't Plan to Be a Witch*
- *Empty Nest Parenting*
- *The Book of Nurturing*
- *A Mother's Book of Secrets*
- *Five Spiritual Solutions for Parents*
- *On The Homefront*

*Brief summaries of each of these books and complete downloads of many of them are available for free at www.EyresFreeBooks.com

APPENDIX III

REFERENCES

CHAPTER ONE

1. Keith A. Owens, "Society Shouldn't Try to Hide behind Fuzzy Family Values," *Sun Sentinel*, November 24, 1990.

CHAPTER TWO

1. Srdjan Mrkić, Tina Johnson and Michael Rose, "The World's Women 2010: Trends and Statistics," *Department of Economic and Social Affairs*, United Nations, (2010): 33.

   Economist, "For Richer, for Smarter," June 23, 2011.

   Pew Social and Demographic Trends, "The Decline of Marriage and the Rise of New Families," *Pew Research Center*, November 18, 2010.

2. Brady Hamilton, Joyce A. Martin and Stephanie J. Ventura, "Births: Preliminary Data for 2012," *National Vital Statistics Report*, 62.3 (2013).

   Michelle Castillo, "Almost Half of First Babies in U.S. Born to Unwed Mothers," *CBS News*, March 15, 2013, http://www.cbsnews.com/news/almost-half-of-first-babies-in-us-born-to-unwed-mothers/.

3. Anna Miller, "Can This Marriage Be Saved?" *American Psychological Association*, April 2013, http://www.apa.org/monitor/2013/04/marriage.aspx.

4. Eric Klinenberg, "One's a Crowd," *New York Times*, February 4, 2012, http://www.nytimes.com/2012/02/05/opinion/sunday/living-alone-means-being-social.html?_r=0.

5. Emily Allen, "Young Women Put Off Starting a Family for Fear It Will Damage Their Looks, Career, and Lifestyle," *Daily Mail Online*, UK. September 14, 2011, http://www.dailymail.co.uk/health/article-2037179/Young-women-putting-starting-family-fearing-damage-looks-career-lifestyle. html#ixzz1YQ0HtiPz.

6.   Meg Jay, "The Downside of Cohabiting Before Marriage," *New York Times*, April 14, 2012, http://www.nytimes.com/2012/04/15/opinion/sunday/the-downside-of-cohabiting-before-marriage.html?pagewanted=all.

"Children in Single-Parent Families by Race," *Kids Count Data Center*, Accessed March 14, 2014, http://datacenter.kidscount.org/data/tables/107-children-in-single-parent-families-by#detailed/1/any/false/868,867,133,38,35/10,168,9,12,1,13,185,11/432,431.

7.   Luke Rosiak, "Fathers Disappear from Households Across America," *The Washington Times*, December 25, 2012, http://www.washingtontimes.com/news/2012/dec/25/fathers-disap-pear-from-households-across-america/?page=all.

8.   Jonathan Vespa, Jamie M. Lewis and Rose M. Kreider, "America's Families and Living Arrangements: 2012." *United States Census Bureau*, 1-2.

Tyjen T Conley, "Australian Fathers' Long Hours Affect Sons More Than Daughters," *Population Reference Bureau*, March 2014, http://www.prb.org/Publications/Articles/2014/australian-fathers-sons.aspx.

9.   Richard V. Reeves, *The Atlantic*, February 13, 2014, http://www.theatlantic.com/business/archive/2014/02/how- to-save-marriage-in-america/283732/.

Wendy Wang, Kim Parker and Paul Taylor, "Breadwinner Moms," *Pew Research*, May 29, 2013, http://www.pewsocialtrends.org/2013/05/29/breadwinner-moms/.

Shelly Lundberg and Robert Pollak, "Cohabitation and the Uneven Retreat from Marriage in the US, 1950-2010," November 2013, http://www.nber.org/chapters/c12896.pdf?new_window=1.

10. "Country Comparison: Total Fertility Rate," *The World Fact Book*, Central Intelligence Agency, 2014.

Max Fisher, "How the World's Populations Are Changing, in One Map," *The Washington Post*, October 13, 2013, https://www.cia.gov/library/publications/the-world-factbook/rankorder/2127rank.html.

Joseph Chamie and Barry Mirkin, "Childless by Choice," *Yale Global Online*, March 2, 2012, http://yaleglobal.yale.edu/content/childless-choice.

11. Pew Social and Demographic Trends, "The Decline of Marriage and the Rise of New Families," *Pew Research Center*, November 18, 2010.

12. Joseph Chamie and Barry Mirkin, "Childless by Choice," Yale Global Online. *MacMillan Center*, March 2, 2012. http://yaleglobal.yale.edu/content/childless-choice.

13. Shelly Lundberg and Robert A. Pollak, *Cohabitation and the Uneven Retreat from Marriage in the U.S.*, 1950-2010; http://www.nber.org/chapters/c12896.pdf?new_window=1.

14. Noelle Knox, "Nordic Family Ties Don't Mean Tying the Knot," *USA Today*, December 16, 2004, www.usatoday.com/news/world.

At the same time, unmarried couples in Scandinavia have somewhat more stable relationships than unmarried US couples, whose cohabiting relationships are shorter than in any other country.

Andrew Cherlin, *The Marriage Go Round* (New York: Random House, 2009).

Sociologist Andrew Cherlin has found that even a child born to married parents in the U.S. is statistically more likely to see his parents break up than is the child of an unmarried couple in Sweden. This statement is from Cherlin's "about the book" summary on RandomHouse.com.

15. US Census Bureau, Current Population Survey, Annual Social and Economic Supplements, 1950 to 2013, https://www.census.gov/hhes/families/files/graphics/FM-1.pdf.

Wendy Wang, Kim Parker and Paul Taylor, "Breadwinner Moms," *Pew Research*, May 29, 2013, http://www.pewsocialtrends.org/2013/05/29/breadwinner-moms/.

Kim Parker and Wendy Wang, "Modern Parenthood: Roles of Moms and Dads Converge as They Balance Work and Family," *Pew Research*, March 14, 2013.

Bradford Wilcox, *The Atlantic*, October 29, 2013, http://www.theatlantic.com/business/archive/2013/10/marriage-makes-our-children-richer-heres-why/280930/.

16. Wayne Parker, "Statistics on Fatherless Children in America," *About.com*, http://fatherhood.about.com/od/fathersrights/a/fatherless_children.htm.

17. Kay S. Hymowitz, "The Fragile Family Effect," *Los Angeles Times*, November 11, 2010, http://articles.latimes.com/2010/nov/11/opinion/la-oe-hymowitz-families-20101111.

18. Sarah Eberspacher, "Everything You Need to Know About Japan's Population Crisis," *The Week*, January 11, 2014, http://theweek.com/article/index/254923/everything-you-need-to-know-about-japans-population-crisis.

19. Eric Klinenberg, "One's a Crowd," *New York Times*, February 4, 2012, http://www.nytimes.com/2012/02/05/opinion/sunday/living-alone-means-being-social.html?_r=0.

20. Joel Kotkin, "The Rise of Post-Familialism: Humanity's Future?" *Newgeography.com*, October 10, 2012, http://www.newgeography.com/content/003133-the-rise-post-familialism-humanitys-future.

21. David Brooks, "The Age of Possibility," *New York Times*, November 15, 2012, http://www.nytimes.com/2012/11/16/opinion/brooks-the-age-of-possibility.html.

22. Ryan Streeter, "Marriage Rates and the Libertarian-Libertine Assault on the American Dream," January 2, 2012.

23. Linda A. Jacobsen, Mary Kent, Marlene Lee and Mark Mather, "Population Bulletin: America's Aging Population," *Population Reference Bureau*, February 2011: 5.

Eduardo Porter, "Maybe We're Not Robbing the Craddle," *New York Times*, April 10, 2005. http://www.nytimes.com/2005/04/10/weekinreview/10porter.html?pagewanted=print.

24. Nick Schultz, *Home Economics: The Consequences of Changing Family Structure*, 2013 American Enterprise Institute for Public Policy Research, Washington, DC.

CHAPTER THREE

1. Paul Tough, *How Children Succeed: Grit, Curiosity, and the Hidden Power of Character* (New York: Mariner Books, 2013), 7.

2. "Youth Violence: National Statistics," *Centers for Disease Control and Prevention*, December 27, 2013, http://www.cdc.gov/VIOLENCEPREVENTION/youthviolence/stats_at-a_glance/.

   "List of School Shootings," *Stop the Shootings*, 2013, http://www.stoptheshootings.org/.

   "Protect Children, Not Guns 2012," *Children Defense Fund*, 2012, http://www.childrensdefense.org/child-research-data-publications/data/protect-children-not-guns-2012.html.

   "School Shootings in America Since Sandy Hook," *Demand Action to End Gun Violence*, University of Delaware College/University, March 23, 2014.

   "Teens and Violence Prevention," *Palo Alto Medical Foundation*, August 2013, http://www.pamf.org/parenting-teens/emotions/violence/violence.html.

3. "America's Children: Key National Indicators of Well-Being," *Child Stats: Forum on Child and Family Statistics*, 2011, http://www.childstats.gov/americaschildren/.

   "Adolescent Pregnancy," *World Health Organization*, May 2012, http://www.who.int/mediacentre/factsheets/fs364/en/.

   B.E. Hamilton, J.A. Martin and S.J. Ventura, "Births: Preliminary data for 2012," Hattsville, MD: National Center for Health Statistics, 2012.

   Sarah Isrealsen-Hartley, "Ubiquitous Assailant: The Dangerous Unasked Questions Surrounding Pornography," *Deseret News*, July 6, 2013, http://www.deseretnews.com/article/865582634/Ubiquitous-assailant-The-dangerous-unasked-questions-surrounding-pornography.html.

   Martin Downs, "Is Pornography Addictive?" *Webmd.com*, http://www.webmd.com/men/features/is-pornography-addictive.

4. "Teens: Alcohol and Other Drugs," *Child & Adolescent Psychiatry*, October 2013, http://www.aacap.org/aacap/Families_and_Youth/Facts_for_Families/Facts_for_Families_Pages/Teens_Alcohol_And_Other_Drugs_03.aspx.

   "Drug Facts: High School and Youth Trends," *National Institute on Drug Abuse*, January 2014, http://www.drugabuse.gov/publications/drugfacts/high-school-youth-trends.

   "Underage Drinking," *National Institute on Alcohol Abuse and Alcoholism*, 2010. http://pubs.niaaa.nih.gov/publications/UnderageDrinking/Underage_Fact.pdf.

   Kyle James, "In Germany, Excessive Drinking by Teens Is on the Rise," *Deutsche Welle*, April 8, 2009, http://www.dw.de/in-germany-excessive-drinking-by-teens-is-on-the-rise/a-4542438-1.

   "International Guide to Minimum Legal Drinking Ages (MLDAs) in 138 Countries," *ProCon.org*, June 6, 2011, http://drinkingage.procon.org/view.resource.php?resourceID=004294.

Hingson RW, Heeren T and Winter MR, "Age at Drinking Onset and Alcohol Dependence: Age at Onset, Duration, and Severity," *Pediatrics* 2006; 160:739–746.

Kyle James, "In Germany, Excessive Drinking by Teens Is on the Rise," *Deutsche Welle*, April 8, 2009, http://www.dw.de/in-germany-excessive-drinking-by-teens-is-on-the-rise/a-4542438-1.

"The Truth About Inhalants: International Statistics," *Drug Free World*, 2014, http://www.drugfreeworld.org/drugfacts/inhalants.html.

5.   National Institutes of Health, National Institute of Mental Health. (n.d.). Any Disorder among Children, 2013.

American Association of Suicidology, (2012), Suicide in the USA Based on 2010 Data, Washington, DC: American Association of Suicidology.

"Teen Suicide." *American Academy of Child & Adolescent Psychiatry*, October 2013.

Petaling Jaya, "Cyberbullying up by 55.6 Percent in a Year," *The Malay Mail*, March 27, 2014, http://manage.mmail.com.my/story/cyberbullying-556-cent-year-75900.

6.   US Department of Education, Institute of Education Sciences, National Center for Education Statistics, (2013) *Public School Graduates and Dropouts from the Common Core of Data: School Year 2009-10*; http://nces.ed.gov/pubs2013/2013309.pdf.

National Center for Education Statistics, (2013), *Statistics in Brief: First Year Undergraduate Remedial Coursetaking: 1999-2000, 2003-04, 2007-08*, Retrieved from http://nces.ed.gov/programs/coe/indicator_rmc.asp#info.

"Children and Watching TV," *American Academy of Child & Adolescent Psychiatry*, December 2011, http://www.aacap.org/AACAP/Families_and_Youth/Facts_for_Families/Facts_for_Families_Pages/Children_And_Wat_54.aspx.

Masuma Ahuja, "Teens Are Spending More Time Consuming Media, on Mobile Devices," *Washington Post*, March 13, 2013, http://www.washingtonpost.com/postlive/teens-are-spending-more-time-consuming-media-on-mobile-devices/2013/03/12/309bb242-8689-11e2-98a3-b3db-6b9ac586_story.html.

Claudio Sanchez, "College Board 'Concerned' about Low SAT Scores," *National Public Radio*, September 26, 2013, http://www.npr.org/2013/09/26/226530184/college-board-concerned-about-low-sat-scores.

7.   "Teenagers with Eating Disorders," *American Academy of Child & Adolescent Psychiatry*, October 2013, http://www.aacap.org/aacap/Families_and_Youth/Facts_for_Families/Facts_for_Families_Pages/Teenagers_With_Eating_Disorders_02.aspx.

"Girls Aged Seven 'Have Anorexia,'" *BBC News*, September 19, 2006. http://news.bbc.co.uk/2/hi/uk_news/england/london/5360768.stm.

Rochelle Finzel, "Homeless and Runaway Youth," *National Conference of State Legislatures*, October 1, 2013, http://www.ncsl.org/research/human-services/homeless-and-runaway-youth.aspx.

Elaine Patricia Cruz, "Mais de 1,2 mil crianças e adolescentes viciadas em crack vivem nas ruas de São Paulo," *Agência Brasil*, October 3, 2013. http://memoria.ebc.com.br/agenciabrasil/noticia/2013-03-10/mais-de-12-mil-criancas-e-adolescentes-viciadas-em-crack-vivem-nas-ruas-de-sao-paulo.

Errol Barnett and Diane McCarthy, "Mama Sunday' Feeds Burundi's Hungry Street Children," *CNN World*, December 9, 2013, http://www.cnn.com/2013/12/09/world/africa/mama-sunday-feeds-burundis/.

Rochelle Finzel, "Homeless and Runaway Youth," *National Conference of State Legislatures*, October 1, 2013, http://www.ncsl.org/research/human-services/homeless-and-runaway-youth.aspx.

"Ethiopia: Focus on Street Children Rehabilitation Project," *IRIN*, March 1, 2004, http://www.irinnews.org/report/48799/ethiopia-focus-on-street-children-rehabilitation-project.

Rochelle Finzel, "Homeless and Runaway Youth," *National Conference of State Legislatures*, October 1, 2013, http://www.ncsl.org/research/human-services/homeless-and-runaway-youth.aspx.

Rochelle Finzel, "Homeless and Runaway Youth," *National Conference of State Legislatures*, October 1, 2013, http://www.ncsl.org/research/human-services/homeless-and-runaway-youth.aspx.

"Child Poverty," *National Center for Children in Poverty*, Columbia University, Mailman School of Public Health and Department of Health Policy & Management, 2013.

CHAPTER FOUR

1. Glenn T. Stanton, "Why Marriage Matters for Children," *Family Institute of Connecticut Action*, Accessed July 11, 2014, http://www.ctfamily.org/why_it_matters.html.

2. Richard V. Reeves, "How to Save a Marriage in America," *The Atlantic*, February 13, 2014, http://www.theatlantic.com/business/archive/2014/02/how-to-save-marriage-in-america/283732/.

3. John W. Santrock, *Adolescence* (Ohio: McGraw-Hill, 2003), 171.

4. Tyjen T Conley, "Australian Fathers' Long Hours Affect Sons More Than Daughters," *Population Reference Bureau*, March 2014, http://www.prb.org/Publications/Articles/2014/australian-fathers-sons.aspx.

5. Rick Nauert and John M. Grohol, "Higher Risk of Suicidal Thought for Children of Divorce," *Psych Central*, University of Toronto, January 20, 2011, http://psychcentral.com/news/2011/01/20/higher-risk-of-suicidal-thoughts-for-children-of-divorce/22807.html.

6. Josh Mitchell, "About Half of Kids with Single Moms Live in Poverty," *The Wall Street Journal*, November 25, 2013, http://blogs.wsj.com/economics/2013/11/25/about-half-of-kids-with-single-moms-live-in-poverty/.

7. "America's Children: Key National Indicators of Well-Being." *Child Stats: Forum on Child and Family Statistics*, 2011, http://www.childstats.gov/americaschildren/.

8. G. Martinez, C. E. Copen and J. C. Abma, (2011), Teenagers in the United States: Sexual activity, contraceptive use, and childbearing, 2006-2010 National Survey of Family Growth: National Center for Health Statistics. Vital Health Stat 23 (31).

9. Frances Kemper Alston, "Latch Key Children," *Education.com*, NYU Child Study Center, July 9, 2010, Web, March 2013, http://www.aboutourkids.org/articles/latch_key_children.

10. Frances Kemper Alston, "Latch Key Children," *Education.com*, NYU Child Study Center, July 9, 2010, Web, March 2013, http://www.aboutourkids.org/articles/latch_key_children.

11. Frances Kemper Alston, "Latch Key Children," *Education.com*, NYU Child Study Center, July 9, 2010, Web, March 2013, http://www.aboutourkids.org/articles/latch_key_children.

12. Ross Douthat, "More Imperfect Unions," *New York Times*, January 25, 3014.

13. Janet Street Porter, "Why GCSEs in Parenting Could Save a Generation," *Daily Mail*, August 9, 2010, http://www.dailymail.co.uk/femail/article-1301373/JANET-STREET-PORTER-Why-GCSEs-parenting-save-generation.html.

14. Barbara Pierce Bush, "Commencement Address," Commencement Address at Wellesley College, Wellesley, MA, June 1, 1990, http://www.americanrhetoric.com/speeches/barbarabushwellesley-commencement.htm.

CHAPTER FIVE

1. David Brooks, "The Age of Possibility," *New York Times*. November 15, 2012, http://www.nytimes.com/2012/11/16/opinion/brooks-the-age-of-possibility.html.

2. Bruce C. Hafen, "Marriage, Family Law, and the Temple," J. Reuben Clark Law Society Annual International Broadcast, Salt Lake City, Utah, January 31, 2014. Publication forthcoming in *The Clark Memorandum*, Fall 2014, BYU Law School.

CHAPTER SIX

1. Lawrence Mishel, "The CEO-to-Worker Compensation Ratio in 2012 of 273 Was Far Above That of the Late 1990s and 14 Times the Ratio of 20.1 in 1965," September 24, 2013, http://www.epi.org/publication/the-ceo-to-worker-compensation-ratio-in-2012-of-273/.

2. Bruce C. Hafen, "Marriage, Family Law, and the Temple," J. Reuben Clark Law Society Annual International Broadcast, Salt Lake City, Utah, January 31, 2014. Publication forthcoming in *The Clark Memorandum*, Fall 2014, BYU Law School.

3. Silvia Ann Hewlett and Cornel West, *The War Against Parents: What We Can Do for America's Beleaguered Moms and Dads* (New York: Mariner Books, 1999).

CHAPTER SEVEN

1. "Number, Timing, and Duration of Marriages and Divorces: 2009." *U.S. Census Bureau*. May 2011: 12.

2. Angus Deatona and Arthur A. Stone, "Evaluative and Hedonic Wellbeing Among Those with and Without Children at Home," *Proceedings of the National Academy of Sciences*, December 11, 2013.

3. "Stay Teen: Stay Informed," last modified 2014, http://stayteen.org/waiting.

4. Francis Collins, *The Language of God: A Scientist Presents Evidence for Belief* (Massachusetts: Free Press, 2007), 30.

CHAPTER EIGHT

1. Richard V. Reeves, "How to Save a Marriage in America," *The Atlantic*, February 13, 2014, http://www.theatlantic.com/business/archive/2014/02/how-to-save-marriage-in-america/283732/.

2. Stewart D. Freedman, *Baby Bust: New Choices for Men and Women in Work and Family* (Pennsylvania: Wharton Digital Press), 2013.

3. Sue Shellenbarger, "Cost of Raising a Child Ticks Up," *The Wall Street Journal*, June 10, 2010, http://blogs.wsj.com/juggle/2010/06/10/cost-of-raising-a-child-ticks-up/.

CHAPTER NINE

1. "Stay Teen: Stay Informed," last modified 2014, http://stayteen.org/waiting.

2. William Wordsworth, "Ode: Intimations of Immortality," 1807, Arthur Quiller-Couch, ed. 1919, *The Oxford Book of English Verse: 1250–1900*.

3. Paul Tough, *How Children Succeed: Grit, Curiosity, and the Hidden Power of Character* (New York: Mariner Books, 2013), 83.

4. Bruce Feiler, "Stories That Bind Us," *New York Times*, 2013.

CHAPTER TEN

1. Jana Kasperkevic, "Why Single People Are Hurting the Economy," *The Guardian*, October 30, 2013, http://www.theguardian.com/money/2013/oct/30/marriage-single-people-hurting-economy.

CHAPTER ELEVEN

1. Louis M. Collins, "President Convenes 'Family-Friendly Workplace' Summit to Consider Policies," *Deseret News: National Edition*, June 25 2014, http://www.deseretnews.com/article/865605725/President-convenes-family-friendly-workplace-summit-to-consider-policies.html.

ACKNOWLEDGMENTS

Thanks to our nine kids—we still call them that, though they are all now thoroughly accomplished adults. They are our motivation for living, as well as for writing, and they have each, in their own way, picked up the torch of our Eyrealm cause to strengthen families through their wide-ranging family organizations, books, blogs, and the creation of stellar families of their own. (You might want to check out www.PowerOfMoms.com and www.71Toes. com as examples.) And to the Inklings, our literary brainstorming group, who have offered input and feedback on many parts of this book, and at many stages.

Thanks to Christopher Robbins and Familius Publishing. We know something about publishers because we have had quite a list of them over the years: Random House, McGraw-Hill, Simon and Schuster, and St. Martin's Press. But we have never felt the loyalty and support and the commonality of objectives that we feel with Familius. We now refer fondly to Christopher as "our publisher" and hope that is what he always will be.

Thanks to our editors, Sheila Curry Oakes and Brooke Jorden, for their brilliant work, and to our dedicated researcher and publicist, Erika Riggs, and our creative designer, David Miles. Finally, thanks to the more than 200,000 parents who have participated in and helped develop the family programs at www.ValuesParenting.com, and whose support and feedback we always value.

ABOUT THE
AUTHORS

Linda is a musician and teacher and the founder of JoySchools.com and ValuesParenting.com. Richard is a Harvard Business School–trained management consultant, former Director of the White House Conference on Parents and Children, Gubernatorial candidate, and a ranked senior tennis player. Together, the Eyres are the authors of forty books, the parents of nine, and the grandparents of twenty-six. They have been guests on most national TV morning and talk shows and for a time had a regular segment on *CBS This Morning*. They now spend full time writing and speaking on family strategies and life-balance to parents, teachers, and business and government leaders throughout the world. When they come home, it is to Park City, Utah, or to their intimate "Eyrealm" compound in Bear Lake, Idaho, where the family gathers each summer.

All of Eyrealm shares the goal of promoting family-centric lifestyles and is trying to help expand and energize the global movement in which society's most powerful engines of change become more involved in fortifying families by celebrating commitment, popularizing parenting, bolstering balance, and validating values.

ABOUT FAMILIUS

VISIT OUR WEBSITE: WWW.FAMILIUS.COM

Our website is a different kind of place. Get inspired, read articles, discover books, watch videos, connect with our family experts, download books and apps and audiobooks, and along the way, discover how values and happy family life go together.

JOIN OUR FAMILY

There are lots of ways to connect with us! Subscribe to our newsletters at www.familius.com to receive uplifting daily inspiration, essays from our Pater Familius, a free ebook every month, and the first word on special discounts and Familius news.

BECOME AN EXPERT

Familius authors and other established writers interested in helping families be happy are invited to join our family and contribute online content. If you have something important to say on the family, join our expert community by applying at:

www.familius.com/apply-to-become-a-familius-expert

GET BULK DISCOUNTS

If you feel a few friends and family might benefit from what you've read, let us know and we'll be happy to provide you with quantity discounts. Simply email us at specialorders@familius.com.

Website: www.familius.com
Facebook: www.facebook.com/paterfamilius
Twitter: @familiustalk, @paterfamilius1
Pinterest: www.pinterest.com/familius

The most important work you ever do will be within the walls of your own home.